Standard Occupational Classification Manual

Based on Information from the U.S. Office of Management and Budget

jist Works

Standard Occupational Classification Manual

© 2002 by JIST Publishing, Inc.

Published by JIST Works, an imprint of JIST Publishing, Inc.
8902 Otis Avenue
Indianapolis, IN 46216-1033

Phone: 1-800-648-JIST   Fax: 1-800-JIST-FAX
E-mail: info@jist.com   Web site: www.jist.com

About Career Materials Published by JIST

For the best information on occupations, many people—including experienced career professionals—rely on JIST. JIST has published information about careers and job search since the 1970s. JIST offers occupational references plus hundreds of other books, videos, assessment devices, and software.

Quantity discounts are available for this reference and other JIST books. Please call 1-800-648-JIST weekdays for details.

Visit www.jist.com to find out about JIST products, get free book chapters, and link to other career-related sites. You can also learn more about JIST authors and JIST training available to professionals.

A free catalog is available to professionals at schools, institutions, and other programs. It presents hundreds of helpful publications on career, job search, self-help, and business topics. Call 1-800-648-JIST or visit www.jist.com.

Editors: Susan Pines, Veda Dickerson
Cover and Interior Design and Layout: Trudy Coler
Proofreader: Jeanne Clark

Printed in the United States of America
06 05 04 03 02 01   9 8 7 6 5 4 3 2 1

Library of Congress Cataloging-in-Publication Data

Standard occupational classification manual : based on information from the U.S. Office of Management and Budget.—2001 ed.

    p. cm.

"Presents the new Standard Occupational Classification (SOC) system ... Restructured and updated for the first time since 1980 ... devised through the cooperative effort of all the federal agencies that use the occupational classification systems"—Pref.

ISBN 1-56370-844-2

1. Occupations—United States—Classification—Handbooks, manuals, etc. 2.Occupations—Classification—Handbooks, manuals, etc. I. United States. Office of Management and Budget. II. JIST Works, Inc.

HB2595 .S7 2001

331.7'0012—dc21   2001038821

We have been careful to provide accurate information throughout this book, but it is possible that errors and omissions have been introduced. Please consider this in making any career plans or other important decisions. Trust your own judgment above all else and in all things.

Trademarks: All brand names and product names used in this book are trade names, service marks, trademarks, or registered trademarks of their respective owners.

O*NET™ 3.1 is a trademark of the U.S. Department of Labor, Education and Training Administration.

WELCOME TO THIS BOOK AND THE SOC

This one convenient volume presents the new Standard Occupational Classification (SOC) system, which organizes all occupations in the nation done for pay or profit by the type of work performed. Restructured and updated for the first time since 1980, the SOC system in this book was devised through the cooperative effort of all federal agencies that use occupational classification systems.

The new SOC structure was developed to address the inconsistent and outdated occupational organization systems used by government agencies. All federal agencies that collect and produce occupational data will implement this one structure over the next few years. Federal agencies' universal adherence to the SOC will make it easier to analyze the educational, demographic, and economic factors related to employment, wages, and other work issues.

With the SOC, everyone who gathers or uses occupational data can benefit from a consistently organized structure of occupations. Employers, schools, industrial and labor relations practitioners, counselors, job seekers, and others will be able to produce and use comparable information efficiently and effectively.

THIS MANUAL IS EASY TO USE

This manual presents the SOC's four-level occupational structure as well as its occupational descriptions. It includes the content found in the government's new SOC release, plus updates and corrections not previously published. To help meet your reference needs, the introduction and several appendixes list the principles of classification, describe the SOC revision process, answer frequently asked questions, and provide a cross-reference to O*NET job titles.

You can use this book to find a SOC code, job group, job title, or job description:

- **For an overview of the SOC structure,** review the list called "The SOC Structure" in the table of contents. It includes, in numerical order, all SOC codes, groups, and job titles, plus page numbers where you can find more detail.

- **If you know an occupation's SOC code,** simply flip through the book until you find the group or job title you're seeking. All information is organized numerically by SOC code.

- **If you know the SOC job title or associated title,** use the alphabetical index to find it. Then turn to the listed page number for more detail.

Credits

The SOC was developed by a committee formed by the Office of Management and Budget and included representatives from the Bureau of Labor Statistics, the Bureau of the Census, the Employment and Training Administration (Department of Labor), the Defense Manpower Data Center (Department of Defense), and the Office of Personnel Management.

In addition, ex-officio members included the National Science Foundation, the National Occupational Information Coordinating Committee, and the Office of Management and Budget. Several other agencies, such as the Department of Education, the Department of Health and Human Services, and the Equal Employment Opportunity Commission, participated in SOC Committee meetings or on the Federal Consultation Group.

TABLE OF CONTENTS

Quick Summary of Sections

Introduction. The introduction explains the SOC structure, includes a sample occupational description with key elements highlighted, and gives the SOC guidelines for classifying occupations. *Begins on page 1.*

SOC Occupational Structure and Definitions. This is the book's main section, and it presents the four-level SOC structure, plus SOC codes, job titles, definitions for the detailed occupations, and associated job titles. *Begins on page 7.*

Appendix A: Frequently Asked Questions About the SOC. Learn about future SOC revisions, the SOC implementation schedule, and other details. *Begins on page 203.*

Appendix B: Revising the SOC. Read background information on why and how the SOC was revised. *Begins on page 207.*

Appendix C: SOC-to-O*NET Cross-Reference Table. Find the O*NET codes and job titles that correspond to the SOC codes and job titles. The O*NET is an occupational information database from the U.S. Department of Labor that includes descriptions of about 1,000 occupations. The SOC is the basis for the O*NET database's structure. Helpful for job seekers, students, counselors, and others. *Begins on page 217.*

Index. This alphabetical list includes all the SOC detailed occupation titles and alternate titles in this book, along with page numbers. *Begins on page 255.*

The SOC Structure

This list shows the SOC structure, including SOC codes and job titles. Refer to the page numbers shown for more details and for descriptions of the detailed occupations.

Table of Contents

Table of Contents

Table of Contents

Table of Contents

Table of Contents

Table of Contents

Table of Contents

Table of Contents

Table of Contents

Table of Contents

INTRODUCTION

This information will help you to understand the SOC and its structure. The text was derived from various sources, including the Standard Occupational Classification User Guide at http://stats.bls.gov/soc/socguide.htm and the Standard Occupational Classification home page at http://stats.bls.gov/soc_home.htm. JIST editors added other details.

The Standard Occupational Classification (SOC) system was developed to meet a growing need for a universal occupational classification system in the United States. This system will allow government agencies and private industry to produce comparable data.

The SOC is designed to cover all occupations in which work is performed for pay or profit, reflecting the current occupational structure in the United States.

In its first revision since 1980, the new SOC presented in this book is the result of a cooperative effort of all federal agencies that use occupational classification systems and will maximize the usefulness of occupational information collected by the federal government.

Who Uses the SOC?

The SOC system will be used by all federal agencies collecting occupational data, allowing occupational data to be easily compared across agencies. Users of this occupational data include government program managers, industrial and labor relations practitioners, students considering career training, job seekers, vocational training schools, counselors, and employers wishing to set salary scales or locate a new plant.

See Appendix A (specifically, questions 7, 9, and 10) for more details on federal agencies using the SOC.

Sample Definition Within the SOC Structure

The following graphic shows one SOC title and definition from this book, within the SOC structure. Explanations of the highlighted elements follow.

Major Group — ## 11-0000 MANAGEMENT OCCUPATIONS

11-1000 Top Executives — Minor Group

11-1010 Chief Executives — Broad Occupation

This broad occupation is the same as the detailed occupation:
11-1011 Chief Executives

11-1011 Chief Executives — Detailed Occupation

Determine and formulate policies and provide the overall direction of companies or private and public sector organizations, within the guidelines set up by a board of directors or similar governing body. Plan, direct, or coordinate operational activities at the highest level of management, with the help of subordinate executives and staff managers. **Examples:** Board Member; Chief Operating Officer; President.

SOC Code — **11-1020 General and Operations Managers**

This broad occupation is the same as the detailed occupation:
11-1021 General and Operations Managers

11-1021 General and Operations Managers

Plan, direct, or coordinate the operations of companies or public and private sector organizations. Formulate policies, manage daily operations, and plan the use of materials and human resources. Perform duties that are too diverse and general in nature to be classified in any one functional area of management or administration such as personnel, purchasing, or administrative services. Includes owners and managers who head small business establishments and whose duties are primarily managerial. Excludes "First-Line Supervisors/Managers of Retail Sales Workers" (41-1011) and workers in other small establishments. **Examples:** Industrial Organization Manager; District Manager; Department Store General Manager.

Definition — [bracket pointing to the above definition paragraph]

Examples of associated job titles — [bracket pointing to the Examples above]

SOC Classification and Coding Structure

The SOC classifies workers at four levels: (1) major group, (2) minor group, (3) broad occupation, and (4) detailed occupation. All occupations are clustered into one of the following 23 major groups:

11-0000	Management Occupations	35-0000	Food Preparation and Serving Related Occupations
13-0000	Business and Financial Operations Occupations	37-0000	Building and Grounds Cleaning and Maintenance Occupations
15-0000	Computer and Mathematical Occupations		
17-0000	Architecture and Engineering Occupations	39-0000	Personal Care and Service Occupations
19-0000	Life, Physical, and Social Science Occupations	41-0000	Sales and Related Occupations
21-0000	Community and Social Services Occupations	43-0000	Office and Administrative Support Occupations
23-0000	Legal Occupations	45-0000	Farming, Fishing, and Forestry Occupations
25-0000	Education, Training, and Library Occupations	47-0000	Construction and Extraction Occupations
27-0000	Arts, Design, Entertainment, Sports, and Media Occupations	49-0000	Installation, Maintenance, and Repair Occupations
29-0000	Healthcare Practitioners and Technical Occupations	51-0000	Production Occupations
31-0000	Healthcare Support Occupations	53-0000	Transportation and Material Moving Occupations
33-0000	Protective Service Occupations	55-0000	Military Specific Occupations

Occupations with similar skills or work activities are grouped at each of the four levels of hierarchy for easier comparisons. Within these 23 major groups are

- **96 minor groups.** For example, Life, Physical and Social Science Occupations (19-0000) is divided into four minor groups: Life Scientists (19-1000), Physical Scientists (19-2000), Social Scientists and Related Workers (19-3000), and Life, Physical and Social Science Technicians (19-4000).

- **449 broad occupations.** For example, Life Scientists contains broad occupations such as Agriculture and Food Scientists (19-1010) and Biological Scientists (19-1020).

- **821 detailed occupations.** For example, the broad occupation Biological Scientists includes detailed occupations such as Biochemists and Biophysicists (19-1021) and Microbiologists (19-1022).

A broad occupation includes detailed occupations with different titles where necessary. For example, the broad occupation of Psychologists includes the more detailed occupation of Industrial-Organizational Psychologists for those requiring further detail. But if there is little confusion about the content of a detailed occupation, it has the same title as the broad occupation (for example, Lawyers).

As you can see from the table below, each item in the hierarchy is designated by a six-digit code. The hyphen between the second and third digits is used only for presentation clarity. The first two digits of the SOC code represent the major group; the third digit represents the minor group; the fourth and fifth digits represent the broad occupation; and the detailed occupation is represented by the sixth digit.

Also, major group codes end with 0000 (for example, 33-0000, Protective Service Occupations), minor groups end with 000 (for example, 33-2000, Fire Fighting and Prevention Workers), and broad occupations end with 0 (for example, 33-2020, Fire Inspectors). Codes not ending in zero are for detailed occupations (for example, 33-2021, Fire Inspectors and Investigators and 33-2022, Forest Fire Inspectors and Prevention Specialists).

SOC Level	Represented by	Example
Major group	first and second digits	**33**-0000 Protective Service Occupations
Minor group	third digit	33-**2**000 Fire Fighting and Prevention Workers
Broad occupation	fourth and fifth digits	33-2**020** Fire Inspectors
Detailed occupation	sixth digit	33-2021 Fire Inspectors and Investigators
Detailed occupation	sixth digit	33-202**2** Forest Fire Inspectors and Prevention Specialists

All residuals ("Other," "Miscellaneous," or "All Other"), whether at the detailed or broad occupation or minor group level, contain a 9 at the level of the residual. Detailed residual occupations end in 9 (for example, 33-9199, Protective Service Workers, All Other); broad occupations that are minor group residuals end in 90 (for example, 33-9190, Miscellaneous Protective Service Workers); and minor groups that are major group residuals end in 9000 (for example, 33-9000, Other Protective Service Workers):

33-0000 Protective Service Occupations
   33-9000 Other Protective Service Workers
      33-9190 Miscellaneous Protective Service Workers
         33-9199 Protective Service Workers, All Other

If there are more than 9 broad occupations in a minor group (or more than 8, if there is no residual), the xx-x090 is skipped (reserved for residuals), the xx-x000 is skipped (reserved for minor groups), and the numbering system goes to xx-x110. The residual broad occupation is then xx-x190 or xx-x290 (for example, 51-9190, Miscellaneous Production Workers).

The SOC occupational groups and detailed occupations are not always consecutively numbered, both to accommodate these coding conventions and to allow for the insertion of additional occupational groups in future revisions of the SOC.

SOC Guidelines for Classifying Workers

To ensure that all users of occupational data classify workers in the same way, the following classification principles are followed:

1. The classification covers all occupations in which work is performed for pay or profit, including work performed in family-operated enterprises by family members who are not directly compensated. It excludes occupations unique to volunteers. Each occupation is assigned to only one occupational category at the lowest level of the classification.

2. Occupations are classified based upon work performed, skills, education, training, and credentials.

3. Supervisors of professional and technical workers usually have a background similar to the workers they supervise and are therefore classified with the workers they supervise. Likewise, team leaders, lead workers, and supervisors of production, sales, and service workers who spend at least 20 percent of their time performing work similar to the workers they supervise are classified with the workers they supervise.

4. First-line managers and supervisors of production, service, and sales workers who spend more than 80 percent of their time performing supervisory activities are classified separately in the appropriate supervisor category, since their work activities are distinct from those of the workers they supervise. First-line managers are generally found in smaller establishments where they perform both supervisory and management functions, such as accounting, marketing, and personnel work.

5. Apprentices and trainees should be classified with the occupations for which they are being trained, while helpers and aides should be classified separately.

6. If an occupation is not included as a distinct detailed occupation in the structure, it is classified in the appropriate residual occupation. Residual occupations contain all occupations within a major, minor, or broad group that are not classified separately.

7. When workers may be classified in more than one occupation, they should be classified in the occupation that requires the highest level of skill. If there is no measurable difference in skill requirements, workers are included in the occupation in which they spend the most time.

8. Data collection and reporting agencies should classify workers at the most detailed level possible. Different agencies may use different levels of aggregation, depending on their ability to collect data and the requirements of users.

Occupational Definitions

Each detailed occupation has a description, called a "definition," that uniquely defines the workers that are included. Definitions begin with tasks that all workers in the occupation are expected to perform. The qualifier "may" precedes duties that only some workers perform. Where a definition includes duties also performed by workers in another occupation, cross-references to the occupation are given.

Examples of Associated Titles

Workers within an occupation may have many different job titles. The associated titles list will be available through the Census Bureau to help users classify workers into the appropriate SOC occupation. Sometimes, however, a job title is not enough to classify a worker, and more information on work activities is needed. When a job title changes classification based on industry, the industries are also included. This book includes examples of associated titles for many occupations, but the listings are not yet complete.

For More Details on the SOC Occupations and Revision

For sources of more information on occupations in the SOC, see Appendix A (question 2) and Appendix C.

For more information on the SOC's background and revision process, see Appendix B.

SOC OCCUPATIONAL STRUCTURE AND DEFINITIONS

This is the book's main section. It shows the four-level SOC structure, plus SOC codes, job titles, definitions for the detailed occupations, and examples of associated job titles.

Refer to the introduction for an explanation of the SOC hierarchy and a sample definition with key elements highlighted.

11-0000 MANAGEMENT OCCUPATIONS

11-1000 Top Executives

11-1010 CHIEF EXECUTIVES

This broad occupation is the same as the detailed occupation:
11-1011 Chief Executives

11-1011 Chief Executives

Determine and formulate policies and provide the overall direction of companies or private and public sector organizations, within the guidelines set up by a board of directors or similar governing body. Plan, direct, or coordinate operational activities at the highest level of management, with the help of subordinate executives and staff managers. **Examples:** Board Member; Chief Operating Officer; President.

11-1020 GENERAL AND OPERATIONS MANAGERS

This broad occupation is the same as the detailed occupation:
11-1021 General and Operations Managers

11-1021 General and Operations Managers

Plan, direct, or coordinate the operations of companies or public and private sector organizations. Formulate policies, manage daily operations, and plan the use of materials and human resources. Perform duties that are too diverse and general in nature to be classified in any one functional area of management or administration such as personnel, purchasing, or administrative services. Includes owners and managers who head small business establishments and whose duties are primarily managerial. Excludes "First-Line Supervisors/Managers of Retail Sales Workers" (41-1011) and workers in other small establishments. **Examples:** Industrial Organization Manager; District Manager; Department Store General Manager.

11-1030 Legislators

This broad occupation is the same as the detailed occupation:
11-1031 Legislators

11-1031 Legislators

Develop laws and statutes at the federal, state, or local level. Includes only elected officials. **Examples:** Representative; Council Member; Senator.

11-2000 Advertising, Marketing, Promotions, Public Relations, and Sales Managers

11-2010 Advertising and Promotions Managers

This broad occupation is the same as the detailed occupation:
11-2011 Advertising and Promotions Managers

11-2011 Advertising and Promotions Managers

Plan and direct advertising policies and programs, or produce collateral materials such as posters, contests, coupons, or give-aways, to create extra interest in the purchase of a product or service for a department, an entire organization, or for one account. **Examples:** Campaign Director; Circulation Director; Media Director.

11-2020 Marketing and Sales Managers

This broad occupation includes the following two detailed occupations:
11-2021 Marketing Managers
11-2022 Sales Managers

11-2021 Marketing Managers

Determine the demand for products and services offered by a firm and its competitors; identify potential customers. Develop pricing strategies, with the goal of maximizing the firm's profits or share of the market while ensuring that the firm's customers are satisfied. Oversee product development; monitor trends that indicate the need for new products and services. **Examples:** Fashion Coordinator; Marketing Director.

11-2022 Sales Managers

Direct the actual distribution or movement of a product or service to the customer. Coordinate sales distribution by establishing sales territories, quotas, and goals; establish training programs for sales representatives. Analyze sales statistics gathered by staff, to determine sales potential and inventory requirements and to monitor the preferences of customers. **Examples:** Director of Sales; Export Manager; Regional Sales Manager.

11-2030 Public Relations Managers

This broad occupation is the same as the detailed occupation:
11-2031 Public Relations Managers

3 1833 04188 4443

11-2031 Public Relations Managers

Plan and direct public relations programs designed to create and maintain a favorable public image for employer or client. If engaged in fundraising, plan and direct activities to solicit and maintain funds for special projects and nonprofit organizations. **Examples:** Fundraising Director; Public Information Director; Publicity Director.

11-3000 Operations Specialties Managers

11-3010 Administrative Services Managers

This broad occupation is the same as the detailed occupation:
11-3011 Administrative Services Managers

11-3011 Administrative Services Managers

Plan, direct, or coordinate supportive services of an organization, such as record-keeping, mail distribution, telephone operator/receptionist, and other office support services. Oversee facilities planning and maintenance and custodial operations. Excludes "Purchasing Managers" (11-3061). **Examples:** Facilities Manager; Space Officer.

11-3020 Computer and Information Systems Managers

This broad occupation is the same as the detailed occupation:
11-3021 Computer and Information Systems Managers

11-3021 Computer and Information Systems Managers

Plan, direct, or coordinate activities in such fields as electronic data processing, information systems, systems analysis, and computer programming. Excludes "Computer Specialists" (15-1011 through 15-1099). **Examples:** Data Processing Manager; Computer Programming Manager; Data Systems Manager.

11-3030 Financial Managers

This broad occupation is the same as the detailed occupation:
11-3031 Financial Managers

11-3031 Financial Managers

Plan, direct, and coordinate accounting, investing, banking, insurance, securities, and other financial activities of a branch office or department of an establishment. **Examples:** Bank Director; Comptroller; Budget Director.

11-3040 Human Resources Managers

This broad occupation includes the following three detailed occupations:
11-3041 Compensation and Benefits Managers
11-3042 Training and Development Managers
11-3049 Human Resources Managers, All Other

11-3041 Compensation and Benefits Managers

Plan, direct, or coordinate compensation and benefits activities and staff of an organization. Includes job analysis and position description managers. **Examples:** Employee Benefits Director; Job Analysis Manager; Wage and Salary Administrator.

11-3042 Training and Development Managers

Plan, direct, or coordinate the training and development activities and staff of an organization. **Examples:** Efficiency Manager; Education and Training Manager; Training Director.

11-3049 Human Resources Managers, All Other

All human resources managers not listed separately. **Examples:** Director of Industrial Relations; Employee Wellness/Fitness Coordinator; Personnel Director.

11-3050 Industrial Production Managers

This broad occupation is the same as the detailed occupation:
11-3051 Industrial Production Managers

11-3051 Industrial Production Managers

Plan, direct, or coordinate the work activities and resources necessary for manufacturing products in accordance with cost, quality, and quantity specifications. **Examples:** Factory Superintendent; Plant Manager; Quality Control Manager.

11-3060 Purchasing Managers

This broad occupation is the same as the detailed occupation:
11-3061 Purchasing Managers

11-3061 Purchasing Managers

Plan, direct, or coordinate the activities of buyers, purchasing officers, and related workers involved in purchasing materials, products, and services. Includes wholesale or retail trade merchandising managers and procurement managers. **Examples:** Director of Purchasing; Merchandise Manager; Procurement Manager.

11-3070 Transportation, Storage, and Distribution Managers

This broad occupation is the same as the detailed occupation:
11-3071 Transportation, Storage, and Distribution Managers

11-3071 Transportation, Storage, and Distribution Managers

Plan, direct, or coordinate transportation, storage, or distribution activities in accordance with governmental policies and regulations. Includes logistics managers. **Examples:** Airport Manager; Schedule Planning Manager; Warehouse Manager.

11-9000 Other Management Occupations

11-9010 Agricultural Managers

This broad occupation includes the following two detailed occupations:
11-9011 Farm, Ranch, and Other Agricultural Managers
11-9012 Farmers and Ranchers

11-9011 Farm, Ranch, and Other Agricultural Managers

Manage farms, ranches, aquacultural operations, greenhouses, nurseries, timber tracts, cotton gins, packing houses, or other agricultural establishments for employers. Carry out production, financial, and marketing decisions relating to the managed operations, following guidelines from the owner. Contract tenant farmers or producers to carry out the day-to-day activities of the managed operation. Supervise planting, cultivating, harvesting, and marketing activities. Prepare cost, production, and other records. Perform physical work and operate machinery. **Examples:** Fruit Grower; Farm Livestock Manager; Nursery and Greenhouse Manager.

11-9012 Farmers and Ranchers

Operate farms, ranches, greenhouses, nurseries, timber tracts, or other agricultural production establishments which produce crops, horticultural specialties, livestock, poultry, finfish, shellfish, or animal specialties, on an ownership or rental basis. Plant, cultivate, harvest, perform post-harvest activities, and market crops and livestock. Hire, train, and supervise farm workers, or supervise a farm labor contractor. Prepare cost, production, and other records. Maintain and operate machinery and perform physical work. Includes operators of cotton gins, packing houses, and other post-harvest operations. **Examples:** Beekeeper; Dairy Farmer; Tobacco Grower.

11-9020 Construction Managers

This broad occupation is the same as the detailed occupation:
11-9021 Construction Managers

11-9021 Construction Managers

Plan, direct, coordinate, or budget, usually through subordinate supervisory personnel, activities concerned with the construction and maintenance of structures, facilities, and systems. Participate in the conceptual development of a construction project; oversee its organization, scheduling, and implementation. Includes managers in specialized construction fields such as carpentry or plumbing. Includes general superintendents, project managers, and constructors who manage, coordinate, and supervise the construction process. **Examples:** Masonry Contractor Administrator; Developer; General Contractor.

11-9030 Education Administrators

This broad occupation includes the following four detailed occupations:
11-9031 Education Administrators, Preschool and Child Care Center/Program
11-9032 Education Administrators, Elementary and Secondary School
11-9033 Education Administrators, Postsecondary
11-9039 Education Administrators, All Other

11-9031 Education Administrators, Preschool and Child Care Center/Program

Plan, direct, or coordinate the academic and nonacademic activities of preschool and child care centers or programs. Excludes "Preschool Teachers" (25-2011). **Examples:** Director of Child Care Center; Head Start Director.

11-9032 Education Administrators, Elementary and Secondary School

Plan, direct, or coordinate the academic, clerical, or auxiliary activities of public or private elementary or secondary level schools. **Examples:** Director of Physical Education; Curriculum Director; School Principal.

11-9033 Education Administrators, Postsecondary

Plan, direct, or coordinate research, instruction, student administration, student services, and other educational activities at postsecondary institutions including universities, colleges, junior colleges, and community colleges. **Examples:** Director of Student Affairs; Dean; Registrar.

11-9039 Education Administrators, All Other

All education administrators not listed separately. **Examples:** Director of Extension Work; Director of Vocational Training; Health Education Director.

11-9040 Engineering Managers

This broad occupation is the same as the detailed occupation:
11-9041 Engineering Managers

11-9041 Engineering Managers

Plan, direct, or coordinate activities in such fields as architecture and engineering. Plan, direct, or coordinate research and development in these fields. Excludes "Natural Sciences Managers" (11-9121). **Examples:** Engineering Research Manager; Safety Director; Technical Director.

11-9050 Food Service Managers

This broad occupation is the same as the detailed occupation:
11-9051 Food Service Managers

11-9051 Food Service Managers

Plan, direct, or coordinate activities of an organization or department that serves food and beverages. **Examples:** Banquet Director; Restaurant Manager; Catering Manager.

11-9060 Funeral Directors

This broad occupation is the same as the detailed occupation:
11-9061 Funeral Directors

11-9061 Funeral Directors

Perform various tasks to arrange and direct funeral services, such as coordinating transportation of body to mortuary for embalming, interviewing family or other authorized person to arrange details, selecting pallbearers, procuring official for religious rites, and providing transportation for mourners. **Examples:** Mortician; Funeral Home Manager; Undertaker.

11-9070 Gaming Managers

This broad occupation is the same as the detailed occupation:
11-9071 Gaming Managers

11-9071 Gaming Managers

Plan, organize, direct, control, or coordinate gaming operations in a casino. Formulate gaming policies for an assigned area of responsibility. **Examples:** Casino Manager; Blackjack Manager; Dice Manager.

11-9080 Lodging Managers

This broad occupation is the same as the detailed occupation:
11-9081 Lodging Managers

11-9081 Lodging Managers

Plan, direct, or coordinate activities of an organization or department that provides lodging and other accommodations. Excludes "Food Service Managers" (11-9051) in lodging establishments. **Examples:** Director of Housing; Innkeeper; Hotel Manager.

11-9110 Medical and Health Services Managers

This broad occupation is the same as the detailed occupation:
11-9111 Medical and Health Services Managers

11-9111 Medical and Health Services Managers

Plan, direct, or coordinate medicine and health services in hospitals, clinics, managed care organizations, public health agencies, or similar organizations. **Examples:** Director of Occupational Therapy; Medical Records Administrator; Public Health Administrator.

11-9120 Natural Sciences Managers

This broad occupation is the same as the detailed occupation:
11-9121 Natural Sciences Managers

11-9121 Natural Sciences Managers

Plan, direct, or coordinate activities in such fields as life sciences, physical sciences, mathematics, and statistics. Plan, direct, or coordinate research and development in these fields. Excludes "Engineering Managers" (11-9041) and "Computer and Information Systems Managers" (11-3021). **Examples:** Geophysical Manager; Research and Development Director; Wildlife Manager.

11-9130 Postmasters and Mail Superintendents

This broad occupation is the same as the detailed occupation:
11-9131 Postmasters and Mail Superintendents

11-9131 Postmasters and Mail Superintendents

Direct and coordinate operational, administrative, management, and supportive services of a U.S. post office. Coordinate activities of workers engaged in postal and related work in assigned post office.

11-9140 Property, Real Estate, and Community Association Managers

This broad occupation is the same as the detailed occupation:
11-9141 Property, Real Estate, and Community Association Managers

11-9141 Property, Real Estate, and Community Association Managers

Plan, direct, or coordinate selling, buying, leasing, or governance activities of commercial, industrial, or residential real estate properties. Includes managers of homeowner and condominium associations, rented or leased housing units, buildings, or land (including rights-of-way). **Examples:** Condominium Association Manager; Trailer Park Manager.

11-9150 Social and Community Service Managers

This broad occupation is the same as the detailed occupation:
11-9151 Social and Community Service Managers

11-9151 Social and Community Service Managers

Plan, organize, or coordinate the activities of a social service program or community outreach organization. Oversee the program or organization's budget and policies regarding participant involvement, program requirements, and benefits. Direct social workers, counselors, or probation officers. **Examples:** Child Welfare Director; Youth Program Director; Director of Casework Services.

11-9190 Miscellaneous Managers

This broad occupation is the same as the detailed occupation:
11-9199 Managers, All Other

11-9199 Managers, All Other

All managers not listed separately. **Examples:** City Clerk; Publisher; Communications Manager.

13-0000 BUSINESS AND FINANCIAL OPERATIONS OCCUPATIONS

13-1000 Business Operations Specialists

13-1010 Agents and Business Managers of Artists, Performers, and Athletes

This broad occupation is the same as the detailed occupation:
13-1011 Agents and Business Managers of Artists, Performers, and Athletes

13-1011 Agents and Business Managers of Artists, Performers, and Athletes

Represent and promote artists, performers, and athletes to prospective employers. Handle contract negotiations and other business matters for clients. **Examples:** Booking Agent; Boxing Promoter; Theatrical Agent.

13-1020 Buyers and Purchasing Agents

This broad occupation includes the following three detailed occupations:
13-1021 Purchasing Agents and Buyers, Farm Products
13-1022 Wholesale and Retail Buyers, Except Farm Products
13-1023 Purchasing Agents, Except Wholesale, Retail, and Farm Products

13-1021 Purchasing Agents and Buyers, Farm Products

Purchase farm products either for further processing or for resale. Includes Christmas tree contractors, grain brokers, market operators, grain buyers, and tobacco buyers. **Examples:** Cotton Broker; Livestock Buyer; Tobacco Buyer.

13-1022 Wholesale and Retail Buyers, Except Farm Products

Buy merchandise or commodities, other than farm products, for resale to consumers at the wholesale or retail level, including both durable and nondurable goods. Analyze past buying trends, sales records, price, and quality of merchandise, to determine value and yield. Select, order, and authorize payment for merchandise according to contractual agreements. Conduct meetings with sales personnel; introduce new products. Includes assistant buyers. **Examples:** Importer; Merchandiser; Wholesale Jobber.

13-1023 Purchasing Agents, Except Wholesale, Retail, and Farm Products

Purchase machinery, equipment, tools, parts, supplies, or services necessary for the operation of an establishment. Purchase raw or semifinished materials for manufacturing. Includes contract specialists, field contractors, purchasers, price analysts, tooling coordinators, and media buyers. Excludes "Purchasing Agents and Buyers, Farm Products" (13-1021) and "Wholesale and Retail Buyers, Except Farm Products" (13-1022). **Examples:** Fuel Buyer; Lumber Buyer; Radio Time Buyer.

13-1030 Claims Adjusters, Appraisers, Examiners, and Investigators

This broad occupation includes the following two detailed occupations:
13-1031 Claims Adjusters, Examiners, and Investigators
13-1032 Insurance Appraisers, Auto Damage

13-1031 Claims Adjusters, Examiners, and Investigators

Review settled claims to determine that payments and settlements have been made in accordance with company practices and procedures and to ensure that proper methods have been followed. Report overpayments, underpayments, and other irregularities. Confer with legal counsel on claims requiring litigation. **Examples:** Health Insurance Adjuster; Arson Investigator; Claims Agent.

13-1032 Insurance Appraisers, Auto Damage

Appraise automobile or other vehicle damage to determine cost of repair for insurance claim settlement. Seek agreement with automotive repair shop on cost of repair. Prepare insurance forms to indicate repair cost, cost estimates, and recommendations. **Example:** Auto Damage Estimator.

13-1040 Compliance Officers, Except Agriculture, Construction, Health and Safety, and Transportation

This broad occupation is the same as the detailed occupation:
13-1041 Compliance Officers, Except Agriculture, Construction, Health and Safety, and Transportation

13-1041 Compliance Officers, Except Agriculture, Construction, Health and Safety, and Transportation

Examine, evaluate, and investigate eligibility for or conformity with laws and regulations governing contract compliance of licenses and permits. Perform other compliance and enforcement inspection activities not classified elsewhere. Excludes "Tax Examiners, Collectors, and Revenue Agents" (13-2081) and "Financial Examiners" (13-2061). **Examples:** Truant Officer; Coroner; Inspector of Weights and Measures.

13-1050 Cost Estimators

This broad occupation is the same as the detailed occupation:
13-1051 Cost Estimators

13-1051 Cost Estimators

Prepare cost estimates for product manufacturing, construction projects, or services, to aid management in bidding on or determining price of product or service. Specialize according to particular service performed or type of product manufactured. **Examples:** Construction Estimator; Crating and Moving Estimator; Job Estimator.

13-1060 Emergency Management Specialists

This broad occupation is the same as the detailed occupation:
13-1061 Emergency Management Specialists

13-1061 Emergency Management Specialists

Coordinate disaster response or crisis management activities; provide disaster preparedness training. Prepare emergency plans and procedures for natural disasters such as hurricanes, floods, and earthquakes; for wartime disasters; for technological disasters such as nuclear power plant emergencies or hazardous materials spills; or for hostage situations. **Examples:** Director of Civil Defense; Public Safety Director.

13-1070 Human Resources, Training, and Labor Relations Specialists

This broad occupation includes the following four detailed occupations:
13-1071 Employment, Recruitment, and Placement Specialists
13-1072 Compensation, Benefits, and Job Analysis Specialists
13-1073 Training and Development Specialists
13-1079 Human Resources, Training, and Labor Relations Specialists, All Other

13-1071 Employment, Recruitment, and Placement Specialists

Recruit and place workers. **Examples:** Employment Interviewer; Personnel Recruiter; Placement Assistant.

13-1072 Compensation, Benefits, and Job Analysis Specialists

Conduct programs of compensation, benefits, and job analysis for employer. Specialize in specific areas such as position classification and pension programs. **Examples:** Occupational Analyst; Relocation Director; Wage Conciliator.

13-1073 Training and Development Specialists

Conduct training and development programs for employees. **Examples:** Training Coordinator; Workforce Development Specialist; Supervisor, Training Personnel.

13-1079 Human Resources, Training, and Labor Relations Specialists, All Other

All human resources, training, and labor relations specialists not listed separately. **Examples:** Personnel Arbitrator; Employee Relations Specialist.

13-1080 Logisticians

This broad occupation is the same as the detailed occupation:
13-1081 Logisticians

13-1081 Logisticians

Analyze and coordinate the logistical functions of a firm or organization. Assume responsibility for the entire life cycle of a product, including acquisition, distribution, internal allocation, delivery, and final disposal of resources. **Examples:** Logistics Engineer; Logistics Analyst; Logistics Planner.

13-1110 Management Analysts

This broad occupation is the same as the detailed occupation:
13-1111 Management Analysts

13-1111 Management Analysts

Conduct organizational studies and evaluations. Design systems and procedures. Conduct work simplifications and measurement studies. Prepare operations and procedures manuals to assist management in operating more efficiently and effectively. Includes program analysts and management consultants. Excludes "Computer Systems Analysts" (15-1051) and "Operations Research Analysts" (15-2031). **Examples:** Business Consultant; Industrial Analyst; Price Analyst.

13-1120 Meeting and Convention Planners

This broad occupation is the same as the detailed occupation:
13-1121 Meeting and Convention Planners

13-1121 Meeting and Convention Planners

Coordinate activities of staff and convention personnel to make arrangements for group meetings and conventions. **Examples:** Conference Planner; Conference Service Coordinator; Convention Manager.

13-0000
Business and
Financial
Operations
Occupations

13-1190 Miscellaneous Business Operations Specialists

This broad occupation is the same as the detailed occupation:
13-1199 Business Operations Specialists, All Other

13-1199 Business Operations Specialists, All Other

All business operations specialists not listed separately. **Examples:** Grant Coordinator; Liaison Officer; Purser.

13-2000 Financial Specialists

13-2010 Accountants and Auditors

This broad occupation is the same as the detailed occupation:
13-2011 Accountants and Auditors

13-2011 Accountants and Auditors

Examine, analyze, and interpret accounting records for the purpose of giving advice or preparing statements. Install or advise on systems of recording costs or other financial and budgetary data. **Examples:** Bursar; Certified Public Accountant; Tax Accountant.

13-2020 Appraisers and Assessors of Real Estate

This broad occupation is the same as the detailed occupation:
13-2021 Appraisers and Assessors of Real Estate

13-2021 Appraisers and Assessors of Real Estate

Appraise real property to determine its fair value. Assess taxes in accordance with prescribed schedules. **Examples:** Building Appraiser; County Assessor; Property Evaluator.

13-2030 Budget Analysts

This broad occupation is the same as the detailed occupation:
13-2031 Budget Analysts

13-2031 Budget Analysts

Examine budget estimates for completeness, accuracy, and conformance with procedures and regulations. Analyze budgeting and accounting reports for the purpose of maintaining expenditure controls. **Examples:** Budget Examiner; Fiscal Agent; Fiscal Officer.

13-2040 Credit Analysts

This broad occupation is the same as the detailed occupation:
13-2041 Credit Analysts

13-2041 Credit Analysts

Analyze current credit data and financial statements of individuals or firms to determine the degree of risk involved in extending credit or lending money. Prepare reports with this credit information, for use in decision making. **Examples:** Credit Negotiator; Escrow Representative; Factorer.

13-2050 Financial Analysts and Advisors

This broad occupation includes the following three detailed occupations:
13-2051 Financial Analysts
13-2052 Personal Financial Advisors
13-2053 Insurance Underwriters

13-2051 Financial Analysts

Conduct quantitative analyses of information affecting investment programs of public or private institutions. **Examples:** Bond Analyst; Investment Analyst; Securities Consultant.

13-2052 Personal Financial Advisors

Advise clients on financial plans, utilizing knowledge of tax and investment strategies, securities, insurance, pension plans, and real estate. Assess clients' assets, liabilities, cash flow, insurance coverage, tax status, and financial objectives, to establish investment strategies. **Examples:** Budget Counselor; Financial Planner; Estate Planner.

13-2053 Insurance Underwriters

Review individual applications for insurance, to evaluate degree of risk involved and to determine acceptance of applications. **Examples:** Bond Underwriter; Insurance Analyst.

13-2060 Financial Examiners

This broad occupation is the same as the detailed occupation:
13-2061 Financial Examiners

13-2061 Financial Examiners

Enforce or ensure compliance with laws and regulations governing financial and securities institutions and governing financial and real estate transactions. Examine, verify correctness of, or establish authenticity of records. **Examples:** Bank Examiner; Payroll Examiner; Pension Examiner.

13-2070 Loan Counselors and Officers

This broad occupation includes the following two detailed occupations:
13-2071 Loan Counselors
13-2072 Loan Officers

13-2071 Loan Counselors

Provide guidance to prospective loan applicants who have problems qualifying for traditional loans. Assist applicants in determining the best type of loan; explain loan requirements or restrictions. **Examples:** Credit Counselor; Farm Mortgage Agent; Financial Aid Counselor.

13-2072 Loan Officers

Evaluate, authorize, or recommend approval of commercial, real estate, or credit loans. Advise borrowers on financial status and methods of payments. Includes mortgage loan officers and agents, collection analysts, loan servicing officers, and loan underwriters. **Examples:** Loan Reviewer; Escrow Officer; Mortgage Consultant.

13-2080 Tax Examiners, Collectors, Preparers, and Revenue Agents

This broad occupation includes the following two detailed occupations:
13-2081 Tax Examiners, Collectors, and Revenue Agents
13-2082 Tax Preparers

13-2081 Tax Examiners, Collectors, and Revenue Agents

Determine tax liability of or collect taxes from individuals or business firms, according to prescribed laws and regulations. **Examples:** Tax Investigator; Revenue Agent; Tax Auditor.

13-2082 Tax Preparers

Prepare tax returns for individuals or small businesses, without having the background or responsibilities of an accredited or certified public accountant. **Examples:** Income Tax Advisor; Income Tax Consultant; Tax Specialist.

13-2090 Miscellaneous Financial Specialists

This broad occupation is the same as the detailed occupation:
13-2099 Financial Specialists, All Other

13-2099 Financial Specialists, All Other

All financial specialists not listed separately. **Examples:** Bail Bondsman; Executor of Estate; Foreign Exchange Trader.

15-0000 COMPUTER AND MATHEMATICAL OCCUPATIONS

15-1000 Computer Specialists

15-1010 Computer and Information Scientists, Research

This broad occupation is the same as the detailed occupation:
15-1011 Computer and Information Scientists, Research

15-1011 Computer and Information Scientists, Research

Conduct research into fundamental computer and information science as theorists, designers, or inventors. Solve or develop solutions to problems in the field of computer hardware and software.

15-1020 Computer Programmers

This broad occupation is the same as the detailed occupation:
15-1021 Computer Programmers

15-1021 Computer Programmers

Convert project specifications and statements of problems and procedures into detailed logical flow charts, for coding into computer language. Develop and write computer programs to store, locate, and retrieve specific documents, data, and information. Program web sites. **Examples:** Computer Programmer Aide; Mainframe Programmer; Systems Programmer.

15-1030 Computer Software Engineers

This broad occupation includes the following two detailed occupations:
15-1031 Computer Software Engineers, Applications
15-1032 Computer Software Engineers, Systems Software

15-1031 Computer Software Engineers, Applications

Develop, create, and modify general computer applications software or specialized utility programs. Analyze user needs and develop software solutions. Design or customize software for client use, with the aim of optimizing operational efficiency. Analyze and design databases within an application area, working individually or coordinating database development as part of a team. Excludes "Computer Hardware Engineers" (17-2061). **Examples:** Applications Developer; Programmer Analyst; Software Designer.

15-1032 Computer Software Engineers, Systems Software

Research, design, develop, and test operating systems-level software, compilers, and network distribution software, for medical, industrial, military, communications, aerospace, business, scientific, and general computing applications. Set operational specifications; formulate and analyze software requirements. Apply principles and techniques of computer science, engineering, and mathematical analysis. **Example:** EDP Systems Engineers.

15-1040 Computer Support Specialists

This broad occupation is the same as the detailed occupation:
15-1041 Computer Support Specialists

15-1041 Computer Support Specialists

Provide technical assistance to computer system users. Answer questions or resolve computer problems for clients in person, via telephone, or from remote location. Provide assistance concerning the use of computer hardware and software, including printing, installation, word processing, electronic mail, and operating systems. Excludes "Network and Computer Systems Administrators" (15-1071). **Examples:** Customer Support Analyst; Help Desk Technician; Work Station Support Specialist.

15-1050 Computer Systems Analysts

This broad occupation is the same as the detailed occupation:
15-1051 Computer Systems Analysts

15-1051 Computer Systems Analysts

Analyze science, engineering, business, and all other data-processing problems, for application to electronic data-processing systems. Analyze user requirements, procedures, and problems, to automate or improve existing systems; review computer system capabilities, workflow, and scheduling limitations. Analyze or recommend commercially available software. Supervise computer programmers. Excludes persons working primarily as "Engineers" (17-2011 through 17-2199), "Mathematicians" (15-2021), or "Scientists" (19-1011 through 19-3099). **Examples:** Health Systems Computer Analyst; Data Processing Systems Project Planner; Information Systems Consultant.

15-1060 Database Administrators

This broad occupation is the same as the detailed occupation:
15-1061 Database Administrators

15-1061 Database Administrators

Coordinate changes to computer databases. Test and implement the database, applying knowledge of database management systems. Plan, coordinate, and implement security measures to safeguard computer databases. **Examples:** Automatic Data Processing Planner; Data Base Design Analyst; Database Security Administrator.

15-1070 Network and Computer Systems Administrators

This broad occupation is the same as the detailed occupation:
15-1071 Network and Computer Systems Administrators

15-1071 Network and Computer Systems Administrators

Install, configure, and support an organization's local area network (LAN), wide area network (WAN), Internet system, or a segment of a network system. Maintain network hardware and software. Monitor network to ensure network availability to all system users; perform necessary maintenance to support network availability. Supervise other network support and client server specialists. Plan, coordinate, and implement network security measures. Excludes "Computer Support Specialists" (15-1041). **Examples:** LAN/WAN Administrator; Network Control Operator; Network Security Administrator.

15-1080 Network Systems and Data Communications Analysts

This broad occupation is the same as the detailed occupation:
15-1081 Network Systems and Data Communications Analysts

15-1081 Network Systems and Data Communications Analysts

Analyze, design, test, and evaluate network systems, such as local area networks (LAN), wide area networks (WAN), Internet, intranet, and other data communications systems. Perform network modeling, analysis, and planning. Research and recommend network and data communications hardware and software. Supervise computer programmers. Includes telecommunications specialists who deal with the interfacing of computer and communications equipment. **Examples:** Internet Developer; Systems Integrator; Webmaster.

15-1090 Miscellaneous Computer Specialists

This broad occupation is the same as the detailed occupation:
15-1099 Computer Specialists, All Other

15-1099 Computer Specialists, All Other

All computer specialists not listed separately. **Example:** Computer Laboratory Technician.

15-2000 Mathematical Science Occupations

15-2010 Actuaries

This broad occupation is the same as the detailed occupation:
15-2011 Actuaries

15-2011 Actuaries

Analyze statistical data such as mortality, accident, sickness, disability, and retirement rates; construct probability tables to forecast risk and liability for payment of future benefits. Ascertain premium rates required and cash reserves necessary to ensure payment of future benefits. **Example:** Actuarial Mathematician.

15-2020 Mathematicians

This broad occupation is the same as the detailed occupation:
15-2021 Mathematicians

15-2021 Mathematicians

Conduct research in fundamental mathematics or in application of mathematical techniques to science, management, and other fields. Solve or direct the solution of problems in various fields, by mathematical methods. **Examples:** Algebraist; Cipher Expert; Cryptographer.

15-2030 Operations Research Analysts

This broad occupation is the same as the detailed occupation:
15-2031 Operations Research Analysts

15-2031 Operations Research Analysts

Formulate and apply mathematical modeling and other optimizing methods, using a computer to develop and interpret information that assists management with decision making, policy formulation, or other managerial functions. Develop related software, service, or products. Concentrate on collecting and analyzing data and developing decision support software. Develop and supply optimal time, cost, or logistics networks for program evaluation, review, or implementation. **Examples:** Procedure Analyst; Method Consultant; Standards Analyst.

15-2040 Statisticians

This broad occupation is the same as the detailed occupation:
15-2041 Statisticians

15-2041 Statisticians

Engage in the development of mathematical theory or apply statistical theory and methods to collect, organize, interpret, and summarize numerical data to provide usable information. May specialize in fields, such as bio-statistics, agricultural statistics, business statistics, economic statistics, or other fields. Includes mathematical statisticians. **Examples:** Biometrician; Sampling Expert; Statistical Analyst.

15-2090 Miscellaneous Mathematical Scientists

This broad occupation includes the following two detailed occupations:
15-2091 Mathematical Technicians
15-2099 Mathematical Scientists, All Other

15-2091 Mathematical Technicians

Apply standardized mathematical formulas, principles, and methodology to technological problems in engineering and physical sciences, in relation to specific industrial and research objectives, processes, equipment, and products.

15-2099 Mathematical Scientists, All Other

All mathematical scientists not listed separately. **Examples:** Geometrician; Harmonic Analyst; Weight Analyst.

15-0000
Computer and
Mathematical
Occupations

17-0000 ARCHITECTURE AND ENGINEERING OCCUPATIONS

17-1000 Architects, Surveyors, and Cartographers

17-1010 Architects, Except Naval

This broad occupation includes the following two detailed occupations:
17-1011 Architects, Except Landscape and Naval
17-1012 Landscape Architects

17-1011 Architects, Except Landscape and Naval

Plan and design structures such as private residences, office buildings, theaters, factories, and other structural property. **Examples:** Architectural Designer; Building Consultant; Site Planner.

17-1012 Landscape Architects

Plan and design land areas for such projects as parks, other recreational facilities, airports, highways, hospitals, schools, land subdivisions, and commercial, industrial, and residential sites. **Examples:** Environmental Planner; Land Planner; Landscape Designer.

17-1020 Surveyors, Cartographers, and Photogrammetrists

This broad occupation includes the following two detailed occupations:
17-1021 Cartographers and Photogrammetrists
17-1022 Surveyors

17-1021 Cartographers and Photogrammetrists

Collect, analyze, and interpret geographic information provided by geodetic surveys, aerial photographs, and satellite data. Research, study, and prepare maps and other spatial data in digital or graphic form, for legal, social, political, educational, and design purposes. Work with Geographic Information Systems (GIS). Design and evaluate algorithms, data structures, and user interfaces for GIS and mapping systems. **Examples:** Field Map Editor; Mapper; Topographer.

17-1022 Surveyors

Make exact measurements and determine property boundaries. Provide data relevant to the shape, contour, gravitation, location, elevation, or dimension of land or land features on or near the earth's surface, for engineering, mapmaking, mining, land evaluation, construction, and other purposes. **Examples:** Geodetic Surveyor; Land Examiner; Mineral Surveyor.

17-2000 Engineers

17-2010 Aerospace Engineers

This broad occupation is the same as the detailed occupation:
17-2011 Aerospace Engineers

17-2011 Aerospace Engineers

Perform a variety of engineering work in designing, constructing, and testing aircraft, missiles, and spacecraft. Conduct basic and applied research to evaluate adaptability of materials and equipment to aircraft design and manufacture. Recommend improvements in testing equipment and techniques. **Examples:** Aerodynamicist; Flight Test Engineer; Aeronautical Engineer.

17-2020 Agricultural Engineers

This broad occupation is the same as the detailed occupation:
17-2021 Agricultural Engineers

17-2021 Agricultural Engineers

Apply knowledge of engineering technology and biological science to agricultural problems concerned with power and machinery, electrification, structures, soil and water conservation, and processing of agricultural products. **Examples:** Farm Equipment Engineer; Agricultural Research Engineer.

17-2030 Biomedical Engineers

This broad occupation is the same as the detailed occupation:
17-2031 Biomedical Engineers

17-2031 Biomedical Engineers

Apply knowledge of engineering, biology, and biomechanical principles to the design, development, and evaluation of biological and health systems and products such as artificial organs, prostheses, instrumentation, medical information systems, and health management and care delivery systems. **Example:** Orthopedic Designer.

17-2040 Chemical Engineers

This broad occupation is the same as the detailed occupation:
17-2041 Chemical Engineers

17-2041 Chemical Engineers

Design chemical plant equipment and devise processes for manufacturing chemicals and products such as gasoline, synthetic rubber, plastics, detergents, cement, paper, and pulp, by applying principles and technology of chemistry, physics, and engineering. **Examples:** Absorption and Adsorption Engineer; Explosives Engineer; Fuels Engineer.

17-2050 Civil Engineers

This broad occupation is the same as the detailed occupation:
17-2051 Civil Engineers

17-2051 Civil Engineers

Perform engineering duties in planning, designing, and overseeing construction and maintenance of building structures and facilities such as roads, railroads, airports, bridges, harbors, channels, dams, irrigation projects, pipelines, power plants, water and sewage systems, and waste disposal units. Includes architectural, structural, traffic, ocean, and geotechnical engineers. Excludes "Hydrologists" (19-2043). **Examples:** Bridge Engineer; Construction Engineer; Concrete Engineer.

17-2060 Computer Hardware Engineers

This broad occupation is the same as the detailed occupation:
17-2061 Computer Hardware Engineers

17-2061 Computer Hardware Engineers

Research, design, develop, and test computer or computer-related equipment for commercial, industrial, military, or scientific use. Supervise the manufacturing and installation of computer or computer-related equipment and components. Excludes "Computer Software Engineers, Applications" (15-1031) and "Computer Software Engineers, Systems Software" (15-1032).

17-2070 Electrical and Electronics Engineers

This broad occupation includes the following two detailed occupations:
17-2071 Electrical Engineers
17-2072 Electronics Engineers, Except Computer

17-2071 Electrical Engineers

Design, develop, test, or supervise the manufacturing and installation of electrical equipment, components, or systems for commercial, industrial, military, or scientific use. Excludes "Computer Hardware Engineers" (17-2061). **Examples:** Power Distribution Engineer; Illuminating Engineer; Relay Engineer.

17-2072 Electronics Engineers, Except Computer

Research, design, develop, and test electronic components and systems for commercial, industrial, military, or scientific use, utilizing knowledge of electronic theory and materials properties. Design electronic circuits and components for use in fields such as telecommunications, aerospace guidance and propulsion control, acoustics, or instruments and controls. Excludes "Computer Hardware Engineers" (17-2061). **Examples:** Communications Engineer; Circuit Design Engineer; Guidance and Control Systems Engineer.

17-2080 Environmental Engineers

This broad occupation is the same as the detailed occupation:
17-2081 Environmental Engineers

17-2081 Environmental Engineers

Design, plan, or perform engineering duties in the prevention, control, and remediation of environmental health hazards, utilizing various engineering disciplines. Design, plan, or perform work involving waste treatment, site remediation, or pollution control technology. **Examples:** Soil Engineer; Industrial Hygiene Engineer; Pollution Control Engineer.

17-2110 Industrial Engineers, Including Health and Safety

This broad occupation includes the following two detailed occupations:
17-2111 Health and Safety Engineers, Except Mining Safety Engineers and Inspectors
17-2112 Industrial Engineers

17-2111 Health and Safety Engineers, Except Mining Safety Engineers and Inspectors

Promote worksite or product safety by applying knowledge of industrial processes, mechanics, chemistry, psychology, and industrial health and safety laws. Includes industrial product safety engineers. **Examples:** Fire-Protection Engineer; Industrial Health Engineer; Product Safety Engineer.

17-2112 Industrial Engineers

Design, develop, test, and evaluate integrated systems for managing industrial production processes, including human work factors, quality control, inventory control, logistics and material flow, cost analysis, and production coordination. Excludes "Health and Safety Engineers, Except Mining Safety Engineers and Inspectors" (17-2111). **Examples:** Packaging Engineer; Time Study Engineer; Plant Engineer.

17-2120 Marine Engineers and Naval Architects

This broad occupation is the same as the detailed occupation:
17-2121 Marine Engineers and Naval Architects

17-2121 Marine Engineers and Naval Architects

Design, develop, and evaluate the operation of marine vessels, ship machinery, and related equipment such as power supply and propulsion systems. **Examples:** Marine Architect; Port Engineer; Ship Surveyor.

17-2130 Materials Engineers

This broad occupation is the same as the detailed occupation:
17-2131 Materials Engineers

17-2131 Materials Engineers

Evaluate materials and develop machinery and processes to manufacture materials for use in products that must meet specialized design and performance specifications. Develop new uses for known materials. Includes those working with composite materials or specializing in one type of material such as graphite, metal and metal alloys, ceramics and glass, plastics and polymers, and naturally occurring materials. Includes metallurgists and metallurgical engineers, ceramic engineers, and welding engineers. **Examples:** Ceramic Engineer; Corrosion Engineer; Metallurgical Engineer.

17-2140 Mechanical Engineers

This broad occupation is the same as the detailed occupation:
17-2141 Mechanical Engineers

17-2141 Mechanical Engineers

Perform engineering duties in planning and designing tools, engines, machines, and other mechanically functioning equipment. Oversee installation, operation, maintenance, and repair of such equipment as centralized heat, gas, water, and steam systems. **Examples:** Combustion Engineer; Plant Equipment Engineer; Hydraulic Engineer.

17-2150 Mining and Geological Engineers, Including Mining Safety Engineers

This broad occupation is the same as the detailed occupation:
17-2151 Mining and Geological Engineers, Including Mining Safety Engineers

17-2151 Mining and Geological Engineers, Including Mining Safety Engineers

Determine the location and plan the extraction of coal, metallic ores, nonmetallic minerals, and building materials such as stone and gravel. Conduct preliminary surveys of deposits or undeveloped mines, and plan their development. Examine deposits or mines to determine whether they can be worked at a profit. Make geological and topographical surveys. Evolve methods of mining best suited to character, type, and size of deposits. Supervise mining operations. **Examples:** Exploration Engineer; Mineral Engineer; Mine Equipment Design Engineer.

17-2160 Nuclear Engineers

This broad occupation is the same as the detailed occupation:
17-2161 Nuclear Engineers

17-2161 Nuclear Engineers

Conduct research on nuclear engineering problems. Apply principles and theory of nuclear science to problems concerned with release, control, and utilization of nuclear energy and nuclear waste disposal. **Examples:** Atomic Process Engineer; Radiation Engineer; Reactor Engineer.

17-2170 Petroleum Engineers

This broad occupation is the same as the detailed occupation:
17-2171 Petroleum Engineers

17-2171 Petroleum Engineers

Devise methods to improve oil and gas well production; determine the need for new or modified tool designs. Oversee drilling; offer technical advice to achieve economical and satisfactory progress. **Examples:** Drilling Engineer; Natural Gas Engineer; Oil Well Surveying Engineer.

17-2190 Miscellaneous Engineers

This broad occupation is the same as the detailed occupation:
17-2199 Engineers, All Other

17-2199 Engineers, All Other

All engineers not listed separately. **Examples:** Optical Engineer; Salvage Engineer; Ordnance Engineer.

17-3000 Drafters, Engineering, and Mapping Technicians

17-3010 Drafters

This broad occupation includes the following four detailed occupations:
17-3011 Architectural and Civil Drafters
17-3012 Electrical and Electronics Drafters
17-3013 Mechanical Drafters
17-3019 Drafters, All Other

17-3011 Architectural and Civil Drafters

Prepare detailed drawings of architectural and structural features of buildings. Prepare drawings and topographical relief maps used in civil engineering projects such as highways, bridges, and public works. Utilize knowledge of building materials, engineering practices, and mathematics to complete drawings. **Example:** Structural Drafter.

17-3012 Electrical and Electronics Drafters

Prepare wiring diagrams, circuit board assembly diagrams, and layout drawings used for manufacture, installation, and repair of electrical equipment, in factories, power plants, and buildings.

17-3013 Mechanical Drafters

Prepare detailed working diagrams of machinery and mechanical devices, including dimensions, fastening methods, and other engineering information. **Examples:** Die Designer; Aeronautical Drafter.

17-3019 Drafters, All Other

All drafters not listed separately. **Examples:** Geological Drafter; Hull Drafter.

17-3020 Engineering Technicians, Except Drafters

This broad occupation includes the following eight detailed occupations:
17-3021 Aerospace Engineering and Operations Technicians
17-3022 Civil Engineering Technicians
17-3023 Electrical and Electronic Engineering Technicians
17-3024 Electro-Mechanical Technicians
17-3025 Environmental Engineering Technicians
17-3026 Industrial Engineering Technicians
17-3027 Mechanical Engineering Technicians
17-3029 Engineering Technicians, Except Drafters, All Other

17-3021 Aerospace Engineering and Operations Technicians

Operate, install, calibrate, and maintain integrated computer/communications systems consoles, simulators, and other data acquisition, test, and measurement instruments and equipment, to launch, track, position, and evaluate air and space vehicles. Record and interpret test data. **Examples:** Wind Tunnel Technician; Flight Data Technician; Altitude Chamber Technician.

17-3022 Civil Engineering Technicians

Apply theory and principles of civil engineering in planning, designing, and overseeing construction and maintenance of structures and facilities, under the direction of engineering staff or physical scientists. **Example:** Highway Technician.

17-3023 Electrical and Electronic Engineering Technicians

Apply electrical and electronic theory and related knowledge, usually under the direction of engineering staff, to design, build, repair, calibrate, and modify electrical components, circuitry, controls, and machinery for subsequent evaluation and use by engineering staff in making engineering design decisions. Excludes "Broadcast Technicians" (27-4012). **Examples:** Calibration Laboratory Technician; Semiconductor Development Technician; Instrumentation Technician.

17-3024 Electro-Mechanical Technicians

Operate, test, and maintain unmanned, automated, servo-mechanical, or electromechanical equipment. Operate unmanned submarines, aircraft, or other equipment at worksites such as oil rigs, deep ocean exploration, or hazardous waste removal. Assist engineers in testing and designing robotics equipment.

17-3025 Environmental Engineering Technicians

Apply theory and principles of environmental engineering to modify, test, and operate equipment and devices used in the prevention, control, and remediation of environmental pollution, including waste treatment and site remediation. Assist in the development of environmental pollution remediation devices, under direction of engineer. **Examples:** Air Analysis Technician; Soil Technician.

17-3026 Industrial Engineering Technicians

Apply engineering theory and principles to problems of industrial layout or manufacturing production, usually under the direction of engineering staff. Study and record time, motion, method, and speed involved in performance of production, maintenance, clerical, and other worker operations, for such purposes as establishing standard production rates or improving efficiency. **Examples:** Methods Study Analyst; Quality Control Technician; Time Study Analyst.

17-3027 Mechanical Engineering Technicians

Apply theory and principles of mechanical engineering, to modify, develop, and test machinery and equipment, under direction of engineering staff or physical scientists. **Examples:** Heat Transfer Technician; Optomechanical Technician; Tool Analyst.

17-3029 Engineering Technicians, Except Drafters, All Other

All engineering technicians, except drafters, not listed separately. **Examples:** Laser Specialist; Metallurgical Technician; Material Stress Tester.

17-3030 Surveying and Mapping Technicians

This broad occupation is the same as the detailed occupation:
17-3031 Surveying and Mapping Technicians

17-3031 Surveying and Mapping Technicians

Perform surveying and mapping duties, usually under the direction of a surveyor, cartographer, or photogrammetrist, to obtain data used for construction, mapmaking, boundary location, mining, or other purposes. Calculate mapmaking information and create maps from source data such as surveying notes, aerial photography, satellite data, or other maps, to show topographical features, political boundaries, and other features. Verify accuracy and completeness of topographical maps. Excludes "Surveyors" (17-1022), "Cartographers and Photogrammetrists" (17-1021), and "Geoscientists, Except Hydrologists and Geographers" (19-2042). **Examples:** Cartographic Technician; Map Drafter; Stereo Map Plotter Operator.

19-0000 LIFE, PHYSICAL, AND SOCIAL SCIENCE OCCUPATIONS

19-1000 Life Scientists

19-1010 Agricultural and Food Scientists

This broad occupation includes the following three detailed occupations:
19-1011 Animal Scientists
19-1012 Food Scientists and Technologists
19-1013 Soil and Plant Scientists

19-1011 Animal Scientists

Conduct research in the genetics, nutrition, reproduction, growth, and development of domestic farm animals. **Examples:** Dairy Scientist; Poultry Scientist.

19-1012 Food Scientists and Technologists

Use chemistry, microbiology, engineering, and other sciences to study the principles underlying the processing and deterioration of foods. Analyze food content to determine levels of vitamins, fat, sugar, and protein. Discover new food sources. Research ways to make processed foods safe, palatable, and healthful. Apply food science knowledge to determine best ways to process, package, preserve, store, and distribute food.

19-1013 Soil and Plant Scientists

Conduct research in breeding, physiology, production, yield, and management of crops and agricultural plants. Conduct research on plants' growth in soils and on the control of pests. Study the chemical, physical, biological, and mineralogical composition of soils as they relate to plant or crop growth. Classify and map soils; investigate effects of alternative practices on soil and crop productivity. **Examples:** Agronomist; Plant Pathologist; Pomologist.

19-1020 Biological Scientists

This broad occupation includes the following four detailed occupations:
19-1021 Biochemists and Biophysicists
19-1022 Microbiologists
19-1023 Zoologists and Wildlife Biologists
19-1029 Biological Scientists, All Other

19-0000
Life,
Physical,
and Social
Science
Occupations

19-1021 Biochemists and Biophysicists

Study the chemical composition and physical principles of living cells and organisms, their electrical and mechanical energy, and related phenomena. Conduct research to further understanding of the complex chemical combinations and reactions involved in metabolism, reproduction, growth, and heredity. Determine the effects of foods, drugs, serums, hormones, and other substances on tissues and vital processes of living organisms.

19-1022 Microbiologists

Investigate the growth, structure, development, and other characteristics of microscopic organisms such as bacteria, algae, or fungi. Includes medical microbiologists who study the relationship between organisms and disease or the effects of antibiotics on microorganisms. **Examples:** Bacteriologist; Cytologist; Virologist.

19-1023 Zoologists and Wildlife Biologists

Study the origins, behavior, diseases, genetics, and life processes of animals and wildlife. Specialize in wildlife research and management, including the collection and analysis of biological data, to determine the environmental effects of present and potential use of land and water areas. **Examples:** Ecologist; Herpetologist; Ornithologist.

19-1029 Biological Scientists, All Other

All biological scientists not listed separately. **Examples:** Geneticist; Paleobotanist; Plant Taxonomist.

19-1030 Conservation Scientists and Foresters

This broad occupation includes the following two detailed occupations:
19-1031 Conservation Scientists
19-1032 Foresters

19-1031 Conservation Scientists

Manage, improve, and protect natural resources to maximize their use without damaging the environment. Conduct soil surveys and develop plans to eliminate soil erosion or to protect rangelands from fire and rodent damage. Instruct farmers, agricultural production managers, or ranchers. Provide instruction in the best ways to use crop rotation, contour plowing, or terracing to conserve soil and water. Provide instruction in the number and kind of livestock and forage plants best suited to particular ranges. Provide instruction in range and farm improvements such as fencing and reservoirs for stock watering. Excludes "Zoologists and Wildlife Biologists" (19-1023) and "Foresters" (19-1032). **Examples:** Range Manager; Conservation Officer.

19-1032 Foresters

Manage forested lands for economic, recreational, and conservation purposes. Inventory the type, amount, and location of standing timber; appraise the timber's worth; negotiate the purchase; draw up contracts for procurement. Determine how to conserve wildlife habitats, creek beds, water quality, and soil stability; determine how best to comply with environmental regulations. Devise plans for planting and growing new trees; monitor trees for healthy growth; determine the best time for harvesting. Develop forest-management plans for public and privately-owned forested lands. **Examples:** Forest Ecologist; Timber Management Specialist.

19-1040 Medical Scientists

This broad occupation includes the following two detailed occupations:
19-1041 Epidemiologists
19-1042 Medical Scientists, Except Epidemiologists

19-1041 Epidemiologists

Investigate and describe the determinants and distribution of disease, disability, and other health outcomes; develop the means for prevention and control. **Example:** Malariologist.

19-1042 Medical Scientists, Except Epidemiologists

Conduct research dealing with the understanding of human diseases and the improvement of human health. Engage in clinical investigation or other research, production, technical writing, or related activities. Includes medical scientists such as physicians, dentists, public health specialists, pharmacologists, and medical pathologists. Excludes practitioners who provide medical or dental care or who dispense drugs. **Examples:** Cancer Researcher; Toxicologist; Virologist.

19-1090 Miscellaneous Life Scientists

This broad occupation is the same as the detailed occupation:
19-1099 Life Scientists, All Other

19-1099 Life Scientists, All Other

All life scientists not listed separately.

19-2000 Physical Scientists

19-2010 Astronomers and Physicists

This broad occupation includes the following two detailed occupations:
19-2011 Astronomers
19-2012 Physicists

19-2011 Astronomers

Observe, research, and interpret celestial and astronomical phenomena to increase basic knowledge; apply such information to practical problems.

19-2012 Physicists

Conduct research into the phases of physical phenomena; develop theories and laws on the basis of observation and experiments; devise methods to apply laws and theories to industry and other fields. **Examples:** Fluid Dynamicist; Rheologist; Thermodynamicist.

19-2020 Atmospheric and Space Scientists

This broad occupation is the same as the detailed occupation:
19-2021 Atmospheric and Space Scientists

19-2021 Atmospheric and Space Scientists

Investigate atmospheric phenomena and interpret meteorological data gathered by surface and air stations, satellites, and radar, to prepare reports and forecasts for public and other uses. Includes weather analysts and forecasters whose functions require the detailed knowledge of a meteorologist. **Examples:** Climatologist; Meteorologist; Weather Forecaster.

19-2030 Chemists and Materials Scientists

This broad occupation includes the following two detailed occupations:
19-2031 Chemists
19-2032 Materials Scientists

19-2031 Chemists

Conduct qualitative and quantitative chemical analyses or chemical experiments in laboratories, to ensure quality or process control or to develop new products or knowledge. Excludes "Geoscientists, Except Hydrologists and Geographers" (19-2042) and "Biochemists and Biophysicists" (19-1021). **Examples:** Inorganic Chemist; Chemical Analyst.

19-2032 Materials Scientists

Research and study the structures and chemical properties of various natural and man-made materials, including metals, alloys, rubber, ceramics, semiconductors, polymers, and glass. Determine ways to strengthen or combine materials, or develop new materials with new or specific properties, for use in a variety of products and applications. Includes glass scientists, ceramic scientists, metallurgical scientists, and polymer scientists.

19-2040 Environmental Scientists and Geoscientists

This broad occupation includes the following three detailed occupations:
19-2041 Environmental Scientists and Specialists, Including Health
19-2042 Geoscientists, Except Hydrologists and Geographers
19-2043 Hydrologists

19-2041 Environmental Scientists and Specialists, Including Health

Conduct research or perform investigation for the purpose of identifying, abating, or eliminating sources of pollutants or hazards that affect either the environment or the health of the population. Utilize knowledge of various scientific disciplines to collect, synthesize, study, report, and take action based on data derived from measurements or observations of air, food, soil, water, and other sources. Excludes "Zoologists and Wildlife Biologists" (19-1023), "Conservation Scientists" (19-1031), "Forest and Conservation Technicians" (19-4093), "Fish and Game Wardens" (33-3031), and "Forest and Conservation Workers" (45-4011). **Examples:** Environmental Analyst; Water Pollution Specialist.

19-2042 Geoscientists, Except Hydrologists and Geographers

Study the composition, structure, and other physical aspects of the earth. Use knowledge of geology, physics, and mathematics in exploration for oil, gas, minerals, or underground water, or in waste disposal, land reclamation, or other environmental problems. Study the earth's internal composition, atmospheres, and oceans. Study the earth's magnetic, electrical, and gravitational forces. Includes mineralogists, crystallographers, paleontologists, stratigraphers, geodesists, and seismologists. **Examples:** Oceanographer; Paleontologist; Seismologist.

19-2043 Hydrologists

Research the distribution, circulation, and physical properties of underground and surface waters. Study the form and intensity of precipitation, its rate of infiltration into the soil, its movement through the earth, and its return to the ocean and atmosphere. **Example:** Hydrogeologist.

19-0000
Life,
Physical,
and Social
Science
Occupations

19-2090 Miscellaneous Physical Scientists

This broad occupation is the same as the detailed occupation:
19-2099 Physical Scientists, All Other

19-2099 Physical Scientists, All Other

All physical scientists not listed separately.

19-3000 Social Scientists and Related Workers

19-3010 Economists

This broad occupation is the same as the detailed occupation:
19-3011 Economists

19-3011 Economists

Conduct research, prepare reports, or formulate plans to aid in solution of economic problems arising from production and distribution of goods and services. Collect and process economic and statistical data using econometric and sampling techniques. Excludes "Market Research Analysts" (19-3021). **Examples:** Econometrician; Economic Research Analyst; Industrial Economist.

19-3020 Market and Survey Researchers

This broad occupation includes the following two detailed occupations:
19-3021 Market Research Analysts
19-3022 Survey Researchers

19-3021 Market Research Analysts

Research market conditions in local, regional, or national areas to determine potential sales of a product or service. Gather information on competitors, prices, sales, and methods of marketing and distribution. Use survey results to create a marketing campaign based on regional preferences and buying habits. **Examples:** Advertising Analyst; Marketing Consultant; Marketing Forecaster.

19-3022 Survey Researchers

Design or conduct surveys. Supervise interviewers who conduct the survey in person or over the telephone. Present survey results to client. Excludes "Statisticians" (15-2041), "Economists" (19-3011), and "Market Research Analysts" (19-3021). **Example:** Pollster.

19-3030 Psychologists

This broad occupation includes the following three detailed occupations:
19-3031 Clinical, Counseling, and School Psychologists
19-3032 Industrial-Organizational Psychologists
19-3039 Psychologists, All Other

19-3031 Clinical, Counseling, and School Psychologists

Diagnose and treat mental disorders, learning disabilities, and cognitive, behavioral, and emotional problems, using individual, child, family, and group therapies. Design and implement behavior modification programs. **Examples:** Vocational Psychologist; Child Psychologist.

19-3032 Industrial-Organizational Psychologists

Apply principles of psychology to personnel, administration, management, sales, and marketing problems. Participate in policy planning, in employee screening, training, and development, and in organizational development and analysis. Work with management to reorganize the work setting to improve worker productivity. **Example:** Engineering Psychologist.

19-3039 Psychologists, All Other

All psychologists not listed separately. **Examples:** Social Psychologist; Psychometrist.

19-3040 Sociologists

This broad occupation is the same as the detailed occupation:
19-3041 Sociologists

19-3041 Sociologists

Study human society and social behavior by examining the groups and social institutions that people form. Study various social, religious, political, and business organizations. Study the behavior and interaction of groups; trace their origin and growth; analyze the influence of group activities on individual members. **Examples:** Criminologist; Penologist; Social Welfare Research Worker.

19-3050 Urban and Regional Planners

This broad occupation is the same as the detailed occupation:
19-3051 Urban and Regional Planners

19-3051 Urban and Regional Planners

Develop comprehensive plans and programs for use of land and physical facilities of local jurisdictions such as towns, cities, counties, and metropolitan areas. **Example:** City Planner.

19-0000
Life,
Physical,
and Social
Science
Occupations

19-3090 Miscellaneous Social Scientists and Related Workers

This broad occupation includes the following five detailed occupations:
19-3091 Anthropologists and Archeologists
19-3092 Geographers
19-3093 Historians
19-3094 Political Scientists
19-3099 Social Scientists and Related Workers, All Other

19-3091 Anthropologists and Archeologists

Study the origin, development, and behavior of humans. Study the way of life, language, or physical characteristics of existing people in various parts of the world. Engage in systematic recovery and examination of material evidence such as tools or pottery remaining from past human cultures, to determine the history, customs, and living habits of earlier civilizations. **Example:** Political Anthropologist.

19-3092 Geographers

Study nature and use of areas of earth's surface, relating and interpreting interactions of physical and cultural phenomena. Conduct research on physical aspects of a region, including land forms, climates, soils, plants, and animals. Conduct research on the spatial implications of human activities within a given area, including social characteristics, economic activities, and political organization. Research interdependence between regions at scales ranging from local to global.

19-3093 Historians

Research, analyze, record, and interpret the past, as recorded in sources such as government and institutional records, newspapers and other periodicals, photographs, interviews, films, and unpublished manuscripts such as personal diaries and letters. **Examples:** Genealogist; Historical Society Director.

19-3094 Political Scientists

Study the origin, development, and operation of political systems. Research a wide range of subjects such as relations between the United States and foreign countries, the beliefs and institutions of foreign nations, or the politics of small towns or a major metropolis. Study topics such as public opinion, political decision making, and ideology. Analyze the structure and operation of governments, as well as various political entities. Conduct public opinion surveys; analyze election results; analyze public documents. **Examples:** Political Analyst; Political Consultant.

19-3099 Social Scientists and Related Workers, All Other

All social scientists and related workers not listed separately. **Examples:** Ethnologist; Linguist; Philologist.

Standard Occupational Classification Manual   © JIST Works

19-4000 Life, Physical, and Social Science Technicians

19-4010 Agricultural and Food Science Technicians

This broad occupation is the same as the detailed occupation:
19-4011 Agricultural and Food Science Technicians

19-4011 Agricultural and Food Science Technicians

Work with agricultural scientists in food, fiber, and animal research, production, and processing. Assist with animal breeding and nutrition work. Conduct tests and experiments, under supervision, to improve yield and quality of crops or to increase the resistance of plants and animals to disease or insects. Includes technicians who assist food scientists or food technologists in the research, development, production technology, quality control, packaging, processing, and use of foods. **Examples:** Inseminator; Feed Research Technician; Dairy Technologist.

19-4020 Biological Technicians

This broad occupation is the same as the detailed occupation:
19-4021 Biological Technicians

19-4021 Biological Technicians

Assist biological and medical scientists in laboratories. Set up, operate, and maintain laboratory instruments and equipment; monitor experiments; make observations; calculate and record results. Analyze organic substances such as blood, food, and drugs. **Examples:** Biotechnologist; Wildlife Technician; Specimen Technician.

19-4030 Chemical Technicians

This broad occupation is the same as the detailed occupation:
19-4031 Chemical Technicians

19-4031 Chemical Technicians

Conduct chemical and physical laboratory tests to assist scientists in making qualitative and quantitative analyses of solids, liquids, and gaseous materials, for purposes such as research and development of new products or processes, quality control, maintenance of environmental standards. Perform other work involving experimental, theoretical, or practical application of chemistry and related sciences. **Examples:** Assayer; Fiber Analyst; Paint Tester.

19-4040 Geological and Petroleum Technicians

This broad occupation is the same as the detailed occupation:
19-4041 Geological and Petroleum Technicians

19-0000
Life,
Physical,
and Social
Science
Occupations

19-4041 Geological and Petroleum Technicians

Assist scientists in the use of electrical, sonic, or nuclear measuring instruments, in both laboratory and production activities, to obtain data indicating potential sources of metallic ore, gas, or petroleum. Analyze mud and drill cuttings. Chart pressure, temperature, and other characteristics of wells or bore holes. Investigate and collect information leading to the possible discovery of new oil fields. **Examples:** Field Scout; Crude Tester; Seismic Observer.

19-4050 Nuclear Technicians

This broad occupation is the same as the detailed occupation:
19-4051 Nuclear Technicians

19-4051 Nuclear Technicians

Assist scientists in both laboratory and production activities by performing technical tasks involving nuclear physics, primarily in operation, maintenance, production, and quality-control support activities. **Examples:** Accelerator Operator; Radiation Monitor.

19-4060 Social Science Research Assistants

This broad occupation is the same as the detailed occupation:
19-4061 Social Science Research Assistants

19-4061 Social Science Research Assistants

Assist social scientists in laboratory, survey, and other social research. Perform publication activities, laboratory analysis, quality control, or data management. Work under the direct supervision of a social scientist; assist in those activities which are more routine. Excludes "Graduate Teaching Assistants" (25-1191) who both teach and do research. **Examples:** City Planning Aide; Economic Research Assistant; Historian Research Assistant.

19-4090 Miscellaneous Life, Physical, and Social Science Technicians

This broad occupation includes the following four detailed occupations:
19-4091 Environmental Science and Protection Technicians, Including Health
19-4092 Forensic Science Technicians
19-4093 Forest and Conservation Technicians
19-4099 Life, Physical, and Social Science Technicians, All Other

19-4091 Environmental Science and Protection Technicians, Including Health

Perform laboratory and field tests to monitor the environment and to investigate sources of pollution, including those that affect health. Under direction of an environmental scientist or specialist, collect samples of gases, soil, water, and other materials for testing; take corrective actions as assigned. **Example:** Pollution Control Technician.

19-4092 Forensic Science Technicians

Collect, identify, classify, and analyze physical evidence related to criminal investigations. Perform tests on weapons or on substances such as fiber, hair, and tissue, to determine significance to investigation. Testify as expert witness on evidence or on crime laboratory techniques. Serve as specialist in area of expertise, such as ballistics, fingerprinting, handwriting, or biochemistry. **Examples:** Ballistic Expert; Fingerprint Classifier; Polygraph Examiner.

19-4093 Forest and Conservation Technicians

Compile data pertaining to size, content, condition, and other characteristics of forest tracts, under direction of foresters. Train and lead forest workers in forest propagation and in fire prevention and suppression. Assist conservation scientists in managing, improving, and protecting rangelands and wildlife habitats. Provide technical assistance regarding the conservation of soil, water, and related natural resources. **Examples:** Grazing Examiner; Soil Tester; Tree Warden.

19-4099 Life, Physical, and Social Science Technicians, All Other

All life, physical, and social science technicians not listed separately. **Examples:** Laser Technician; Radiographer; Meteorological Aide.

19-0000 Life, Physical, and Social Science Occupations

21-0000 COMMUNITY AND SOCIAL SERVICES OCCUPATIONS

21-1000 Counselors, Social Workers, and Other Community and Social Service Specialists

21-1010 Counselors

This broad occupation includes the following six detailed occupations:
21-1011 Substance Abuse and Behavioral Disorder Counselors
21-1012 Educational, Vocational, and School Counselors
21-1013 Marriage and Family Therapists
21-1014 Mental Health Counselors
21-1015 Rehabilitation Counselors
21-1019 Counselors, All Other

21-1011 Substance Abuse and Behavioral Disorder Counselors

Counsel and advise individuals with alcohol, tobacco, or drug problems, or with other problems such as gambling and eating disorders. Counsel individuals, families, or groups. Engage in prevention programs. Excludes "Social Workers" (21-1021 through 21-1029), "Psychologists" (19-3031 through 19-3039), and "Mental Health Counselors" (21-1014) providing these services. **Examples:** Addiction Counselor; Chemical Dependency Counselor; Drug Counselor.

21-1012 Educational, Vocational, and School Counselors

Counsel individuals and provide group educational and vocational guidance services. **Examples:** Curriculum Counselor; Guidance Counselor; Educational Adviser.

21-1013 Marriage and Family Therapists

Diagnose and treat mental and emotional disorders, whether cognitive, affective, or behavioral, within the context of marriage and family systems. Apply psychotherapeutic and family-systems theories and techniques, in the delivery of professional services to individuals, couples, and families, for the purpose of treating such diagnosed nervous and mental disorders. Excludes "Social Workers" (21-1021 through 21-1029) and "Psychologists" of all types (19-3031 through 19-3039). **Examples:** Family Counselor; Marriage Counselor.

21-1014 Mental Health Counselors

Counsel, with emphasis on prevention. Work with individuals and groups to promote optimum mental health. Help individuals deal with addictions and substance abuse, with family, parenting, and marital problems, with suicide, with stress management, with self-esteem problems, and with issues associated with aging and with mental and emotional health. Excludes "Social Workers" (21-1021 through 21-1029), "Psychiatrists" (29-1066), and "Psychologists" (19-3031 through 19-3039).

21-1015 Rehabilitation Counselors

Counsel individuals coping with personal, social, and vocational difficulties that result from birth defects, illness, disease, accidents, or the stress of daily life, to maximize the persons' independence and employability. Coordinate activities for residents of care and treatment facilities. Assess client needs; design and implement rehabilitation programs that include personal and vocational counseling, training, and job placement. **Examples:** Coordinator of Rehabilitation Services; Homemaking Rehabilitation Consultant.

21-1019 Counselors, All Other

All counselors not listed separately. **Examples:** Mental Hygienist; Race Relations Adviser.

21-1020 Social Workers

This broad occupation includes the following four detailed occupations:
21-1021 Child, Family, and School Social Workers
21-1022 Medical and Public Health Social Workers
21-1023 Mental Health and Substance Abuse Social Workers
21-1029 Social Workers, All Other

21-1021 Child, Family, and School Social Workers

Provide social services and assistance to improve the social and psychological functioning of children and their families and to maximize the family well-being and the academic functioning of children. Assist single parents, arrange adoptions, and find foster homes for abandoned or abused children. Address such problems as teenage pregnancy, misbehavior, and truancy, in schools. Advise teachers on how to deal with problem children. **Examples:** Adoption Agent; Child Abuse Worker; Foster Care Worker.

21-1022 Medical and Public Health Social Workers

Provide persons, families, or vulnerable populations with the psychosocial support needed to cope with chronic, acute, or terminal illnesses such as Alzheimer's, cancer, or AIDS. Advise family care givers, provide patient education and counseling, and make necessary referrals for other social services. **Examples:** Bereavement Counselor; Hospice Social Worker; Medical Caseworker.

21-1023 Mental Health and Substance Abuse Social Workers

Assess and treat individuals with mental, emotional, or substance abuse problems, including abuse of alcohol, tobacco, and/or other drugs. Provide individual and

21-0000
Community
and
Social
Services
Occupations

group therapy, crisis intervention, case management, client advocacy, prevention, and education. **Examples:** Community Mental Health Worker; Psychiatric Social Worker.

21-1029 Social Workers, All Other

All social workers not listed separately. **Examples:** Case Worker; Case Supervisor; Welfare Investigator.

21-1090 Miscellaneous Community and Social Service Specialists

This broad occupation includes the following four detailed occupations:
21-1091 Health Educators
21-1092 Probation Officers and Correctional Treatment Specialists
21-1093 Social and Human Service Assistants
21-1099 Community and Social Service Specialists, All Other

21-1091 Health Educators

Promote, maintain, and improve individual and community health by assisting individuals and communities to adopt healthy behaviors. Collect and analyze data to identify community needs; plan, implement, monitor, and evaluate programs designed to encourage healthy lifestyles, policies, and environments. Serve as a resource to assist individuals, professionals, or the community. Administer fiscal resources for health education programs. **Examples:** Public Health Advisor; Public Health Representative.

21-1092 Probation Officers and Correctional Treatment Specialists

Provide social services to assist in rehabilitation of law offenders who are in custody or who are on probation or parole. Make recommendations for actions involving formulation of rehabilitation plan and treatment of offender, including conditional release and education and employment stipulations. **Examples:** Attendance Officer; Parole Officer; Truant Officer.

21-1093 Social and Human Service Assistants

Assist professionals from a wide variety of fields, such as psychology, rehabilitation, or social work, to provide client services and family support. Assist clients in identifying available benefits and social and community services; help clients obtain benefits and services. Assist social workers with developing, organizing, and conducting programs to prevent and resolve problems relevant to substance abuse, human relationships, rehabilitation, or adult daycare. Excludes "Rehabilitation Counselors" (21-1015), "Personal and Home Care Aides" (39-9021), "Eligibility Interviewers, Government Programs" (43-4061), and "Psychiatric Technicians" (29-2053). **Examples:** Case Aide; Home Visitor; Human Services Worker.

21-1099 Community and Social Service Specialists, All Other

All community and social service specialists not listed separately. **Examples:** Community Organization Worker; Veteran's Service Officer.

21-2000 Religious Workers

21-2010 Clergy

This broad occupation is the same as the detailed occupation:
21-2011 Clergy

21-2011 Clergy

Conduct religious worship and perform other spiritual functions associated with beliefs and practices of religious faith or denomination. Provide spiritual and moral guidance and assistance to members. **Examples:** Bishop; Parish Priest; Rabbi.

21-2020 Directors, Religious Activities and Education

This broad occupation is the same as the detailed occupation:
21-2021 Directors, Religious Activities and Education

21-2021 Directors, Religious Activities and Education

Direct and coordinate activities of a denominational group designed to meet religious needs of students. Plan, direct, or coordinate church school programs designed to promote religious education among church membership. Provide counseling and guidance relative to marital, health, financial, and religious problems. **Examples:** Director of Religious Education; Minister of Education; Youth Director.

21-2090 Miscellaneous Religious Workers

This broad occupation is the same as the detailed occupation:
21-2099 Religious Workers, All Other

21-2099 Religious Workers, All Other

All religious workers not listed separately. **Examples:** Religious Healer; Ecclesiastical Worker; Missionary.

21-0000
Community
and
Social
Services
Occupations

23-0000 LEGAL OCCUPATIONS

23-1000 Lawyers, Judges, and Related Workers

23-1010 Lawyers

This broad occupation is the same as the detailed occupation:
23-1011 Lawyers

23-1011 Lawyers

Represent clients in criminal and civil litigation and other legal proceedings. Draw up legal documents. Manage or advise clients on legal transactions. Specialize in a single area or practice broadly in many areas of law. **Examples:** Attorney; Real Estate Attorney; Corporate Counsel.

23-1020 Judges, Magistrates, and Other Judicial Workers

This broad occupation includes the following three detailed occupations:
23-1021 Administrative Law Judges, Adjudicators, and Hearing Officers
23-1022 Arbitrators, Mediators, and Conciliators
23-1023 Judges, Magistrate Judges, and Magistrates

23-1021 Administrative Law Judges, Adjudicators, and Hearing Officers

Conduct hearings to decide or recommend decisions on claims concerning government programs or other government-related matters; prepare decisions. Determine penalties or the existence and amount of liability. Recommend the acceptance or rejection of claims; compromise settlements. **Examples:** Adjudicator; Traffic Court Referee.

23-1022 Arbitrators, Mediators, and Conciliators

Facilitate negotiation and conflict resolution through dialogue. Resolve conflicts outside the court system, by mutual consent of parties involved. **Example:** Ombudsman.

23-1023 Judges, Magistrate Judges, and Magistrates

Arbitrate, advise, adjudicate, or administer justice in a court of law. Sentence defendant in criminal cases according to government statutes. Determine liability of defendant in civil cases. Issue marriage licenses; perform wedding ceremonies. **Examples:** Circuit Court Judge; Jurist; Justice.

23-2000 Legal Support Workers

23-2010 Paralegals and Legal Assistants

This broad occupation is the same as the detailed occupation:
23-2011 Paralegals and Legal Assistants

23-2011 Paralegals and Legal Assistants

Assist lawyers by researching legal precedent, investigating facts, or preparing legal documents. Conduct research to support a legal proceeding, to formulate a defense, or to initiate legal action. **Examples:** Legal Assistant; Legal Investigator.

23-2090 Miscellaneous Legal Support Workers

This broad occupation includes the following four detailed occupations:
23-2091 Court Reporters
23-2092 Law Clerks
23-2093 Title Examiners, Abstractors, and Searchers
23-2099 Legal Support Workers, All Other

23-2091 Court Reporters

Use verbatim methods and equipment to capture, store, retrieve, and transcribe pretrial and trial proceedings or other information. Includes stenocaptioners who operate computerized stenographic captioning equipment to provide captions of live or prerecorded broadcasts for hearing-impaired viewers. **Examples:** Court Transcriber; Stenocaptioner; Mask Reporter.

23-2092 Law Clerks

Assist lawyers or judges by researching or preparing legal documents. Meet with clients; assist lawyers and judges in court. Excludes "Lawyers" (23-1011) and "Paralegals and Legal Assistants" (23-2011). **Example:** Legal Clerk.

23-2093 Title Examiners, Abstractors, and Searchers

Search real estate records, examine titles, or summarize pertinent legal or insurance details for a variety of purposes. Compile lists of mortgages, contracts, and other instruments pertaining to titles, by searching public and private records, for law firms, real estate agencies, or title insurance companies. **Examples:** Abstract Clerk; Escrow Officer; Lien Searcher.

23-2099 Legal Support Workers, All Other

All legal support workers not listed separately. **Examples:** Brief Writer; Legislative Aide; Patent Examiner.

25-0000 EDUCATION, TRAINING, AND LIBRARY OCCUPATIONS

25-1000 Postsecondary Teachers

25-1010 Business Teachers, Postsecondary

This broad occupation is the same as the detailed occupation:
25-1011 Business Teachers, Postsecondary

25-1011 Business Teachers, Postsecondary

Teach courses in business administration and management, such as accounting, finance, human resources, labor relations, marketing, and operations research. Includes both teachers primarily engaged in teaching and those who do a combination of teaching and research. **Examples:** Accounting Teacher; Marketing Teacher; Shorthand Teacher.

25-1020 Math and Computer Teachers, Postsecondary

This broad occupation includes the following two detailed occupations:
25-1021 Computer Science Teachers, Postsecondary
25-1022 Mathematical Science Teachers, Postsecondary

25-1021 Computer Science Teachers, Postsecondary

Teach courses in computer science. Specialize in a field of computer science, such as the design and function of computers, or in operations and research analysis. Includes both teachers primarily engaged in teaching and those who do a combination of teaching and research.

25-1022 Mathematical Science Teachers, Postsecondary

Teach courses pertaining to mathematical concepts, statistics, and actuarial science and to the application of original and standardized mathematical techniques in solving specific problems and situations. Includes both teachers primarily engaged in teaching and those who do a combination of teaching and research. **Examples:** Actuarial Science Teacher; Calculus Teacher; Geometry Teacher.

25-1030 Engineering and Architecture Teachers, Postsecondary

This broad occupation includes the following two detailed occupations:
25-1031 Architecture Teachers, Postsecondary
25-1032 Engineering Teachers, Postsecondary

25-1031 Architecture Teachers, Postsecondary

Teach courses in architecture and architectural design, such as architectural environmental design, interior architecture/design, and landscape architecture. Includes both teachers primarily engaged in teaching and those who do a combination of teaching and research. **Example:** Landscape Architecture Teacher.

25-1032 Engineering Teachers, Postsecondary

Teach courses pertaining to the application of the physical laws and principles of engineering, for the development of machines, materials, instruments, processes, and services. Includes teachers of subjects such as chemical, civil, electrical, industrial, mechanical, mineral, and petroleum engineering. Includes both teachers primarily engaged in teaching and those who do a combination of teaching and research. Excludes "Computer Science Teachers, Postsecondary" (25-1021). **Examples:** Aeronautics Engineering Teacher; Civil Engineering Teacher; Electrical Engineering Teacher.

25-1040 Life Sciences Teachers, Postsecondary

This broad occupation includes the following three detailed occupations:
25-1041 Agricultural Sciences Teachers, Postsecondary
25-1042 Biological Science Teachers, Postsecondary
25-1043 Forestry and Conservation Science Teachers, Postsecondary

25-1041 Agricultural Sciences Teachers, Postsecondary

Teach courses in the agricultural sciences. Includes teachers of agronomy, dairy sciences, fisheries management, horticultural sciences, poultry sciences, range management, and agricultural soil conservation. Includes both teachers primarily engaged in teaching and those who do a combination of teaching and research. **Examples:** Dairy Science Teacher; Farm Management Teacher; Agricultural Soil Conservation Teacher.

25-1042 Biological Science Teachers, Postsecondary

Teach courses in biological sciences. Includes both teachers primarily engaged in teaching and those who do a combination of teaching and research. **Examples:** Bacteriology Teacher; Biochemistry Teacher; Genetics Teacher.

25-1043 Forestry and Conservation Science Teachers, Postsecondary

Teach courses in environmental and conservation science. Includes both teachers primarily engaged in teaching and those who do a combination of teaching and research. Excludes "Agricultural Science Teachers" (25-1041). **Examples:** Forest Management Teacher; Forest Pathology Teacher.

25-1050 Physical Sciences Teachers, Postsecondary

This broad occupation includes the following four detailed occupations:
25-1051 Atmospheric, Earth, Marine, and Space Sciences Teachers, Postsecondary
25-1052 Chemistry Teachers, Postsecondary
25-1053 Environmental Science Teachers, Postsecondary
25-1054 Physics Teachers, Postsecondary

25-1051 Atmospheric, Earth, Marine, and Space Sciences Teachers, Postsecondary

Teach courses in the physical sciences, except chemistry and physics. Includes both teachers primarily engaged in teaching and those who do a combination of teaching and research. **Examples:** Climatology Teacher; Geology Teacher; Oceanography Teacher.

25-1052 Chemistry Teachers, Postsecondary

Teach courses pertaining to the chemical and physical properties and compositional changes of substances. Provide instruction in the methods of qualitative and quantitative chemical analysis. Includes both teachers primarily engaged in teaching and those who do a combination of teaching and research. Excludes "Biological Science Teachers, Postsecondary" (25-1042) who teach biochemistry. **Examples:** Food Technology Teacher; Pharmacognosy Teacher.

25-1053 Environmental Science Teachers, Postsecondary

Teach courses in environmental science. Includes both teachers primarily engaged in teaching and those who do a combination of teaching and research.

25-1054 Physics Teachers, Postsecondary

Teach courses pertaining to the laws of matter and energy. Includes both teachers primarily engaged in teaching and those who do a combination of teaching and research. **Examples:** Aerodynamics Teacher; Ballistics Teacher; Thermodynamics Teacher.

25-1060 Social Sciences Teachers, Postsecondary

This broad occupation includes the following eight detailed occupations:
25-1061 Anthropology and Archeology Teachers, Postsecondary
25-1062 Area, Ethnic, and Cultural Studies Teachers, Postsecondary
25-1063 Economics Teachers, Postsecondary
25-1064 Geography Teachers, Postsecondary
25-1065 Political Science Teachers, Postsecondary
25-1066 Psychology Teachers, Postsecondary
25-1067 Sociology Teachers, Postsecondary
25-1069 Social Sciences Teachers, Postsecondary, All Other

25-1061 Anthropology and Archeology Teachers, Postsecondary

Teach courses in anthropology or archeology. Includes both teachers primarily engaged in teaching and those who do a combination of teaching and research. **Example:** Paleology Teacher.

25-1062 Area, Ethnic, and Cultural Studies Teachers, Postsecondary

Teach courses pertaining to the culture and development of an area (for example, Latin American studies), an ethnic group, or any other group (for example, women's studies, urban affairs). Includes both teachers primarily engaged in teaching and those who do a combination of teaching and research. **Example:** Ethnology Teacher.

25-1063 Economics Teachers, Postsecondary

Teach courses in economics. Includes both teachers primarily engaged in teaching and those who do a combination of teaching and research. **Examples:** Agricultural Economics Teacher; Industrial Economics Teacher.

25-1064 Geography Teachers, Postsecondary

Teach courses in geography. Includes both teachers primarily engaged in teaching and those who do a combination of teaching and research. **Example:** Cartography Teacher.

25-1065 Political Science Teachers, Postsecondary

Teach courses in political science, international affairs, and international relations. Includes both teachers primarily engaged in teaching and those who do a combination of teaching and research. **Examples:** Government Teacher; International Relations Teacher; Public Policy Teacher.

25-1066 Psychology Teachers, Postsecondary

Teach courses in psychology, such as child, clinical, and developmental psychology. Teach courses in psychological counseling. Includes both teachers primarily engaged in teaching and those who do a combination of teaching and research. **Examples:** Child Development Teacher; Human Relations Teacher; Applied Psychology Teacher.

25-1067 Sociology Teachers, Postsecondary

Teach courses in sociology. Includes both teachers primarily engaged in teaching and those who do a combination of teaching and research.

25-1069 Social Sciences Teachers, Postsecondary, All Other

All postsecondary social sciences teachers not listed separately. **Examples:** Urban Planning Teacher; Labor Relations Teacher; Survey Research Teacher.

25-1070 Health Teachers, Postsecondary

This broad occupation includes the following two detailed occupations:
25-1071 Health Specialties Teachers, Postsecondary
25-1072 Nursing Instructors and Teachers, Postsecondary

25-1071 Health Specialties Teachers, Postsecondary

Teach courses in health specialties such as veterinary medicine, dentistry, pharmacy, therapy, laboratory technology, and public health. Excludes "Nursing Instructors and Teachers, Postsecondary" (25-1072) and "Biological Science Teachers, Postsecondary" (25-1042) who teach medical science. **Examples:** Pharmacology Teacher; Dentistry Teacher; Nutrition Teacher.

25-1072 Nursing Instructors and Teachers, Postsecondary

Demonstrate and teach patient care in classroom and clinical units to nursing students. Includes both teachers primarily engaged in teaching and those who do a combination of teaching and research. **Examples:** Registered Nursing Instructor; Practical Nursing Instructor; Nurses Aides Instructors.

25-1080 Education and Library Science Teachers, Postsecondary

This broad occupation includes the following two detailed occupations:
25-1081 Education Teachers, Postsecondary
25-1082 Library Science Teachers, Postsecondary

25-1081 Education Teachers, Postsecondary

Teach courses pertaining to education, such as counseling, curriculum, guidance, instruction, teacher education, and teaching English as a second language. Includes both teachers primarily engaged in teaching and those who do a combination of teaching and research.

25-1082 Library Science Teachers, Postsecondary

Teach courses in library science. Includes both teachers primarily engaged in teaching and those who do a combination of teaching and research. **Example:** Teacher of Medical Record Librarians.

25-1110 Law, Criminal Justice, and Social Work Teachers, Postsecondary

This broad occupation includes the following three detailed occupations:
25-1111 Criminal Justice and Law Enforcement Teachers, Postsecondary
25-1112 Law Teachers, Postsecondary
25-1113 Social Work Teachers, Postsecondary

25-1111 Criminal Justice and Law Enforcement Teachers, Postsecondary

Teach courses in criminal justice, corrections, and law enforcement administration. Includes both teachers primarily engaged in teaching and those who do a combination of teaching and research. **Examples:** Criminology Teacher; Penology Teacher.

25-1112 Law Teachers, Postsecondary

Teach courses in law. Includes both teachers primarily engaged in teaching and those who do a combination of teaching and research.

25-1113 Social Work Teachers, Postsecondary

Teach courses in social work. Includes both teachers primarily engaged in teaching and those who do a combination of teaching and research.

25-1120 Arts, Communications, and Humanities Teachers, Postsecondary

This broad occupation includes the following six detailed occupations:
25-1121 Art, Drama, and Music Teachers, Postsecondary
25-1122 Communications Teachers, Postsecondary
25-1123 English Language and Literature Teachers, Postsecondary
25-1124 Foreign Language and Literature Teachers, Postsecondary
25-1125 History Teachers, Postsecondary
25-1126 Philosophy and Religion Teachers, Postsecondary

25-1121 Art, Drama, and Music Teachers, Postsecondary

Teach courses in drama, music, and the arts, including fine and applied art such as painting and sculpture, or design and crafts. Includes both teachers primarily engaged in teaching and those who do a combination of teaching and research. **Examples:** Photography Teacher; Piano Teacher; Music Director.

25-1122 Communications Teachers, Postsecondary

Teach courses in communications, such as organizational communications, public relations, radio/television broadcasting, and journalism. Includes both teachers primarily engaged in teaching and those who do a combination of teaching and research. **Examples:** Journalism Teacher; Public Speaking Teacher.

25-1123 English Language and Literature Teachers, Postsecondary

Teach courses in English language and literature, including linguistics and comparative literature. Includes both teachers primarily engaged in teaching and those who do a combination of both teaching and research. **Examples:** Classics Teacher; Etymology Teacher; Creative Writing Teacher.

25-0000
Education,
Training,
and Library
Occupations

25-1124 Foreign Language and Literature Teachers, Postsecondary

Teach courses in foreign (that is, other than English) languages and literature. Includes both teachers primarily engaged in teaching and those who do a combination of teaching and research. **Examples:** Arabic Teacher; Russian Teacher; Spanish Teacher.

25-1125 History Teachers, Postsecondary

Teach courses in human history and historiography. Includes both teachers primarily engaged in teaching and those who do a combination of teaching and research.

25-1126 Philosophy and Religion Teachers, Postsecondary

Teach courses in philosophy, religion, and theology. Includes both teachers primarily engaged in teaching and those who do a combination of teaching and research. **Examples:** Divinity Teacher; Metaphysics Teacher; Theology Teacher.

25-1190 Miscellaneous Postsecondary Teachers

This broad occupation includes the following five detailed occupations:
25-1191 Graduate Teaching Assistants
25-1192 Home Economics Teachers, Postsecondary
25-1193 Recreation and Fitness Studies Teachers, Postsecondary
25-1194 Vocational Education Teachers, Postsecondary
25-1199 Postsecondary Teachers, All Other

25-1191 Graduate Teaching Assistants

Assist department chairperson, faculty members, or other professional staff members in college or university by performing teaching or teaching-related duties such as teaching lower-level courses, developing teaching materials, preparing and giving examinations, and grading examinations or papers. Must be enrolled in a graduate school program. Excludes graduate assistants who primarily perform nonteaching duties such as laboratory research, as these are to be reported in the occupational category related to the work performed.

25-1192 Home Economics Teachers, Postsecondary

Teach courses in child care, family relations, finance, nutrition, and related subjects pertaining to home management. Includes both teachers primarily engaged in teaching and those who do a combination of teaching and research. **Examples:** Food and Nutrition Teacher; Sewing Teacher.

25-1193 Recreation and Fitness Studies Teachers, Postsecondary

Teach courses pertaining to recreation, leisure, and fitness studies, including exercise physiology and facilities management. Includes both teachers primarily engaged in teaching and those who do a combination of teaching and research. **Examples:** Swimming Teacher; Leisure Studies Instructor.

25-1194 Vocational Education Teachers, Postsecondary

Teach or instruct vocational or occupational subjects at the postsecondary level (but at less than the baccalaureate level) to students who have graduated or left high school. Teach in public or private schools whose primary business is education or in a school associated with an organization whose primary business is other than education. Includes correspondence school instructors and industrial, commercial and government training instructors. Includes adult education teachers and instructors who prepare persons to operate industrial machinery and equipment, and transportation and communications equipment. **Examples:** Real Estate Instructor; Auto Mechanics Teacher; Barbering Teacher.

25-0000
Education,
Training,
and Library
Occupations

25-1199 Postsecondary Teachers, All Other

All postsecondary teachers not listed separately. **Examples:** Interior Design Teacher; Military Science Teacher.

25-2000 Primary, Secondary, and Special Education School Teachers

25-2010 Preschool and Kindergarten Teachers

This broad occupation includes the following two detailed occupations:
25-2011 Preschool Teachers, Except Special Education
25-2012 Kindergarten Teachers, Except Special Education

25-2011 Preschool Teachers, Except Special Education

Instruct children (normally up to 5 years of age) in preschool, daycare center, or other child development facility. Provide instruction in activities designed to promote social, physical, and intellectual growth needed for primary school. Hold any required state certification. Excludes "Child Care Workers" (39-9011) and "Special Education Teachers" (25-2041 through 25-2043). **Examples:** Head Start Teacher; Childhood Development Teacher; Nursery School Teacher.

25-2012 Kindergarten Teachers, Except Special Education

Teach elemental, natural, and social science, personal hygiene, music, art, and literature to children from 4 to 6 years of age. Promote physical, mental, and social development. Hold any required state certification. Excludes "Special Education Teachers" (25-2041 through 25-2043).

25-2020 Elementary and Middle School Teachers

This broad occupation includes the following three detailed occupations:
25-2021 Elementary School Teachers, Except Special Education
25-2022 Middle School Teachers, Except Special and Vocational Education
25-2023 Vocational Education Teachers, Middle School

25-2021 Elementary School Teachers, Except Special Education

Teach pupils in public or private schools at the elementary level basic academic, social, and other formative skills. Excludes "Special Education Teachers" (25-2041 through 25-2043).

25-2022 Middle School Teachers, Except Special and Vocational Education

Teach students in public or private schools in one or more subjects at the middle, intermediate, or junior-high level, which falls between elementary and senior high school, as defined by applicable state laws and regulations. Excludes "Middle School Vocational Education Teachers" (25-2023) and "Special Education Teachers" (25-2041 through 25-2043). **Example:** Junior High School Teacher.

25-2023 Vocational Education Teachers, Middle School

Teach or instruct vocational or occupational subjects at the middle-school level. Excludes "Special Education Teachers" (25-2041 through 25-2043).

25-2030 Secondary School Teachers

This broad occupation includes the following two detailed occupations:
25-2031 Secondary School Teachers, Except Special and Vocational Education
25-2032 Vocational Education Teachers, Secondary School

25-2031 Secondary School Teachers, Except Special and Vocational Education

Instruct students in secondary public or private schools in one or more subjects such as English, mathematics, or social studies. Provide instruction in a designated subject matter specialty, such as typing instructors, commercial teachers, or English teachers. Excludes "Vocational Education Secondary School Teachers" (25-2032) and "Special Education Teachers" (25-2041 through 25-2043). **Example:** High School Teacher.

25-2032 Vocational Education Teachers, Secondary School

Teach or instruct vocational or occupational subjects at the secondary-school level.

25-2040 Special Education Teachers

This broad occupation includes the following three detailed occupations:
25-2041 Special Education Teachers, Preschool, Kindergarten, and Elementary School
25-2042 Special Education Teachers, Middle School
25-2043 Special Education Teachers, Secondary School

25-2041 Special Education Teachers, Preschool, Kindergarten, and Elementary School

Teach elementary and preschool school subjects to educationally and physically handicapped students. Includes teachers who specialize and work with audibly and visually handicapped students and those who teach basic academic and life processes skills to the mentally impaired.

25-2042 Special Education Teachers, Middle School

Teach middle school subjects to educationally and physically handicapped students. Includes teachers who specialize and work with audibly and visually handicapped students and those who teach basic academic and life processes skills to the mentally impaired.

25-2043 Special Education Teachers, Secondary School

Teach secondary school subjects to educationally and physically handicapped students. Includes teachers who specialize and work with audibly and visually handicapped students and those who teach basic academic and life processes skills to the mentally impaired.

25-3000 Other Teachers and Instructors

25-3010 Adult Literacy, Remedial Education, and GED Teachers and Instructors

This broad occupation is the same as the detailed occupation:
25-3011 Adult Literacy, Remedial Education, and GED Teachers and Instructors

25-3011 Adult Literacy, Remedial Education, and GED Teachers and Instructors

Teach or instruct out-of-school youths and adults in remedial education classes, in preparatory classes for the General Educational Development test, in literacy, or in English as a second language. Teaching may or may not take place in a traditional educational institution. **Example:** Adult Education Teacher.

25-3020 Self-Enrichment Education Teachers

This broad occupation is the same as the detailed occupation:
25-3021 Self-Enrichment Education Teachers

25-3021 Self-Enrichment Education Teachers

Teach or instruct students in courses other than those that normally lead to an occupational objective or degree, including self-improvement, nonvocational, and nonacademic subjects. Teaching may or may not take place in a traditional educational institution. **Examples:** Art Teacher; Flying Teacher; Citizenship Teacher.

25-3090 Miscellaneous Teachers and Instructors

This broad occupation is the same as the detailed occupation:
25-3099 Teachers and Instructors, All Other

25-3099 Teachers and Instructors, All Other

All teachers and instructors not listed separately. **Examples:** Consumer Education Specialist; Lecturer; Private Tutor.

25-4000 Librarians, Curators, and Archivists

25-4010 Archivists, Curators, and Museum Technicians

This broad occupation includes the following three detailed occupations:
25-4011 Archivists
25-4012 Curators
25-4013 Museum Technicians and Conservators

25-4011 Archivists

Appraise, edit, and direct safekeeping of permanent records and historically valuable documents. Participate in research activities based on archival materials. **Example:** Docent Coordinator.

25-4012 Curators

Administer affairs of museum and conduct research programs. Direct instructional, research, and public service activities of institution. **Examples:** Art Gallery Director; Museum Director.

25-4013 Museum Technicians and Conservators

Prepare specimens, such as fossils, skeletal parts, lace, and textiles, for museum collection and exhibits. May restore documents or install, arrange, and exhibit materials. **Example:** Museum Registrar.

25-4020 Librarians

This broad occupation is the same as the detailed occupation:
25-4021 Librarians

25-4021 Librarians

Administer libraries and perform related library services. Work in a variety of settings, including public libraries, schools, colleges and universities, museums, corporations, government agencies, law firms, nonprofit organizations, and healthcare provider organizations. Select, acquire, catalog, classify, circulate, and maintain library materials. Furnish reference, bibliographical, and readers' advisory services. Perform in-depth, strategic research. Synthesize, analyze, edit, and filter information. Set up or work with databases and information systems to catalogue and access information. **Examples:** School Library Media Specialist; Circulation Manager.

25-4030 Library Technicians

This broad occupation is the same as the detailed occupation:
25-4031 Library Technicians

25-4031 Library Technicians

Assist librarians by helping readers in the use of library catalogs, databases, and indexes to locate books and other materials. Answer questions that require only brief consultation of standard reference. Compile records; sort and shelve books; remove or repair damaged books; register patrons; check materials in and out of the circulation process. Replace materials in shelving area (stacks) or files. Includes bookmobile drivers who operate bookmobiles or light trucks that pull trailers to specific locations on a predetermined schedule and who assist with providing services in mobile libraries. **Examples:** Assistant Librarian; Bookmobile Driver.

25-9000 Other Education, Training, and Library Occupations

25-9010 Audio-Visual Collections Specialists

This broad occupation is the same as the detailed occupation:
25-9011 Audio-Visual Collections Specialists

25-9011 Audio-Visual Collections Specialists

Prepare, plan, and operate audio-visual teaching aids for use in education. Record, catalogue, and file audio-visual materials.

25-9020 Farm and Home Management Advisors

This broad occupation is the same as the detailed occupation:
25-9021 Farm and Home Management Advisors

25-9021 Farm and Home Management Advisors

Advise, instruct, and assist individuals and families engaged in agriculture, agricultural-related processes, or home-economics activities. Demonstrate procedures and apply research findings to solve problems. Instruct and train in product development, sales, and the utilization of machinery and equipment to promote general welfare. Includes county agricultural agents, feed and farm management advisers, home economists, and extension service advisors. **Examples:** Agricultural Extension Agent; Feed Adviser; Home Economic Extension Worker.

25-9030 Instructional Coordinators

This broad occupation is the same as the detailed occupation:
25-9031 Instructional Coordinators

25-9031 Instructional Coordinators

Develop instructional material, coordinate educational content, and incorporate current technology in specialized fields that provide guidelines to educators and instructors for developing curricula and conducting courses. Includes educational consultants and specialists and instructional material directors. **Examples:** Curriculum Specialist; Director of Instructional Materials; Educational Consultant.

25-9040 Teacher Assistants

This broad occupation is the same as the detailed occupation:
25-9041 Teacher Assistants

25-9041 Teacher Assistants

Perform duties that are instructional in nature or that deliver direct services to students or parents. Serve in a position for which a teacher or another professional has ultimate responsibility for the design and implementation of educational programs and services. **Examples:** Examination Proctor; Paper Grader; Paraprofessional Teacher Aides.

25-9090 Miscellaneous Education, Training, and Library Workers

This broad occupation is the same as the detailed occupation:
25-9099 Education, Training, and Library Workers, All Other

25-9099 Education, Training, and Library Workers, All Other

All education, training, and library workers not listed separately.

27-0000 ARTS, DESIGN, ENTERTAINMENT, SPORTS, AND MEDIA OCCUPATIONS

27-1000 Art and Design Workers

27-1010 Artists and Related Workers

This broad occupation includes the following five detailed occupations:
27-1011 Art Directors
27-1012 Craft Artists
27-1013 Fine Artists, Including Painters, Sculptors, and Illustrators
27-1014 Multi-Media Artists and Animators
27-1019 Artists and Related Workers, All Other

27-1011 Art Directors

Formulate design concepts and presentation approaches. Direct workers engaged in art work, layout design, and copy writing for visual communications media such as magazines, books, newspapers, and packaging.

27-1012 Craft Artists

Create or reproduce handmade objects for sale and exhibition, using a variety of techniques such as welding, weaving, pottery, and needlecraft. **Examples:** Architectural Modeler; Furniture Reproducer; Ivory Carver.

27-1013 Fine Artists, Including Painters, Sculptors, and Illustrators

Create original artwork using any of a wide variety of mediums and techniques such as painting and sculpture. **Examples:** Art Restorer; Cartoonist; Statue Maker.

27-1014 Multi-Media Artists and Animators

Create special effects, animation, or other visual images, using film, video, computers, or other electronic tools and media, for use in products or creations such as computer games, movies, music videos, and commercials. **Examples:** Computer Artist; Computer Graphics Illustrator; Special Effects Specialist.

27-1019 Artists and Related Workers, All Other

All artists and related workers not listed separately. **Examples:** Art Appraiser; Calligrapher; Inker and Opaquer.

27-1020 Designers

This broad occupation includes the following eight detailed occupations:
27-1021 Commercial and Industrial Designers

27-1022 Fashion Designers
27-1023 Floral Designers
27-1024 Graphic Designers
27-1025 Interior Designers
27-1026 Merchandise Displayers and Window Trimmers
27-1027 Set and Exhibit Designers
27-1029 Designers, All Other

27-1021 Commercial and Industrial Designers

Develop and design manufactured products such as cars, home appliances, and children's toys. Combine artistic talent with research on product use, marketing, and materials, to create the most functional and appealing product design. **Examples:** Body Stylist; Color Consultant; Jewelry Designer.

27-1022 Fashion Designers

Design clothing and accessories. Create original garments or design garments that follow well established fashion trends. Develop the line of color and kinds of materials. **Examples:** Costume Designer; Custom Furrier; Stylist.

27-1023 Floral Designers

Design, cut, and arrange live, dried, or artificial flowers and foliage. **Examples:** Corsage Maker; Florist; Flower Arranger.

27-1024 Graphic Designers

Design or create graphics to meet a client's specific commercial or promotional needs, such as packaging, displays, or logos. Use a variety of mediums to achieve artistic or decorative effects. **Examples:** Catalogue Illustrator; Graphic Artist; Layout Artist.

27-1025 Interior Designers

Plan, design, and furnish interiors of residential, commercial, or industrial buildings. Formulate design which is practical, aesthetic, and conducive to intended purposes, such as raising productivity, selling merchandise, or improving life style. Specialize in a particular field, style, or phase of interior design. Excludes "Merchandise Displayers and Window Trimmers" (27-1026). **Examples:** Decorator; Furniture Arranger; Home Lighting Adviser.

27-1026 Merchandise Displayers and Window Trimmers

Plan and erect commercial displays such as those in windows and interiors of retail stores and those at trade exhibitions. **Examples:** Mannequin Decorator; Display Artist; Model Dresser.

27-1027 Set and Exhibit Designers

Design special exhibits and movie, television, and theater sets. Study scripts; confer with directors; conduct research to determine appropriate architectural styles. **Examples:** Set Decorator; Stage Scenery Designer.

27-1029 Designers, All Other

All designers not listed separately. **Examples:** Copyist; Frame Stylist.

27-2000 Entertainers and Performers, Sports and Related Workers

27-2010 Actors, Producers, and Directors

This broad occupation includes the following two detailed occupations:
27-2011 Actors
27-2012 Producers and Directors

27-0000
Arts, Design,
Entertain-
ment, Sports,
and Media
Occupations

27-2011 Actors

Play parts in stage, television, radio, video, or motion picture productions for entertainment, information, or instruction. Interpret serious or comic role by speech, gesture, and body movement, to entertain or inform audience. Dance and sing. **Examples:** Elocutionist; Extra; Dramatic Reader.

27-2012 Producers and Directors

Produce or direct stage, television, radio, video, or motion picture productions for entertainment, information, or instruction. Assume responsibility for creative decisions such as interpretation of script, choice of guests, set design, sound, special effects, and choreography. **Examples:** Independent Film Maker; Stage Manager; Program Arranger.

27-2020 Athletes, Coaches, Umpires, and Related Workers

This broad occupation includes the following three detailed occupations:
27-2021 Athletes and Sports Competitors
27-2022 Coaches and Scouts
27-2023 Umpires, Referees, and Other Sports Officials

27-2021 Athletes and Sports Competitors

Compete in athletic events. **Examples:** Ball Player; Jockey; Racing Car Driver.

27-2022 Coaches and Scouts

Instruct or coach groups or individuals in the fundamentals of sports. Demonstrate techniques and methods of participation. Evaluate athletes' strengths and weaknesses to determine possible recruits or to improve the athletes' technique and prepare them for competition. Excludes coaches and scouts who are required to hold teaching degrees, as those are to be reported in the appropriate teaching category. Excludes "Athletic Trainers" (29-9091). **Examples:** Boxing Trainer; Horse Trainer; Baseball Club Manager.

27-2023 Umpires, Referees, and Other Sports Officials

Officiate at competitive athletic or sporting events. Detect infractions of rules and decide penalties, according to established regulations. Includes all sporting officials, referees, and competition judges. **Examples:** Handicapper; Paddock Judge; Athletic Events Scorer.

27-2030 Dancers and Choreographers

This broad occupation includes the following two detailed occupations:
27-2031 Dancers
27-2032 Choreographers

27-2031 Dancers

Perform dances. Sing or act.

27-2032 Choreographers

Create and teach dance. Direct and stage presentations. **Example:** Dance Director.

27-2040 Musicians, Singers, and Related Workers

This broad occupation includes the following two detailed occupations:
27-2041 Music Directors and Composers
27-2042 Musicians and Singers

27-2041 Music Directors and Composers

Conduct, direct, plan, and lead instrumental or vocal performances by musical groups such as orchestras, choirs, and glee clubs. Includes arrangers, composers, choral directors, and orchestrators. **Examples:** Choirmaster; Orchestra Conductor.

27-2042 Musicians and Singers

Play one or more musical instruments, or entertain by singing songs, in recital, in accompaniment, or as a member of an orchestra, band, or other musical group. Entertain on stage, radio, TV, film, or video; record in studios. Excludes "Dancers" (27-2031). **Examples:** Cantor; Church Organist; Instrumentalist.

27-2090 Miscellaneous Entertainers and Performers, Sports and Related Workers

This broad occupation is the same as the detailed occupation:
27-2099 Entertainers and Performers, Sports and Related Workers, All Other

27-2099 Entertainers and Performers, Sports and Related Workers, All Other

All entertainers and performers, sports and related workers, not listed separately. **Examples:** Circus Performer; Comedian; Magician.

27-3000 Media and Communication Workers

27-3010 Announcers

This broad occupation includes the following two detailed occupations:
27-3011 Radio and Television Announcers
27-3012 Public Address System and Other Announcers

27-3011 Radio and Television Announcers

Talk on radio or television. Interview guests, act as master of ceremonies, read news flashes, identify station by giving call letters, or announce song title and artist. **Examples:** Broadcaster; Radio Disk Jockey.

27-3012 Public Address System and Other Announcers

Make announcements over loud speaker at sporting or other public events. Act as master of ceremonies or as disc jockey at weddings, parties, clubs, or other gathering places. **Examples:** Ringmaster; Train Caller.

27-3020 News Analysts, Reporters and Correspondents

This broad occupation includes the following two detailed occupations:
27-3021 Broadcast News Analysts
27-3022 Reporters and Correspondents

27-3021 Broadcast News Analysts

Analyze, interpret, and broadcast news received from various sources. **Examples:** News Anchor; Commentator; Newscaster.

27-3022 Reporters and Correspondents

Collect and analyze facts about newsworthy events by interview, investigation, or observation. Report and write stories for newspaper, news magazine, radio, or television. Excludes "Broadcast News Analysts" (27-3021). **Examples:** Columnist; Critic; Foreign Correspondent.

27-3030 Public Relations Specialists

This broad occupation is the same as the detailed occupation:
27-3031 Public Relations Specialists

27-3031 Public Relations Specialists

Engage in promoting or creating goodwill for individuals, groups, or organizations by writing or selecting favorable publicity material and releasing it through various communications media. Prepare and arrange displays. Make speeches. **Examples:** Lobbyist; Press Secretary; Publicist.

27-3040 Writers and Editors

This broad occupation includes the following three detailed occupations:
27-3041 Editors
27-3042 Technical Writers
27-3043 Writers and Authors

27-3041 Editors

Perform variety of editorial duties such as laying out, indexing, and revising content of written materials, in preparation for final publication. Includes technical editors. **Examples:** Copy Editor; Censor; Reviewer.

27-3042 Technical Writers

Write technical materials such as equipment manuals, appendices, or operating and maintenance instructions. Assist in layout work. **Examples:** Documentation Writer; Assembly Instructions Writer; Specifications Writer.

27-3043 Writers and Authors

Originate and prepare written material such as scripts, stories, advertisements, and other material. Excludes "Public Relations Specialists" (27-3031) and "Technical Writers" (27-3042). **Examples:** Crossword Puzzle Maker; Copy Writer; Playwright.

27-3090 Miscellaneous Media and Communication Workers

This broad occupation includes the following two detailed occupations:
27-3091 Interpreters and Translators
27-3099 Media and Communication Workers, All Other

27-3091 Interpreters and Translators

Translate or interpret written, oral, or sign language text into another language for others. **Examples:** Braille Translator; Deaf Interpreter; Language Translator.

27-3099 Media and Communication Workers, All Other

All media and communication workers not listed separately. **Examples:** Graphologist; Stage Technician.

27-4000 Media and Communication Equipment Workers

27-4010 Broadcast and Sound Engineering Technicians and Radio Operators

This broad occupation includes the following four detailed occupations:
27-4011 Audio and Video Equipment Technicians
27-4012 Broadcast Technicians
27-4013 Radio Operators
27-4014 Sound Engineering Technicians

27-4011 Audio and Video Equipment Technicians

Set up, or set up and operate, audio and video equipment, including microphones, sound speakers, video screens, projectors, video monitors, recording equipment, connecting wires and cables, sound and mixing boards, and related electronic equipment, for concerts, sports events, meetings, conventions, presentations, and news conferences. Set up and operate associated spotlights and other custom lighting systems. Excludes "Sound Engineering Technicians" (27-4014). **Examples:** Video Control Operator; Audio Visual Production Specialist.

27-4012 Broadcast Technicians

Set up, operate, and maintain the electronic equipment used to transmit radio and television programs. Control audio equipment to regulate volume level and quality of sound during radio and television broadcasts. Operate radio transmitter to broadcast radio and television programs. **Examples:** Control Room Technician; Audio Engineer.

27-4013 Radio Operators

Receive and transmit communications using radiotelegraph or radiotelephone equipment in accordance with government regulations. Repair equipment. **Example:** Radio Officer.

27-4014 Sound Engineering Technicians

Operate machines and equipment to record, synchronize, mix, or reproduce music, voices, or sound effects, in sporting arenas, theater productions, recording studios, or movie and video productions. **Examples:** Film Recordist; Sound Editor; Sound Effects Person.

27-4020 Photographers

This broad occupation is the same as the detailed occupation:
27-4021 Photographers

27-4021 Photographers

Photograph persons, subjects, merchandise, or other commercial products. Develop negatives and produce finished prints. Includes scientific photographers, aerial photographers, and photojournalists. **Examples:** Camera Operator; Photojournalist.

27-4030 Television, Video, and Motion Picture Camera Operators and Editors

This broad occupation includes the following two detailed occupations:
27-4031 Camera Operators, Television, Video, and Motion Picture
27-4032 Film and Video Editors

27-4031 Camera Operators, Television, Video, and Motion Picture

Operate television, video, or motion picture camera to photograph images or scenes for various purposes, such as TV broadcasts, advertising, video production, or motion pictures. **Example:** Cinematographer.

27-4032 Film and Video Editors

Edit motion picture soundtracks, film, and video. **Examples:** Cue Selector; Video Tape Duplicator.

27-4090 Miscellaneous Media and Communication Equipment Workers

This broad occupation is the same as the detailed occupation:
27-4099 Media and Communication Equipment Workers, All Other

27-4099 Media and Communication Equipment Workers, All Other

All media and communication equipment workers not listed separately. **Examples:** Radar Operator; Light Technician.

29-0000 HEALTHCARE PRACTITIONERS AND TECHNICAL OCCUPATIONS

29-1000 Health Diagnosing and Treating Practitioners

29-1010 Chiropractors

This broad occupation is the same as the detailed occupation:
29-1011 Chiropractors

29-1011 Chiropractors

Adjust spinal column and other articulations of the body to correct abnormalities of the human body caused by interference with the nervous system. Examine patient to determine nature and extent of disorder. Manipulate spine or other involved area. Utilize supplementary measures such as exercise, rest, water, light, heat, and nutritional therapy.

29-1020 Dentists

This broad occupation includes the following five detailed occupations:
29-1021 Dentists, General
29-1022 Oral and Maxillofacial Surgeons
29-1023 Orthodontists
29-1024 Prosthodontists
29-1029 Dentists, All Other Specialists

29-1021 Dentists, General

Diagnose and treat diseases, injuries, and malformations of teeth, gums, and related oral structures. Treat diseases of nerve, pulp, and other dental tissues affecting vitality of teeth. Excludes "Prosthodontists" (29-1024), "Orthodontists" (29-1023), "Oral and Maxillofacial Surgeons" (29-1022) and "Dentists, All Other Specialists" (29-1029).

29-1022 Oral and Maxillofacial Surgeons

Perform surgery on mouth, jaws, and related head and neck structure, to execute difficult and multiple extractions of teeth, to remove tumors and other abnormal growths, to correct abnormal jaw relations by mandibular or maxillary revision, to prepare mouth for insertion of dental prosthesis, or to treat fractured jaws.
Example: Dental Surgeon.

29-0000
Healthcare
Practitioners
and
Technical
Occupations

29-1023 Orthodontists

Examine, diagnose, and treat dental malocclusions and oral cavity anomalies. Design and fabricate appliances for realigning teeth and jaws, to produce and maintain normal function and to improve appearance.

29-1024 Prosthodontists

Construct oral prostheses for replacing missing teeth and other oral structures, to correct natural and acquired deformation of mouth and jaws, to restore and maintain oral functions such as chewing and speaking, and to improve appearance.

29-1029 Dentists, All Other Specialists

All dentists not listed separately. **Examples:** Endodontist; Periodontist; Oral Pathologist.

29-1030 Dietitians and Nutritionists

This broad occupation is the same as the detailed occupation:
29-1031 Dietitians and Nutritionists

29-1031 Dietitians and Nutritionists

Plan and conduct food service or nutritional programs to assist in the promotion of health and in the control of disease. Supervise activities of a department providing quantity food services; counsel individuals; conduct nutritional research. **Examples:** Public Health Dietitian; Nutrition Director; Research Dietitian.

29-1040 Optometrists

This broad occupation is the same as the detailed occupation:
29-1041 Optometrists

29-1041 Optometrists

Diagnose, manage, and treat conditions and diseases of the human eye and visual system. Examine eyes and visual system; diagnose problems or impairments; prescribe corrective lenses; provide treatment. Prescribe therapeutic drugs to treat specific eye conditions. **Example:** Doctor of Optometry.

29-1050 Pharmacists

This broad occupation is the same as the detailed occupation:
29-1051 Pharmacists

29-1051 Pharmacists

Dispense drugs prescribed by physicians and other health practitioners. Provide information to patients about medications and their use. Advise physicians and other health practitioners on the selection, dosage, interactions, and side effects of medications. **Examples:** Apothecary; Druggist; Industrial Pharmacist.

29-1060 Physicians and Surgeons

This broad occupation includes the following eight detailed occupations:
29-1061 Anesthesiologists
29-1062 Family and General Practitioners
29-1063 Internists, General
29-1064 Obstetricians and Gynecologists
29-1065 Pediatricians, General
29-1066 Psychiatrists
29-1067 Surgeons
29-1069 Physicians and Surgeons, All Other

29-1061 Anesthesiologists

Administer anesthetics during surgery or other medical procedures.

29-1062 Family and General Practitioners

Diagnose, treat, and help prevent diseases and injuries that commonly occur in the general population.

29-1063 Internists, General

Diagnose and provide nonsurgical treatment of diseases and injuries of internal organ systems. Provide care mainly for adults who have a wide range of problems associated with the internal organs. Include subspecialists such as cardiologists and gastroenterologists with "All Other Physicians" (29-1069).

29-1064 Obstetricians and Gynecologists

Diagnose, treat, and help prevent diseases of women, especially those affecting the reproductive system and the process of childbirth. **Example:** OB/Gyn.

29-1065 Pediatricians, General

Diagnose, treat, and help prevent children's diseases and injuries.

29-1066 Psychiatrists

Diagnose, treat, and help prevent disorders of the mind. **Examples:** Psychoanalyst; Neuropsychiatrist.

29-1067 Surgeons

Treat diseases, injuries, and deformities by invasive methods such as manual manipulation or use of instruments and appliances. **Examples:** Orthopedic Surgeon; Cardiovascular Surgeon; Plastic Surgeon.

29-0000
Healthcare
Practitioners
and
Technical
Occupations

29-1069 Physicians and Surgeons, All Other

All physicians and surgeons not listed separately. **Examples:** Cardiologist; Dermatologist; Ophthalmologist.

29-1070 Physician Assistants

This broad occupation is the same as the detailed occupation:
29-1071 Physician Assistants

29-1071 Physician Assistants

Provide healthcare services typically performed by a physician, under the supervision of a physician. Conduct complete physicals, provide treatment, and counsel patients. Prescribe medication, in some cases. Graduate from an accredited educational program for physician assistants. Excludes "Emergency Medical Technicians and Paramedics" (29-2041), "Medical Assistants" (31-9092), and "Registered Nurses" (29-1111). **Example:** Anesthesiologist Assistant.

29-1080 Podiatrists

This broad occupation is the same as the detailed occupation:
29-1081 Podiatrists

29-1081 Podiatrists

Diagnose and treat diseases and deformities of the human foot. **Examples:** Podiatric Surgeon; Foot Orthopedist; Pododermatologist.

29-1110 Registered Nurses

This broad occupation is the same as the detailed occupation:
29-1111 Registered Nurses

29-1111 Registered Nurses

Assess patient health problems and needs; develop and implement nursing care plans; maintain medical records. Administer nursing care to ill, injured, convalescent, or disabled patients. Advise patients on health maintenance and disease prevention; provide case management. Obtain required licensing or registration. Includes advance practice nurses such as nurse practitioners, clinical nurse specialists, certified nurse midwives, and certified registered nurse anesthetists. Provide advanced-practice nursing, using specialized, formal, post-basic education and functioning in highly autonomous and specialized roles. **Examples:** Nursing Supervisor; Nurse Midwife; Nurse Practitioner.

29-1120 Therapists

This broad occupation includes the following eight detailed occupations:
29-1121 Audiologists
29-1122 Occupational Therapists
29-1123 Physical Therapists
29-1124 Radiation Therapists
29-1125 Recreational Therapists
29-1126 Respiratory Therapists
29-1127 Speech-Language Pathologists
29-1129 Therapists, All Other

29-1121 Audiologists

Assess and treat persons with hearing and related disorders. Fit hearing aids; provide auditory training. Perform research related to hearing problems. **Example:** Hearing Therapist.

29-1122 Occupational Therapists

Assess, plan, organize, and participate in rehabilitative programs that help restore vocational, homemaking, and daily living skills, as well as general independence, to disabled persons.

29-1123 Physical Therapists

Assess, plan, organize, and participate in rehabilitative programs that improve mobility, relieve pain, increase strength, and decrease or prevent deformity of patients suffering from disease or injury. **Examples:** Physiotherapist; Pulmonary Physical Therapist.

29-1124 Radiation Therapists

Provide radiation therapy to patients as prescribed by a radiologist, according to established practices and standards. Review prescription and diagnosis. Act as liaison with physician and supportive-care personnel. Prepare equipment such as immobilization, treatment, and protection devices. Maintain records, reports, and files. Assist in dosimetry procedures and tumor localization. **Examples:** Dosimetrist; Radiation Therapy Technologist.

29-1125 Recreational Therapists

Plan, direct, or coordinate medically approved recreation programs for patients in hospitals, nursing homes, or other institutions. Plan, direct, or coordinate sports, trips, dramatics, social activities, and arts and crafts. Assess patient's condition and recommend appropriate recreational activity. **Example:** Therapeutic Recreation Specialist.

29-0000
Healthcare
Practitioners
and
Technical
Occupations

29-1126 Respiratory Therapists

Assess, treat, and care for patients with breathing disorders. Assume primary responsibility for all respiratory care modalities, including the supervision of respiratory therapy technicians. Initiate and conduct therapeutic procedures. Maintain patient records. Select, assemble, check, and operate equipment. **Examples:** Inhalation Therapist; Respiratory Care Practitioner; Oxygen Therapist.

29-1127 Speech-Language Pathologists

Assess and treat persons with speech, language, voice, and fluency disorders. Select alternative communication systems and teach their use. Perform research related to speech and language problems. **Examples:** Oral Therapist; Speech Clinician; Speech Therapist.

29-1129 Therapists, All Other

All therapists not listed separately. **Examples:** Corrective and Manual Arts Therapist; Hydrotherapist; Music Therapist.

29-1130 Veterinarians

This broad occupation is the same as the detailed occupation:
29-1131 Veterinarians

29-1131 Veterinarians

Diagnose and treat diseases and dysfunctions of animals. Engage in a particular function such as research and development, consultation, administration, technical writing, sale or production of commercial products, or rendering of technical services to commercial firms or other organizations. Includes veterinarians who inspect livestock. **Examples:** Animal Pathologist; Animal Surgeon; Veterinary Bacteriologist.

29-1190 Miscellaneous Health Diagnosing and Treating Practitioners

This broad occupation is the same as the detailed occupation:
29-1199 Health Diagnosing and Treating Practitioners, All Other

29-1199 Health Diagnosing and Treating Practitioners, All Other

All health diagnosing and treating practitioners not listed separately. **Examples:** Acupuncturist; Homeopathic Doctor; Hypnotherapist.

29-2000 Health Technologists and Technicians

29-2010 Clinical Laboratory Technologists and Technicians

This broad occupation includes the following two detailed occupations:
29-2011 Medical and Clinical Laboratory Technologists
29-2012 Medical and Clinical Laboratory Technicians

29-2011 Medical and Clinical Laboratory Technologists

Perform complex medical laboratory tests for diagnosis, treatment, and prevention of disease. Train or supervise staff. **Examples:** Blood Bank Technologist; Cytotechnologist; Immunohematologist.

29-2012 Medical and Clinical Laboratory Technicians

Perform routine medical laboratory tests for the diagnosis, treatment, and prevention of disease. Work under the supervision of a medical technologist. **Examples:** Blood Bank Technician; Cytotechnician; Serology Technician.

29-2020 Dental Hygienists

This broad occupation is the same as the detailed occupation:
29-2021 Dental Hygienists

29-2021 Dental Hygienists

Clean teeth and examine oral areas, head, and neck for signs of oral disease. Educate patients on oral hygiene; take and develop X rays; apply fluoride or sealants. **Example:** Oral Hygienist.

29-2030 Diagnostic Related Technologists and Technicians

This broad occupation includes the following four detailed occupations:
29-2031 Cardiovascular Technologists and Technicians
29-2032 Diagnostic Medical Sonographers
29-2033 Nuclear Medicine Technologists
29-2034 Radiologic Technologists and Technicians

29-2031 Cardiovascular Technologists and Technicians

Conduct tests on pulmonary or cardiovascular systems of patients for diagnostic purposes. Conduct or assist in electrocardiograms, cardiac catheterizations, pulmonary function tests, lung capacity tests, and similar tests. Includes vascular technologists. **Examples:** Cardiographer; Cardiopulmonary Technologist; E.K.G. Technician.

29-0000
Healthcare
Practitioners
and
Technical
Occupations

29-2032 Diagnostic Medical Sonographers

Produce ultrasonic recordings of internal organs for use by physicians. **Examples:** Ultrasonic Tester; Ultrasound Technologist.

29-2033 Nuclear Medicine Technologists

Prepare, administer, and measure radioactive isotopes in therapeutic, diagnostic, and tracer studies, using a variety of radioisotope equipment. Prepare stock solutions of radioactive materials; calculate doses to be administered by radiologists. Subject patients to radiation. Execute studies of blood volume, red cell survival, and fat absorption, following standard laboratory techniques. **Example:** Radioisotope Technician.

29-2034 Radiologic Technologists and Technicians

Take X rays and CAT scans; administer nonradioactive materials into patient's blood stream for diagnostic purposes. Includes technologists who specialize in other modalities such as computed tomography and magnetic resonance. Includes workers whose primary duties are to demonstrate portions of the human body on X-ray film or fluoroscopic screen. **Examples:** CAT Scan Operator; Skiagrapher; X-Ray Technician.

29-2040 Emergency Medical Technicians and Paramedics

This broad occupation is the same as the detailed occupation:
29-2041 Emergency Medical Technicians and Paramedics

29-2041 Emergency Medical Technicians and Paramedics

Assess injuries; administer emergency medical care; extricate trapped individuals. Transport injured or sick persons to medical facilities. **Example:** E.M.T.

29-2050 Health Diagnosing and Treating Practitioner Support Technicians

This broad occupation includes the following six detailed occupations:
29-2051 Dietetic Technicians
29-2052 Pharmacy Technicians
29-2053 Psychiatric Technicians
29-2054 Respiratory Therapy Technicians
29-2055 Surgical Technologists
29-2056 Veterinary Technologists and Technicians

29-2051 Dietetic Technicians

Assist dietitians in the provision of food service and nutritional programs. Plan and produce meals based on established guidelines, teach principles of food and nutrition, or counsel individuals, all under the supervision of dietitians.

29-2052 Pharmacy Technicians

Prepare medications, under the direction of a pharmacist. Measure, mix, count out, label, and record amounts and dosages of medications.

29-2053 Psychiatric Technicians

Care for mentally impaired or emotionally disturbed individuals, following physician instructions and hospital procedures. Monitor patients' physical and emotional well-being; report to medical staff. Participate in rehabilitation and treatment programs; help with personal hygiene; administer oral medications and hypodermic injections. **Example:** Mental Health Technician.

29-2054 Respiratory Therapy Technicians

Provide specific, well-defined respiratory-care procedures, under the direction of respiratory therapists and physicians. **Example:** Oxygen Therapy Technician.

29-2055 Surgical Technologists

Assist in operations, under the supervision of surgeons, registered nurses, or other surgical personnel. Help set up operating room; prepare and transport patients for surgery; adjust lights and equipment. Pass instruments and other supplies to surgeons and surgeons' assistants; hold retractors; cut sutures; help count sponges, needles, supplies, and instruments. **Examples:** Operating Room Technician; Scrub Technician; Surgical Orderly.

29-2056 Veterinary Technologists and Technicians

Perform medical tests in a laboratory environment for use in the treatment and diagnosis of diseases in animals. Prepare vaccines and serums for prevention of diseases. Prepare tissue samples; take blood samples; execute laboratory tests such as urinalysis and blood counts. Clean and sterilize instruments and materials; maintain equipment and machines. **Examples:** Animal Technician; Veterinary X-ray Operator.

29-0000
Healthcare
Practitioners
and
Technical
Occupations

29-2060 Licensed Practical and Licensed Vocational Nurses

This broad occupation is the same as the detailed occupation:
29-2061 Licensed Practical and Licensed Vocational Nurses

29-2061 Licensed Practical and Licensed Vocational Nurses

Care for ill, injured, convalescent, or disabled persons in hospitals, nursing homes, clinics, private homes, group homes, and similar institutions. Work under the supervision of a registered nurse. Obtain required licensing. **Example:** Licensed Attendant.

29-2070 Medical Records and Health Information Technicians

This broad occupation is the same as the detailed occupation:
29-2071 Medical Records and Health Information Technicians

29-2071 Medical Records and Health Information Technicians

Compile, process, and maintain medical records of hospital and clinic patients in a manner consistent with medical, administrative, ethical, legal, and regulatory requirements of the heathcare system. Process, maintain, compile, and report patient information for health requirements and standards. **Examples:** Disability Rater; Medical Records Specialist; Medical Library Historian.

29-2080 Opticians, Dispensing

This broad occupation is the same as the detailed occupation:
29-2081 Opticians, Dispensing

29-2081 Opticians, Dispensing

Design, measure, fit, and adapt lenses and frames for client, according to written optical prescription or specification. Assist client with selecting frames. Measure customer for size of eyeglasses; coordinate frames with facial and eye measurements and with optical prescription. Prepare work order for optical laboratory, including instructions for grinding and mounting lenses in frames. Verify exactness of finished lens spectacles. Adjust frame and lens position to fit client. Shape or reshape frames. Includes contact lens opticians. **Examples:** Contact Lens Fitter; Eyeglass Fitter.

29-2090 Miscellaneous Health Technologists and Technicians

This broad occupation includes the following two detailed occupations:
29-2091 Orthotists and Prosthetists
29-2099 Health Technologists and Technicians, All Other

29-2091 Orthotists and Prosthetists

Fit and prepare orthopedic braces or prostheses, to assist patients with disabling conditions of limbs and spine or with partial or total absence of limb. **Examples:** Artificial Limb Fitter; Orthopedic Mechanic.

29-2099 Health Technologists and Technicians, All Other

All health technologists and technicians not listed separately. **Examples:** Dialysis Technician; Encephalographer; Hearing Aid Specialist.

29-9000 Other Healthcare Practitioners and Technical Occupations

29-9010 Occupational Health and Safety Specialists and Technicians

This broad occupation includes the following two detailed occupations:
29-9011 Occupational Health and Safety Specialists
29-9012 Occupational Health and Safety Technicians

29-9011 Occupational Health and Safety Specialists

Review, evaluate, and analyze work environments. Design programs and procedures to control, eliminate, and prevent disease or injury caused by chemical, physical, and biological agents or ergonomic factors. Conduct inspections; enforce adherence to laws and regulations governing the health and safety of individuals. Work in either the public or private sector. Includes environmental protection officers. **Examples:** Health Sanitarian; Industrial Hygienist; Health Inspector.

29-9012 Occupational Health and Safety Technicians

Collect data on work environments for analysis by occupational health and safety specialists. Implement and conduct evaluation of programs designed to limit chemical, physical, biological, and ergonomic risks to workers. **Example:** Mine Examiner.

29-9090 Miscellaneous Health Practitioners and Technical Workers

This broad occupation includes the following two detailed occupations:
29-9091 Athletic Trainers
29-9099 Healthcare Practitioners and Technical Workers, All Other

29-9091 Athletic Trainers

Evaluate, advise, and treat athletes, to help them recover from injury, avoid injury, or maintain peak physical fitness.

29-9099 Healthcare Practitioners and Technical Workers, All Other

All healthcare practitioners and technical workers not listed separately.

29-0000
Healthcare
Practitioners
and
Technical
Occupations

31-0000 HEALTHCARE SUPPORT OCCUPATIONS

31-1000 Nursing, Psychiatric, and Home Health Aides

31-1010 Nursing, Psychiatric, and Home Health Aides

This broad occupation includes the following three detailed occupations:
31-1011 Home Health Aides
31-1012 Nursing Aides, Orderlies, and Attendants
31-1013 Psychiatric Aides

31-1011 Home Health Aides

Provide routine, personal healthcare, such as bathing, dressing, or grooming, to elderly, convalescent, or disabled persons, in the homes of patients or in a residential care facility. **Example:** Home Attendant.

31-1012 Nursing Aides, Orderlies, and Attendants

Provide basic patient care, under direction of nursing staff. Feed, bathe, dress, groom, or move patients; change linens. Excludes "Home Health Aides" (31-1011) and "Psychiatric Aides" (31-1013). **Examples:** Certified Nursing Assistant; Hospital Aide; Infirmary Attendant.

31-1013 Psychiatric Aides

Assist mentally impaired or emotionally disturbed patients, under direction of nursing and medical staff. **Examples:** Charge Attendant; Psychiatric Orderly.

31-2000 Occupational and Physical Therapist Assistants and Aides

31-2010 Occupational Therapist Assistants and Aides

This broad occupation includes the following two detailed occupations:
31-2011 Occupational Therapist Assistants
31-2012 Occupational Therapist Aides

31-2011 Occupational Therapist Assistants

Assist occupational therapists in providing occupational therapy treatments and procedures. Assist in development of treatment plans, carry out routine functions, direct activity programs, and document the progress of treatments, all in accordance with state laws. Obtain required formal training. **Example:** Occupational Therapy Technician.

31-2012 Occupational Therapist Aides

Work under close supervision of an occupational therapist or occupational therapy assistant. Perform only delegated, selected, or routine tasks in specific situations, including preparing the patient and the treatment room.

31-2020 Physical Therapist Assistants and Aides

This broad occupation includes the following two detailed occupations:
31-2021 Physical Therapist Assistants
31-2022 Physical Therapist Aides

31-2021 Physical Therapist Assistants

Assist physical therapists in providing physical therapy treatments and procedures. In accordance with state laws, assist in the development of treatment plans, carry out routine functions, and document the progress of treatment. Modify specific treatments, in accordance with patient status and within the scope of the treatment plans established by a physical therapist. Obtain required formal training. **Example:** Corrective Therapy Assistant.

31-2022 Physical Therapist Aides

Work under close supervision of a physical therapist or physical therapy assistant. Perform only delegated, selected, or routine tasks in specific situations, including preparing the patient and the treatment area. **Example:** Physiotherapy Aide.

31-9000 Other Healthcare Support Occupations

31-9010 Massage Therapists

This broad occupation is the same as the detailed occupation:
31-9011 Massage Therapists

31-9011 Massage Therapists

Massage customers for hygienic or remedial purposes. **Examples:** Masseuse; Masseur; Rubber.

31-9090 Miscellaneous Healthcare Support Occupations

This broad occupation includes the following seven detailed occupations:
31-9091 Dental Assistants
31-9092 Medical Assistants
31-9093 Medical Equipment Preparers
31-9094 Medical Transcriptionists
31-9095 Pharmacy Aides
31-9096 Veterinary Assistants and Laboratory Animal Caretakers
31-9099 Healthcare Support Workers, All Other

31-0000
Healthcare
Support
Occupations

31-9091 Dental Assistants

Assist dentist, prepare patient, set up equipment, and keep records.

31-9092 Medical Assistants

Perform administrative duties under the direction of physician, including scheduling appointments, maintaining medical records, billing, and coding for insurance purposes. Perform clinical duties under the direction of physician, including taking and recording vital signs and medical histories, preparing patients for examination, drawing blood, and administering medications. Excludes "Physician Assistants" (29-1071). **Examples:** Morgue Attendant; Ophthalmic Aide; Physicians Aide.

31-9093 Medical Equipment Preparers

Prepare, sterilize, install, or clean laboratory or healthcare equipment. Perform routine laboratory tasks. Operate or inspect equipment. **Examples:** Bandage Maker; Hot Packer; Sterilizer.

31-9094 Medical Transcriptionists

Use transcribing machines with headset and foot pedal, to listen to recordings by physicians and other healthcare professionals who dictate a variety of medical reports, such as emergency room visits, diagnostic imaging studies, operations, chart reviews, and final summaries. Transcribe dictated reports. Translate medical jargon and abbreviations into their expanded forms. Edit as necessary; return reports in either printed or electronic form to the dictator for review and signature or for correction. **Example:** Medical Stenographer.

31-9095 Pharmacy Aides

Record drugs delivered to the pharmacy; store incoming merchandise; inform supervisor of stock needs. Operate cash register; accept prescriptions for filling. **Examples:** Dispensary Attendant; Prescription Clerk.

31-9096 Veterinary Assistants and Laboratory Animal Caretakers

Feed, water, and examine pets and other nonfarm animals for signs of illness, disease, or injury, in laboratories and in animal hospitals and clinics. Clean and disinfect cages and work areas; sterilize laboratory and surgical equipment. Provide routine post-operative care; administer medication orally or topically; prepare samples for laboratory examination, under the supervision of veterinary or laboratory animal technologists or technicians, veterinarians, or scientists. Excludes "Nonfarm Animal Caretakers" (39-2021).

31-9099 Healthcare Support Workers, All Other

All healthcare support workers not listed separately. **Examples:** Phlebotomist; Reducing Salon Attendant.

33-0000 PROTECTIVE SERVICE OCCUPATIONS

33-1000 First-Line Supervisors/Managers, Protective Service Workers

33-1010 First-Line Supervisors/Managers, Law Enforcement Workers

This broad occupation includes the following two detailed occupations:
33-1011 First-Line Supervisors/Managers of Correctional Officers
33-1012 First-Line Supervisors/Managers of Police and Detectives

33-1011 First-Line Supervisors/Managers of Correctional Officers

Supervise and coordinate activities of correctional officers and jailers. **Examples:** Prison Guard Supervisor; Prison Warden.

33-1012 First-Line Supervisors/Managers of Police and Detectives

Supervise and coordinate activities of members of police force. **Examples:** Chief of Police; Precinct Captain.

33-1020 First-Line Supervisors/Managers, Fire Fighting and Prevention Workers

This broad occupation is the same as the detailed occupation:
33-1021 First-Line Supervisors/Managers of Fire Fighting and Prevention Workers

33-1021 First-Line Supervisors/Managers of Fire Fighting and Prevention Workers

Supervise and coordinate activities of workers engaged in fire fighting and in fire prevention and control. **Examples:** Fire Captain; Fire Chief; Fire Marshal.

33-1090 Miscellaneous First-Line Supervisors/Managers, Protective Service Workers

This broad occupation is the same as the detailed occupation:
33-1099 First-Line Supervisors/Managers, Protective Service Workers, All Other

33-1099 First-Line Supervisors/Managers, Protective Service Workers, All Other

All protective service supervisors not listed separately. **Examples:** Security Director; Supervisor Animal Cruelty Investigation; Supervisor Plant Protection.

33-0000
Protective
Service
Occupations

33-2000 Fire Fighting and Prevention Workers

33-2010 Fire Fighters

This broad occupation is the same as the detailed occupation:
33-2011 Fire Fighters

33-2011 Fire Fighters

Control and extinguish fires; respond to emergency situations where life, property, or the environment is at risk. Participate in fire prevention, emergency medical service, hazardous material response, search and rescue, and disaster management. **Examples:** Explosive Ordnance Disposal Technician; Fireboat Operator; Smoke Jumper.

33-2020 Fire Inspectors

This broad occupation includes the following two detailed occupations:
33-2021 Fire Inspectors and Investigators
33-2022 Forest Fire Inspectors and Prevention Specialists

33-2021 Fire Inspectors and Investigators

Inspect buildings to detect fire hazards and to enforce local ordinances and state laws. Investigate and gather facts to determine cause of fires and explosions. **Example:** Arson Investigator.

33-2022 Forest Fire Inspectors and Prevention Specialists

Enforce fire regulations and inspect for forest fire hazards. Report forest fires and weather conditions. **Examples:** Forest Fire Control Officer; District Ranger; Fire Ranger.

33-3000 Law Enforcement Workers

33-3010 Bailiffs, Correctional Officers, and Jailers

This broad occupation includes the following two detailed occupations:
33-3011 Bailiffs
33-3012 Correctional Officers and Jailers

33-3011 Bailiffs

Maintain order in courts of law. **Examples:** Court Officer; Sergeant at Arms.

33-3012 Correctional Officers and Jailers

Guard inmates in penal or rehabilitative institution, in accordance with established regulations and procedures. Guard prisoners in transit between jail, courtroom, prison, or other point. Includes deputy sheriffs and police who spend the majority of their time guarding prisoners in correctional institutions. **Examples:** Convict Guard; Custodial Officer; Prison Guard.

33-3020 Detectives and Criminal Investigators

This broad occupation is the same as the detailed occupation:
33-3021 Detectives and Criminal Investigators

33-3021 Detectives and Criminal Investigators

Conduct investigations related to suspected violations of federal, state, or local laws, to prevent or solve crimes. Excludes "Private Detectives and Investigators" (33-9021). **Examples:** Police Inspector; Deputy United States Marshal; Narcotics Agent.

33-3030 Fish and Game Wardens

This broad occupation is the same as the detailed occupation:
33-3031 Fish and Game Wardens

33-3031 Fish and Game Wardens

Patrol assigned area to prevent fish and game law violations. Investigate reports of damage to crops or property by wildlife. Compile biological data. **Examples:** State Game Protector; Wildlife Control Agent; Wildlife Officer.

33-3040 Parking Enforcement Workers

This broad occupation is the same as the detailed occupation:
33-3041 Parking Enforcement Workers

33-3041 Parking Enforcement Workers

Patrol an assigned area such as a public parking lot or a section of a city, to issue tickets to overtime parking violators and illegally parked vehicles. **Examples:** Parking Enforcement Officer; Parking Meter Checker.

33-3050 Police Officers

This broad occupation includes the following two detailed occupations:
33-3051 Police and Sheriff's Patrol Officers
33-3052 Transit and Railroad Police

33-3051 Police and Sheriff's Patrol Officers

Maintain order, enforce laws and ordinances, and protect life and property in an assigned patrol district. Perform combination of following duties: patrol a specific area on foot or in a vehicle; direct traffic; issue traffic summonses; investigate accidents; apprehend and arrest suspects, or serve legal processes of courts. **Examples:** Border Guard; Campus Police; City Constable.

33-3052 Transit and Railroad Police

Protect and police railroad and transit property, employees, or passengers. **Examples:** Railroad Detective; Track Patrol.

33-9000 Other Protective Service Workers

33-9010 Animal Control Workers

This broad occupation is the same as the detailed occupation:
33-9011 Animal Control Workers

33-9011 Animal Control Workers

Handle animals, to investigate reports of mistreatment or to control abandoned, dangerous, or unattended animals. **Examples:** Animal Warden; Dog Catcher; Humane Officer.

33-9020 Private Detectives and Investigators

This broad occupation is the same as the detailed occupation:
33-9021 Private Detectives and Investigators

33-9021 Private Detectives and Investigators

Detect occurrences of unlawful acts or infractions of rules, in private establishment. Seek, examine, and compile information for client. **Example:** House Detective.

33-9030 Security Guards and Gaming Surveillance Officers

This broad occupation includes the following two detailed occupations:
33-9031 Gaming Surveillance Officers and Gaming Investigators
33-9032 Security Guards

33-9031 Gaming Surveillance Officers and Gaming Investigators

Act as oversight and security agent for management and customers. Observe casino or casino hotel operation for irregular activities such as cheating or theft, by employees or patrons. Use one-way mirrors above the casino floor, in the cashier's cage, and at the desk. Use audio-video equipment to observe operation of the business. Provide verbal and written reports of all violations and suspicious behavior to supervisor. **Examples:** Casino Surveillance Officer; Casino Investigator.

33-9032 Security Guards

Guard, patrol, or monitor premises, to prevent theft, violence, or infractions of rules. **Examples:** Bodyguard; Bouncer; Watchguard.

33-9090 Miscellaneous Protective Service Workers

This broad occupation includes the following three detailed occupations:
33-9091 Crossing Guards
33-9092 Lifeguards, Ski Patrol, and Other Recreational Protective Service Workers
33-9099 Protective Service Workers, All Other

33-9091 Crossing Guards

Guide or control vehicular or pedestrian traffic at streets, schools, railroad crossings, construction sites, or other locations. **Examples:** Flagger; Gate Operator; School Patrol.

33-9092 Lifeguards, Ski Patrol, and Other Recreational Protective Service Workers

Monitor recreational areas such as pools, beaches, or ski slopes, to provide assistance and protection to participants.

33-9099 Protective Service Workers, All Other

All protective service workers not listed separately. **Examples:** Park Ranger; Surveillance-System Monitor; Bus Monitor.

35-0000 FOOD PREPARATION AND SERVING RELATED OCCUPATIONS

35-1000 Supervisors, Food Preparation and Serving Workers

35-1010 First-Line Supervisors/Managers, Food Preparation and Serving Workers

This broad occupation includes the following two detailed occupations:
35-1011 Chefs and Head Cooks
35-1012 First-Line Supervisors/Managers of Food Preparation and Serving Workers

35-1011 Chefs and Head Cooks

Direct the preparation, seasoning, and cooking of salads, soups, fish, meats, vegetables, desserts, or other foods. Plan and price menu items; order supplies; keep records and accounts. Cook. **Examples:** Executive Chef; Pastry Chef; Sous Chef.

35-1012 First-Line Supervisors/Managers of Food Preparation and Serving Workers

Supervise workers engaged in preparing and serving food. **Examples:** Cafeteria Manager; Caterer; Bar Manager.

35-2000 Cooks and Food Preparation Workers

35-2010 Cooks

This broad occupation includes the following six detailed occupations:
35-2011 Cooks, Fast Food
35-2012 Cooks, Institution and Cafeteria
35-2013 Cooks, Private Household
35-2014 Cooks, Restaurant
35-2015 Cooks, Short Order
35-2019 Cooks, All Other

35-2011 Cooks, Fast Food

Prepare and cook food in a fast food restaurant with a limited menu. Prepare a few basic items, using large-volume, single-purpose cooking equipment. **Examples:** Fry Cook; Pizza Maker.

35-2012 Cooks, Institution and Cafeteria

Prepare and cook large quantities of food for institutions such as schools, hospitals, or cafeterias. **Examples:** Camp Cook; Mess Cook; Galley Cook.

35-2013 Cooks, Private Household

Prepare meals in private homes.

35-2014 Cooks, Restaurant

Prepare, season, and cook soups, meats, vegetables, desserts, or other food stuffs in restaurants. Order supplies; keep records and accounts; price items on menu; plan menu. **Examples:** Broiler Cook; Specialty Foreign Food Cook; Garde-Manger.

35-2015 Cooks, Short Order

Prepare and cook to order a variety of foods that require only a short preparation time. Take customers' orders and serve patrons at counters or tables. Excludes "Fast Food Cooks" (35-2011). **Examples:** Barbecue Cook; Griddle Cook.

35-2019 Cooks, All Other

All cooks not listed separately.

35-2020 Food Preparation Workers

This broad occupation is the same as the detailed occupation:
35-2021 Food Preparation Workers

35-2021 Food Preparation Workers

Perform a variety of food preparation duties other than cooking, such as preparing cold foods and shellfish, slicing meat, and brewing coffee or tea. **Examples:** Coffee Maker; Kitchen Helper; Sandwich Maker.

35-3000 Food and Beverage Serving Workers

35-3010 Bartenders

This broad occupation is the same as the detailed occupation:
35-3011 Bartenders

35-3011 Bartenders

Mix and serve drinks to patrons, directly or through waitstaff. **Examples:** Barkeeper; Taproom Attendant.

35-3020 Fast Food and Counter Workers

This broad occupation includes the following two detailed occupations:
35-3021 Combined Food Preparation and Serving Workers, Including Fast Food
35-3022 Counter Attendants, Cafeteria, Food Concession, and Coffee Shop

35-3021 Combined Food Preparation and Serving Workers, Including Fast Food

Perform duties which combine both food preparation and food service. **Examples:** Caterers Aide; Deli Clerk; Mess Attendant.

35-3022 Counter Attendants, Cafeteria, Food Concession, and Coffee Shop

Serve food to diners at counter or from a steam table. Include counter attendants who also wait tables with "Waiters and Waitresses" (35-3031). **Examples:** Canteen Operator; Snack Bar Attendant; Hot Dog Attendant.

35-3030 Waiters and Waitresses

This broad occupation is the same as the detailed occupation:
35-3031 Waiters and Waitresses

35-3031 Waiters and Waitresses

Take orders and serve food and beverages to patrons at tables in dining establishment. Excludes "Counter Attendants, Cafeteria, Food Concession, and Coffee Shop" (35-3022). **Examples:** Cocktail Waiter; Wine Steward; Head Waitress.

35-3040 Food Servers, Nonrestaurant

This broad occupation is the same as the detailed occupation:
35-3041 Food Servers, Nonrestaurant

35-3041 Food Servers, Nonrestaurant

Serve food to patrons outside of a restaurant environment, such as in hotels, hospital rooms, or cars. Excludes "Door-to-Door Sales Workers, News and Street Vendors, and Related Workers" (41-9091) and "Counter Attendants, Cafeteria, Food Concession, and Coffee Shop" (35-3022). **Examples:** Curb Attendant; Hospital Tray-Service Worker; Room Service Clerk.

35-9000 Other Food Preparation and Serving Related Workers

35-0000
Food
Preparation
and Serving
Related
Occupations

35-9010 Dining Room and Cafeteria Attendants and Bartender Helpers

This broad occupation is the same as the detailed occupation:
35-9011 Dining Room and Cafeteria Attendants and Bartender Helpers

35-9011 Dining Room and Cafeteria Attendants and Bartender Helpers

Facilitate food service. Clean tables; carry dirty dishes; replace soiled table linens; set tables. Replenish supply of clean linens, silverware, glassware, and dishes. Supply service bar with food; serve water, butter, and coffee to patrons. **Examples:** Busser; Lunchroom Attendant; Tray Setter.

35-9020 Dishwashers

This broad occupation is the same as the detailed occupation:
35-9021 Dishwashers

35-9021 Dishwashers

Clean dishes, kitchen, food preparation equipment, or utensils. **Examples:** Kitchen Cleaner; Glass Washer; Pot Washer.

35-9030 Hosts and Hostesses, Restaurant, Lounge, and Coffee Shop

This broad occupation is the same as the detailed occupation:
35-9031 Hosts and Hostesses, Restaurant, Lounge, and Coffee Shop

35-9031 Hosts and Hostesses, Restaurant, Lounge, and Coffee Shop

Welcome patrons and seat them at tables or in lounge. Help ensure quality of facilities and service. **Examples:** Maitre D'; Dining Room Host.

35-9090 Miscellaneous Food Preparation and Serving Related Workers

This broad occupation is the same as the detailed occupation:
35-9099 Food Preparation and Serving Related Workers, All Other

35-9099 Food Preparation and Serving Related Workers, All Other

All food preparation and serving related workers not listed separately. **Examples:** Vending Machine Attendant; Cafeteria Line Runner.

37-0000 BUILDING AND GROUNDS CLEANING AND MAINTENANCE OCCUPATIONS

37-1000 Supervisors, Building and Grounds Cleaning and Maintenance Workers

37-1010 First-Line Supervisors/Managers, Building and Grounds Cleaning and Maintenance Workers

This broad occupation includes the following two detailed occupations:
37-1011 First-Line Supervisors/Managers of Housekeeping and Janitorial Workers
37-1012 First-Line Supervisors/Managers of Landscaping, Lawn Service, and Groundskeeping Workers

37-1011 First-Line Supervisors/Managers of Housekeeping and Janitorial Workers

Supervise work activities of cleaning personnel in hotels, hospitals, offices, and other establishments. **Examples:** Building Superintendent; Household Manager; Housekeeping Supervisor.

37-1012 First-Line Supervisors/Managers of Landscaping, Lawn Service, and Groundskeeping Workers

Plan, organize, direct, or coordinate activities of workers engaged in landscaping or groundskeeping activities such as planting and maintaining ornamental trees, shrubs, flowers, and lawns and applying fertilizers, pesticides, and other chemicals. Follow contract specifications. Coordinate activities of workers engaged in terracing hillsides, building retaining walls, constructing pathways, installing patios, and similar activities, following a landscape design plan. Review contracts to ascertain service, machine, and workforce requirements. Answer inquiries from potential customers regarding methods, materials, and price ranges. Prepare estimates according to labor, material, and machine costs. **Examples:** Landscape Contractor; Golf Course Superintendent; Nursery Supervisor.

37-2000 Building Cleaning and Pest Control Workers

37-2010 Building Cleaning Workers

This broad occupation includes the following three detailed occupations:
37-2011 Janitors and Cleaners, Except Maids and Housekeeping Cleaners

37-2012 Maids and Housekeeping Cleaners
37-2019 Building Cleaning Workers, All Other

37-2011 Janitors and Cleaners, Except Maids and Housekeeping Cleaners

Keep buildings in clean and orderly condition. Perform heavy cleaning duties such as cleaning floors, shampooing rugs, washing walls and glass, and removing rubbish. Tend furnace and boiler; perform routine maintenance activities; notify management of need for repairs; clean snow or debris from sidewalk. **Examples:** Floor Cleaner; Building Custodian; Window Washer.

37-2012 Maids and Housekeeping Cleaners

Perform any combination of light cleaning duties, to maintain private households or commercial establishments such as hotels, restaurants, and hospitals in a clean and orderly manner. Perform duties such as making beds, replenishing linens, cleaning rooms and halls, and vacuuming. **Examples:** Bed Maker; Chamber Maid; Housekeeper.

37-2019 Building Cleaning Workers, All Other

All building cleaning workers not listed separately. **Examples:** Chimney Sweep; Air Purifier Servicer.

37-2020 Pest Control Workers

This broad occupation is the same as the detailed occupation:
37-2021 Pest Control Workers

37-2021 Pest Control Workers

Spray or release chemical solutions or toxic gases and set traps, to kill pests and vermin such as mice, termites, and roaches that infest buildings and surrounding areas. **Examples:** Exterminator; Exterminator Helper; Fumigator.

37-3000 Grounds Maintenance Workers

37-3010 Grounds Maintenance Workers

This broad occupation includes the following four detailed occupations:
37-3011 Landscaping and Groundskeeping Workers
37-3012 Pesticide Handlers, Sprayers, and Applicators, Vegetation
37-3013 Tree Trimmers and Pruners
37-3019 Grounds Maintenance Workers, All Other

37-3011 Landscaping and Groundskeeping Workers

Landscape or maintain grounds of property, using hand or power tools or equipment. Perform a variety of tasks, including sod laying, mowing, trimming, planting, watering, fertilizing, digging, raking, sprinkler installation, and installation of mortarless segmental concrete masonry wall units. Excludes "Farmworkers and Laborers, Crop, Nursery, and Greenhouse" (45-2092). **Examples:** Landscape Gardener; Outdoor Sprinkler Installer; Greenskeeper.

37-3012 Pesticide Handlers, Sprayers, and Applicators, Vegetation

Mix or apply pesticides, herbicides, fungicides, or insecticides, through sprays, dusts, vapors, soil incorporation, or by chemical application on trees, shrubs, lawns, or botanical crops. Obtain required specific training and state or federal certification. Excludes "Commercial Pilots" (53-2012) who operate aviation equipment to dust or spray crops. **Examples:** Fruit Sprayer; Weed Controller.

37-3013 Tree Trimmers and Pruners

Cut away dead or excess branches from trees or shrubs, to maintain right-of-way for roads, sidewalks, or utilities, or to improve appearance, health, and value of trees. Prune or treat trees or shrubs, using handsaws, pruning hooks, sheers, and clippers. Use truck-mounted lifts and power pruners. Fill cavities in trees, to promote healing and to prevent deterioration. Excludes workers who primarily perform duties of "Pesticide Handlers, Sprayers, and Applicators, Vegetation" (37-3012) and "Landscaping and Groundskeeping Workers" (37-3011). **Examples:** Tree Doctor; Grape Vine Pruner.

37-3019 Grounds Maintenance Workers, All Other

All grounds maintenance workers not listed separately.

39-0000 PERSONAL CARE AND SERVICE OCCUPATIONS

39-1000 Supervisors, Personal Care and Service Workers

39-1010 First-Line Supervisors/Managers of Gaming Workers

This broad occupation includes the following two detailed occupations:
39-1011 Gaming Supervisors
39-1012 Slot Key Persons

39-1011 Gaming Supervisors

Supervise gaming operations and personnel in an assigned area. Circulate among tables and observe operations. Ensure that stations and games are covered for each shift. Explain and interpret operating rules of house to patrons. Plan and organize activities and create friendly atmosphere for guests in hotels or casinos. Adjust service complaints. Excludes "Slot Key Persons" (39-1012). **Examples:** Executive Casino Host; Table Games Supervisor; Pit Boss.

39-1012 Slot Key Persons

Coordinate or supervise functions of slot department workers, to provide service to patrons. Handle and settle complaints of players. Verify and pay off jackpots. Reset slot machines after payoffs. Make minor repairs or adjustments to slot machines. Recommend removal of slot machines for repair. Report hazards and enforces safety rules. **Example:** Slot Floor Person.

39-1020 First-Line Supervisors/Managers of Personal Service Workers

This broad occupation is the same as the detailed occupation:
39-1021 First-Line Supervisors/Managers of Personal Service Workers

39-1021 First-Line Supervisors/Managers of Personal Service Workers

Supervise and coordinate activities of personal service workers such as supervisors of flight attendants, hairdressers, or caddies. **Examples:** Caddymaster; Barber Shop Manager; Health Club Manager.

39-2000 Animal Care and Service Workers

39-2010 Animal Trainers

This broad occupation is the same as the detailed occupation:
39-2011 Animal Trainers

39-2011 Animal Trainers

Train animals for riding, harness, security, performance, or obedience, or for assisting persons with disabilities. Accustom animals to human voice and contact; condition animals to respond to commands. Train animals according to prescribed standards for show or competition. Train animals to carry pack loads or to work as part of pack team. **Examples:** Dog Trainer; Horse Breaker; Lion Trainer.

39-2020 Nonfarm Animal Caretakers

This broad occupation is the same as the detailed occupation:
39-2021 Nonfarm Animal Caretakers

39-2021 Nonfarm Animal Caretakers

Feed, water, groom, bathe, exercise, or otherwise care for pets and other nonfarm animals such as dogs, cats, ornamental fish or birds, zoo animals, and mice. Work in settings such as kennels, animal shelters, zoos, circuses, and aquariums. Keep records of feedings, treatments, and animals received or discharged. Clean, disinfect, and repair cages, pens, or fish tanks. Excludes "Veterinary Assistants and Laboratory Animal Caretakers" (31-9096). **Examples:** Dog Groomer; Kennel Worker; Stable Attendant.

39-3000 Entertainment Attendants and Related Workers

39-3010 Gaming Services Workers

This broad occupation includes the following three detailed occupations:
39-3011 Gaming Dealers
39-3012 Gaming and Sports Book Writers and Runners
39-3019 Gaming Service Workers, All Other

39-3011 Gaming Dealers

Operate table games. Stand or sit behind table and operate games of chance, by dispensing the appropriate number of cards or blocks to players or by operating other gaming equipment. Compare the house's hand against players' hands; pay off or collect players' money or chips. **Examples:** Blackjack Dealers; Roulette Dealers; Craps Dealers.

39-3012 Gaming and Sports Book Writers and Runners

Assist in the operation of games such as keno and bingo. Scan winning tickets presented by patrons; calculate amount of winnings; pay patrons. Operate keno and bingo equipment. Start gaming equipment that randomly selects numbers. Announce number selected until total numbers specified for each game are selected. Pick up tickets from players; collect bets; receive, verify, and record patrons' cash wagers. **Examples:** Sheet Writer; Keno Writers; Keno Runners.

39-3019 Gaming Service Workers, All Other

All gaming service workers not listed separately. **Examples:** Shill; Chip Mucker; Pit Clerk.

39-3020 Motion Picture Projectionists

This broad occupation is the same as the detailed occupation:
39-3021 Motion Picture Projectionists

39-3021 Motion Picture Projectionists

Set up and operate motion picture projection and related sound reproduction equipment. **Examples:** Chief Projectionist; Film Projector Operator.

39-3030 Ushers, Lobby Attendants, and Ticket Takers

This broad occupation is the same as the detailed occupation:
39-3031 Ushers, Lobby Attendants, and Ticket Takers

39-3031 Ushers, Lobby Attendants, and Ticket Takers

Assist patrons at entertainment events by performing duties such as collecting admission tickets and passes from patrons. Assist patrons in finding seats, in searching for lost articles, and in locating such facilities as rest rooms and telephones. **Examples:** Door Attendant; Ticket Collector.

39-3090 Miscellaneous Entertainment Attendants and Related Workers

This broad occupation includes the following four detailed occupations:
39-3091 Amusement and Recreation Attendants
39-3092 Costume Attendants
39-3093 Locker Room, Coatroom, and Dressing Room Attendants
39-3099 Entertainment Attendants and Related Workers, All Other

39-3091 Amusement and Recreation Attendants

Perform variety of attending duties at amusement or recreation facility. Schedule use of recreation facilities; maintain and provide equipment to participants of sporting events or recreational pursuits; operate amusement concessions and rides. **Examples:** Arcade Attendant; Golf Course Starter; Caddy.

39-3092 Costume Attendants

Select, fit, and take care of costumes for cast members. Aid entertainers. **Examples:** Wardrobe Custodian; Dresser.

39-3093 Locker Room, Coatroom, and Dressing Room Attendants

Provide personal items to patrons or customers in locker rooms, dressing rooms, or coatrooms. **Examples:** Bathhouse Attendant; Jockey Valet.

39-3099 Entertainment Attendants and Related Workers, All Other

All entertainment attendants and related workers not listed separately. **Example:** Department Store Greeter.

39-4000 Funeral Service Workers

39-4010 Embalmers

This broad occupation is the same as the detailed occupation:
39-4011 Embalmers

39-4011 Embalmers

Prepare bodies for interment, in conformity with legal requirements.

39-4020 Funeral Attendants

This broad occupation is the same as the detailed occupation:
39-4021 Funeral Attendants

39-4021 Funeral Attendants

Perform variety of tasks during funeral, such as placing casket in parlor or chapel prior to service, arranging floral offerings or lights around casket, directing or escorting mourners, closing casket, and issuing and storing funeral equipment. **Examples:** Mortician Helper; Pallbearer.

39-5000 Personal Appearance Workers

39-5010 Barbers and Cosmetologists

This broad occupation includes the following two detailed occupations:
39-5011 Barbers
39-5012 Hairdressers, Hairstylists, and Cosmetologists

39-5011 Barbers

Provide barbering services such as cutting, trimming, shampooing, and styling hair, trimming beards, or giving shaves. **Examples:** Barber Apprentice; Hair Cutter.

39-5012 Hairdressers, Hairstylists, and Cosmetologists

Provide beauty services such as shampooing, cutting, coloring, and styling hair and massaging and treating scalp. Apply makeup; dress wigs; perform hair removal; provide nail and skin care services. **Examples:** Beautician; Wig Stylist; Electrologist.

39-5090 Miscellaneous Personal Appearance Workers

This broad occupation includes the following four detailed occupations:
39-5091 Makeup Artists, Theatrical and Performance
39-5092 Manicurists and Pedicurists
39-5093 Shampooers
39-5094 Skin Care Specialists

39-5091 Makeup Artists, Theatrical and Performance

Apply makeup to performers, to reflect period, setting, and situation of their roles.

39-5092 Manicurists and Pedicurists

Clean and shape customers' fingernails and toenails. Polish or decorate nails. **Example:** Fingernail Sculptor.

39-5093 Shampooers

Shampoo and rinse customers' hair. **Example:** Scalp Treatment Operator.

39-5094 Skin Care Specialists

Provide skin care treatments to face and body to enhance an individual's appearance. **Example:** Esthetician.

39-6000 Transportation, Tourism, and Lodging Attendants

39-6010 Baggage Porters, Bellhops, and Concierges

This broad occupation includes the following two detailed occupations:
39-6011 Baggage Porters and Bellhops
39-6012 Concierges

39-6011 Baggage Porters and Bellhops

Handle baggage for travelers at transportation terminals or for guests at hotels or similar establishments. **Examples:** Baggage Handler; Lobby Porter; Skycap.

39-6012 Concierges

Assist patrons at hotel, apartment, or office building with personal services. Take messages; arrange or give advice on transportation, business services, or entertainment; monitor guest requests for housekeeping and maintenance.

39-6020 Tour and Travel Guides

This broad occupation includes the following two detailed occupations:
39-6021 Tour Guides and Escorts
39-6022 Travel Guides

39-6021 Tour Guides and Escorts

Escort individuals or groups on sightseeing tours or through places of interest such as industrial establishments, public buildings, and art galleries. **Examples:** Page; Sightseeing Guide.

39-6022 Travel Guides

Plan, organize, and conduct long distance cruises, tours, and expeditions, for individuals and groups. **Examples:** Cruise Director; Tour Director.

39-6030 Transportation Attendants

This broad occupation includes the following two detailed occupations:
39-6031 Flight Attendants
39-6032 Transportation Attendants, Except Flight Attendants and Baggage Porters

39-6031 Flight Attendants

Provide personal services to ensure the safety and comfort of airline passengers during flight. Greet passengers, verify tickets, explain use of safety equipment, and serve food or beverages. **Examples:** Flight Steward; Airline Stewardess.

39-6032 Transportation Attendants, Except Flight Attendants and Baggage Porters

Provide services to ensure the safety and comfort of passengers aboard ships, buses, or trains or within the station or terminal. Perform duties such as greeting passengers, explaining the use of safety equipment, serving meals or beverages, or answering questions related to travel. **Examples:** Club Car Attendant; Ground Attendant; Subway Conductor.

39-9000 Other Personal Care and Service Workers

39-9010 Child Care Workers

This broad occupation is the same as the detailed occupation:
39-9011 Child Care Workers

39-9011 Child Care Workers

Attend to children at schools, businesses, private households, and child care institutions. Perform a variety of tasks such as dressing, feeding, bathing, and overseeing play. Excludes "Preschool Teachers" (25-2011) and "Teacher Assistants" (25-9041). **Examples:** Baby Sitter; Governess; Nanny.

39-9020 Personal and Home Care Aides

This broad occupation is the same as the detailed occupation:
39-9021 Personal and Home Care Aides

39-9021 Personal and Home Care Aides

Assist elderly or disabled adults with daily living activities, at the persons' homes or in a daytime nonresidential facility. Keep house, make beds, do laundry, wash dishes, and prepare meals, at a place of residence. Provide meals and supervised activities, at nonresidential care facilities. Advise families, the elderly, and the disabled on such things as nutrition, cleanliness, and household utilities. **Examples:** Blind Escort; Caregiver; Geriatric Aide.

39-9030 Recreation and Fitness Workers

This broad occupation includes the following two detailed occupations:
39-9031 Fitness Trainers and Aerobics Instructors
39-9032 Recreation Workers

39-9031 Fitness Trainers and Aerobics Instructors

Instruct or coach groups or individuals in exercise activities and the fundamentals of sports. Demonstrate techniques and methods of participation. Observe participants and inform them of corrective measures necessary to improve their skills. Excludes fitness trainers and aerobics instructors who are required to hold teaching degrees, as those are to be reported in the appropriate teaching category. Excludes "Athletic Trainers" (29-9091). **Examples:** Exercise Teacher; Personal Trainer; Yoga Teacher.

39-9032 Recreation Workers

Conduct recreation activities with groups, in public, private, or volunteer agencies or recreation facilities. Organize and promote activities such as arts and crafts, sports, games, music, dramatics, social recreation, camping, and hobbies, taking

39-0000
Personal
Care and
Service
Occupations

into account the needs and interests of individual members. **Examples:** Camp Counselor; Playground Director; Activities Director.

39-9040 Residential Advisors

This broad occupation is the same as the detailed occupation:
39-9041 Residential Advisors

39-9041 Residential Advisors

Coordinate activities for residents of boarding schools, college fraternities or sororities, college dormitories, or similar establishments. Order supplies; determine need for maintenance, repairs, and furnishings. Maintain household records and assign rooms. Refer residents to counseling resources if needed. **Examples:** Dormitory Supervisor; House Parent.

39-9090 Miscellaneous Personal Care and Service Workers

This broad occupation is the same as the detailed occupation:
39-9099 Personal Care and Service Workers, All Other

39-9099 Personal Care and Service Workers, All Other

All personal care and service workers not listed separately. **Examples:** Shoe Shiner; Chaperone; Servant.

41-0000 SALES AND RELATED OCCUPATIONS

41-1000 Supervisors, Sales Workers

41-1010 First-Line Supervisors/Managers, Sales Workers

This broad occupation includes the following two detailed occupations:
41-1011 First-Line Supervisors/Managers of Retail Sales Workers
41-1012 First-Line Supervisors/Managers of Non-Retail Sales Workers

41-1011 First-Line Supervisors/Managers of Retail Sales Workers

Directly supervise sales workers in a retail establishment or department. Perform management functions such as purchasing, budgeting, accounting, and personnel work, in addition to supervisory duties. **Examples:** Department Manager; Flower Shop Manager; Supervisor of Cashiers.

41-1012 First-Line Supervisors/Managers of Non-Retail Sales Workers

Directly supervise and coordinate activities of sales workers other than retail sales workers. Perform duties such as budgeting, accounting, and personnel work, in addition to supervisory duties. **Examples:** District Sales Manager; Dry Cleaning Manager; Blood-Donor Recruiter Supervisor.

41-2000 Retail Sales Workers

41-2010 Cashiers

This broad occupation includes the following two detailed occupations:
41-2011 Cashiers
41-2012 Gaming Change Persons and Booth Cashiers

41-2011 Cashiers

Receive and disburse money in establishments other than financial institutions. Use electronic scanners, cash registers, or related equipment. Process credit or debit card transactions; validate checks. **Examples:** Auction Clerk; Toll Collector; Disbursement Clerk.

41-2012 Gaming Change Persons and Booth Cashiers

Exchange coins and tokens for patrons' money. Issue payoffs; obtain customer's signature on receipt when winnings exceed the amount held in the slot machine. Operate a booth in the slot machine area; furnish change persons with money

41-0000
Sales and
Related
Occupations

bank at the start of the shift; count and audit money in drawers. **Examples:** Carousel Attendant; Slot Attendant.

41-2020 Counter and Rental Clerks and Parts Salespersons

This broad occupation includes the following two detailed occupations:
41-2021 Counter and Rental Clerks
41-2022 Parts Salespersons

41-2021 Counter and Rental Clerks

Receive orders for repairs, rentals, and services. Describe available options, compute cost, and accept payment. **Examples:** Airplane-Charter Clerk; Car Rental Agent; Skate Shop Attendant.

41-2022 Parts Salespersons

Sell spare and replacement parts and equipment in repair shop or parts store. **Examples:** Parts Clerk; Auto Parts Salesperson; Electronic Parts Salesperson.

41-2030 Retail Salespersons

This broad occupation is the same as the detailed occupation:
41-2031 Retail Salespersons

41-2031 Retail Salespersons

Sell merchandise such as furniture, motor vehicles, appliances, or apparel, in a retail establishment. Excludes "Cashiers" (41-2011). **Examples:** Car Dealer; Haberdasher; Wallpaper Salesperson.

41-3000 Sales Representatives, Services

41-3010 Advertising Sales Agents

This broad occupation is the same as the detailed occupation:
41-3011 Advertising Sales Agents

41-3011 Advertising Sales Agents

Sell or solicit advertising, including graphic art, advertising space in publications, custom-made signs, or TV and radio advertising time. Obtain leases for outdoor advertising sites. Persuade retailer to use sales promotion display items. **Examples:** Radio Time Salesperson; Yellow Pages Salesperson; Leasing Agent Outdoor Advertising.

41-3020 Insurance Sales Agents

This broad occupation is the same as the detailed occupation:
41-3021 Insurance Sales Agents

41-3021 Insurance Sales Agents

Sell life, property, casualty, health, automotive, or other types of insurance. Refer clients to independent brokers; work as independent broker; be employed by an insurance company. **Examples:** Insurance Broker; Insurance Solicitor; Pension Agent.

41-3030 Securities, Commodities, and Financial Services Sales Agents

This broad occupation is the same as the detailed occupation:
41-3031 Securities, Commodities, and Financial Services Sales Agents

41-3031 Securities, Commodities, and Financial Services Sales Agents

Buy and sell securities in investment and trading firms; call upon businesses and individuals to sell financial services. Provide financial services such as loan, tax, and securities counseling. Advise securities customers about such things as stocks, bonds, and market conditions. **Examples:** Investment Banker; Stock Broker; Stock Trader.

41-3040 Travel Agents

This broad occupation is the same as the detailed occupation:
41-3041 Travel Agents

41-3041 Travel Agents

Plan and sell transportation and accommodations for travel agency customers. Determine destination, modes of transportation, travel dates, costs, and accommodations required. **Examples:** Travel Consultant; Travel Counselor.

41-3090 Miscellaneous Sales Representatives, Services

This broad occupation is the same as the detailed occupation:
41-3099 Sales Representatives, Services, All Other

41-3099 Sales Representatives, Services, All Other

All services sales representatives not listed separately. **Examples:** Crating-And-Moving Estimator; Data Processing Sales Representative; Telecommunications Consultant.

41-4000 Sales Representatives, Wholesale and Manufacturing

41-4010 Sales Representatives, Wholesale and Manufacturing

This broad occupation includes the following two detailed occupations:
41-4011 Sales Representatives, Wholesale and Manufacturing, Technical and Scientific Products
41-4012 Sales Representatives, Wholesale and Manufacturing, Except Technical and Scientific Products

41-4011 Sales Representatives, Wholesale and Manufacturing, Technical and Scientific Products

Sell goods for wholesalers or manufacturers where technical or scientific knowledge is required, in areas such as biology, engineering, chemistry, and electronics, normally obtained from at least 2 years of post-secondary education. **Examples:** Electronics Sales Representative; Oilfield Equipment Sales Representative; Pharmaceutical Representative.

41-4012 Sales Representatives, Wholesale and Manufacturing, Except Technical and Scientific Products

Sell goods for wholesalers or manufacturers, to businesses or groups of individuals. Possess substantial knowledge of items sold. **Examples:** Diamond Broker; Oil Distributor; Wool Merchant.

41-9000 Other Sales and Related Workers

41-9010 Models, Demonstrators, and Product Promoters

This broad occupation includes the following two detailed occupations:
41-9011 Demonstrators and Product Promoters
41-9012 Models

41-9011 Demonstrators and Product Promoters

Demonstrate merchandise and answer questions, for the purpose of creating public interest in buying the product. Sell demonstrated merchandise. **Examples:** Home Demonstrator; Exhibit-Display Representative.

41-9012 Models

Model garments and other apparel, to display clothing before prospective buyers at fashion shows, private showings, retail establishments, or photographer. Pose for photos to be used for advertising purposes. Pose as subject for paintings, sculptures, and other types of artistic expression. **Examples:** Fashion Model; Mannequin; Photographer's Model.

41-9020 Real Estate Brokers and Sales Agents

This broad occupation includes the following two detailed occupations:
41-9021 Real Estate Brokers
41-9022 Real Estate Sales Agents

41-9021 Real Estate Brokers

Operate real estate office or work for commercial real estate firm, overseeing real estate transactions. Sell real estate; rent properties; arrange loans.

41-9022 Real Estate Sales Agents

Rent, buy, or sell property for clients. Perform duties such as studying property listings, interviewing prospective clients, accompanying clients to property site, discussing conditions of sale, and drawing up real estate contracts. Includes agents who represent buyer. **Examples:** Apartment Rental Agent; Land Agent; Right of Way Agent.

41-9030 Sales Engineers

This broad occupation is the same as the detailed occupation:
41-9031 Sales Engineers

41-9031 Sales Engineers

Sell business goods or services, the selling of which requires a technical background equivalent to a baccalaureate degree in engineering. Excludes "Engineers" (17-2011 through 17-2199) whose primary function is not marketing or sales. **Examples:** Aeronautical Products Sales Engineer; Industrial Machinery Sales Engineer; Nuclear Equipment Sales Engineer.

41-9040 Telemarketers

This broad occupation is the same as the detailed occupation:
41-9041 Telemarketers

41-9041 Telemarketers

Solicit orders for goods or services over the telephone. **Examples:** Telephone Salesperson; Telephone Solicitor.

41-9090 Miscellaneous Sales and Related Workers

This broad occupation includes the following two detailed occupations:
41-9091 Door-To-Door Sales Workers, News and Street Vendors, and Related Workers
41-9099 Sales and Related Workers, All Other

41-9091 Door-To-Door Sales Workers, News and Street Vendors, and Related Workers

Sell goods or services door to door or on the street. **Examples:** Peddler; Direct Selling.

41-9099 Sales and Related Workers, All Other

All sales and related workers not listed separately. **Examples:** Bridal Consultant; Fund Raiser; Auctioneer.

43-0000 OFFICE AND ADMINISTRATIVE SUPPORT OCCUPATIONS

43-1000 Supervisors, Office and Administrative Support Workers

43-1010 First-Line Supervisors/Managers of Office and Administrative Support Workers

This broad occupation is the same as the detailed occupation:
43-1011 First-Line Supervisors/Managers of Office and Administrative Support Workers

43-1011 First-Line Supervisors/Managers of Office and Administrative Support Workers

Supervise and coordinate the activities of clerical and administrative support workers. **Examples:** Claims Supervisor; Stock Room Manager; Teller Supervisor.

43-2000 Communications Equipment Operators

43-2010 Switchboard Operators, Including Answering Service

This broad occupation is the same as the detailed occupation:
43-2011 Switchboard Operators, Including Answering Service

43-2011 Switchboard Operators, Including Answering Service

Operate telephone business systems equipment or switchboards to relay incoming, outgoing, and interoffice calls. Supply information to callers and record messages. **Examples:** Communication Center Operator; Exchange Operator; Telephone Answering Service Operator.

43-0000
Office and Administra-
tive Support
Occupations

43-2020 Telephone Operators

This broad occupation is the same as the detailed occupation:
43-2021 Telephone Operators

43-2021 Telephone Operators

Provide information by accessing alphabetical and geographical directories. Assist customers with special billing requests such as charges to a third party and credits or refunds for incorrectly dialed numbers or bad connections. Handle emergency calls; help children or people with physical disabilities make telephone calls.

Examples: Directory Assistance Operator; Long Distance Operator; Routing Operator.

43-2090 Miscellaneous Communications Equipment Operators

This broad occupation is the same as the detailed occupation:
43-2099 Communications Equipment Operators, All Other

43-2099 Communications Equipment Operators, All Other

All communications equipment operators not listed separately. **Example:** Telegraph Operator.

43-3000 Financial Clerks

43-3010 Bill and Account Collectors

This broad occupation is the same as the detailed occupation:
43-3011 Bill and Account Collectors

43-3011 Bill and Account Collectors

Locate and notify customers of delinquent accounts, by mail, telephone, or personal visit to solicit payment. Receive payment and post amount to customer's account; prepare statements to credit department if customer fails to respond; initiate repossession proceedings or service disconnection; keep records of collection and status of accounts. **Examples:** Payment Collector; Collection Clerk; Installment Agent.

43-3020 Billing and Posting Clerks and Machine Operators

This broad occupation is the same as the detailed occupation:
43-3021 Billing and Posting Clerks and Machine Operators

43-3021 Billing and Posting Clerks and Machine Operators

Compile, compute, and record billing, accounting, statistical, and other numerical data for billing purposes. Prepare billing invoices for services rendered or for delivery or shipment of goods. **Examples:** Calculating Machine Operator; Invoice Control Clerk; Rating Clerk.

43-3030 Bookkeeping, Accounting, and Auditing Clerks

This broad occupation is the same as the detailed occupation:
43-3031 Bookkeeping, Accounting, and Auditing Clerks

43-3031 Bookkeeping, Accounting, and Auditing Clerks

Compute, classify, and record numerical data to keep financial records complete. Perform routine calculating, posting, and verifying duties, to obtain primary financial data for use in maintaining accounting records. Check the accuracy of figures, calculations, and postings pertaining to business transactions recorded by other workers. **Examples:** Accounts Receivable Clerk; Ledger Clerk; Voucher Examiner.

43-3040 Gaming Cage Workers

This broad occupation is the same as the detailed occupation:
43-3041 Gaming Cage Workers

43-3041 Gaming Cage Workers

Conduct financial transactions for patrons in a gaming establishment. Reconcile daily summaries of transactions to balance books. Accept patron's credit application and verify credit references, to provide check-cashing authorization or to establish house credit accounts. Sell gambling chips, tokens, or tickets to patrons, or to other workers for resale to patrons. Convert gaming chips, tokens, or tickets to currency upon patron's request. Use a cash register or computer to record transaction.

43-3050 Payroll and Timekeeping Clerks

This broad occupation is the same as the detailed occupation:
43-3051 Payroll and Timekeeping Clerks

43-3051 Payroll and Timekeeping Clerks

Compile and post employee time and payroll data. Compute employees' time worked, production, and commission. Compute and post wages and deductions. Prepare paychecks. **Examples:** Attendance Clerk; Payroll Bookkeeper; Timekeeper.

43-3060 Procurement Clerks

This broad occupation is the same as the detailed occupation:
43-3061 Procurement Clerks

43-3061 Procurement Clerks

Compile information and records to draw up purchase orders for procurement of materials and services. **Examples:** Property and Supply Officer; Purchasing Clerk.

43-3070 Tellers

This broad occupation is the same as the detailed occupation:
43-3071 Tellers

**43-0000
Office and
Administrative Support
Occupations**

43-3071 Tellers

Receive and pay out money. Keep records of money and negotiable instruments involved in a financial institution's various transactions. **Examples:** Foreign Exchange Clerk; Money Order Clerk; Securities Teller.

43-4000 Information and Record Clerks

43-4010 Brokerage Clerks

This broad occupation is the same as the detailed occupation:
43-4011 Brokerage Clerks

43-4011 Brokerage Clerks

Perform clerical duties involving the purchase or sale of securities. Write orders for stock purchases and sales; compute transfer taxes; verify stock transactions; accept and deliver securities; track stock price fluctuations; compute equity; distribute dividends; keep records of daily transactions and holdings. **Examples:** Portfolio Assistant; Dividend Clerk; Telephone Quotation Clerk.

43-4020 Correspondence Clerks

This broad occupation is the same as the detailed occupation:
43-4021 Correspondence Clerks

43-4021 Correspondence Clerks

Compose letters pertaining to requests for merchandise, damage claims, credit and other information, delinquent accounts, incorrect billings, or unsatisfactory services. Gather data to formulate reply; type correspondence. **Examples:** Collection Correspondent; Fan Mail Editor.

43-4030 Court, Municipal, and License Clerks

This broad occupation is the same as the detailed occupation:
43-4031 Court, Municipal, and License Clerks

43-4031 Court, Municipal, and License Clerks

Perform clerical duties in courts of law, municipalities, and governmental licensing agencies and bureaus. Prepare docket of cases to be called; secure information for judges and court; prepare draft agendas or bylaws for town or city council; answer official correspondence; keep fiscal records and accounts; issue licenses or permits; record data; administer tests; collect fees. Include chief clerks with "Managers, All Other" (11-9199). **Examples:** Circuit Court Clerk; Warrant Clerk.

43-4040 Credit Authorizers, Checkers, and Clerks

This broad occupation is the same as the detailed occupation:
43-4041 Credit Authorizers, Checkers, and Clerks

43-4041 Credit Authorizers, Checkers, and Clerks

Authorize credit charges against customers' accounts. Investigate history and credit standing of individuals or business establishments applying for credit. Interview applicants to obtain personal and financial data; determine credit worthiness; process applications; and notify customers of acceptance or rejection of credit. **Examples:** Credit Interviewer; Credit Rating Inspector; Loan Adjuster.

43-4050 Customer Service Representatives

This broad occupation is the same as the detailed occupation:
43-4051 Customer Service Representatives

43-4051 Customer Service Representatives

Interact with customers to provide information in response to inquiries about products and services and to handle and resolve complaints. Excludes individuals whose duties are primarily sales or repair. **Examples:** Complaint Adjuster; Passenger Relations Representative; Telephone Service Adviser.

43-4060 Eligibility Interviewers, Government Programs

This broad occupation is the same as the detailed occupation:
43-4061 Eligibility Interviewers, Government Programs

43-4061 Eligibility Interviewers, Government Programs

Determine eligibility of persons applying to receive assistance from government programs and agency resources such as welfare, unemployment benefits, social security, and public housing. **Examples:** Unemployment Benefits Claims Taker; County Service Officer; Welfare Interviewer.

43-4070 File Clerks

This broad occupation is the same as the detailed occupation:
43-4071 File Clerks

43-4071 File Clerks

File correspondence, cards, invoices, receipts, and other records in alphabetical or numerical order or according to the filing system used. Locate and remove material from file when requested. **Examples:** Computer Tape Librarian; Document Clerk; Records Custodian.

43-0000
Office and
Administrative Support
Occupations

43-4080 Hotel, Motel, and Resort Desk Clerks

This broad occupation is the same as the detailed occupation:
43-4081 Hotel, Motel, and Resort Desk Clerks

43-4081 Hotel, Motel, and Resort Desk Clerks

Accommodate hotel, motel, and resort patrons by registering and assigning rooms to guests, issuing room keys, transmitting and receiving messages, keeping records of occupied rooms and guests' accounts, making and confirming reservations, and presenting statements to and collecting payments from departing guests. **Examples:** Register Clerk; Room Clerk.

43-4110 Interviewers, Except Eligibility and Loan

This broad occupation is the same as the detailed occupation:
43-4111 Interviewers, Except Eligibility and Loan

43-4111 Interviewers, Except Eligibility and Loan

Interview persons by telephone, by mail, in person, or by other means, for the purpose of completing forms, applications, or questionnaires. Ask specific questions, record answers, and assist persons with completing form. Sort, classify, and file forms. **Examples:** Census Taker; Market Research Interviewer; Out-patient Admitting Clerk.

43-4120 Library Assistants, Clerical

This broad occupation is the same as the detailed occupation:
43-4121 Library Assistants, Clerical

43-4121 Library Assistants, Clerical

Compile records; sort and shelve books; issue and receive library materials such as pictures, cards, slides and microfilm. Locate library materials for loan; replace material in shelving area, stacks, or files, according to identification number and title. Register patrons to permit them to borrow books, periodicals, and other library materials. **Examples:** Braille and Talking Books Clerk; Circulation Clerk; Microfilm Clerk.

43-4130 Loan Interviewers and Clerks

This broad occupation is the same as the detailed occupation:
43-4131 Loan Interviewers and Clerks

43-4131 Loan Interviewers and Clerks

Interview loan applicants to elicit information; investigate applicants' backgrounds; verify references; prepare loan request papers; forward findings, reports, and documents to appraisal department. Review loan papers to ensure completeness; complete transactions between loan establishment, borrowers, and sellers upon approval of loan. **Examples:** Loan Closer; Loan Processor; Mortgage Clerk.

43-4140 New Accounts Clerks

This broad occupation is the same as the detailed occupation:
43-4141 New Accounts Clerks

43-4141 New Accounts Clerks

Interview persons desiring to open bank accounts. Explain banking services available to prospective customers; assist customers in preparing application form. **Example:** Banking Services Clerk.

43-4150 Order Clerks

This broad occupation is the same as the detailed occupation:
43-4151 Order Clerks

43-4151 Order Clerks

Receive and process incoming orders for materials, for merchandise, for classified ads, or for services such as repairs, installations, or rental of facilities. Inform customers of receipt, prices, shipping dates, and delays; prepare contracts; handle complaints. Excludes "Dispatchers, Except Police, Fire, and Ambulance" (43-5032) who both dispatch and take orders for services. **Examples:** Catalogue Clerk; Subscription Clerk; Classified Advertisement Clerk.

43-4160 Human Resources Assistants, Except Payroll and Timekeeping

This broad occupation is the same as the detailed occupation:
43-4161 Human Resources Assistants, Except Payroll and Timekeeping

43-4161 Human Resources Assistants, Except Payroll and Timekeeping

Compile and keep personnel records. Record data for each employee, such as address, weekly earnings, absences, amount of sales or production, supervisory reports on ability, and date of and reason for termination. Compile and type reports from employment records. File employment records. Search employee files and furnish information to authorized persons. **Example:** Personnel Clerk.

43-4170 Receptionists and Information Clerks

This broad occupation is the same as the detailed occupation:
43-4171 Receptionists and Information Clerks

43-4171 Receptionists and Information Clerks

Answer inquiries and obtain information for general public, customers, visitors, and other interested parties. Provide information regarding activities conducted at establishment, regarding location of departments and offices, and regarding employees within organization. Excludes "Switchboard Operators, Including Answering Service" (43-2011). **Examples:** Appointment Clerk; Front Desk Clerk; Referral and Information Aide.

43-4180 Reservation and Transportation Ticket Agents and Travel Clerks

This broad occupation is the same as the detailed occupation:
43-4181 Reservation and Transportation Ticket Agents and Travel Clerks

43-4181 Reservation and Transportation Ticket Agents and Travel Clerks

Make and confirm reservations; sell tickets to passengers for large hotel or motel chains. Check baggage; direct passengers to designated concourse, pier, or track; make reservations; deliver tickets; arrange for visas; contact individuals and groups to inform them of package tours; provide tourists with travel information such as points of interest, restaurants, rates, and emergency service. Excludes "Travel Agents" (41-3041), "Hotel, Motel, and Resort Desk Clerks" (43-4081), and "Cashiers" (41-2011) who sell tickets for local transportation. **Examples:** Ticket Clerk; Hotel Reservationist; Gate Agent.

43-4190 Miscellaneous Information and Record Clerks

This broad occupation is the same as the detailed occupation:
43-4199 Information and Record Clerks, All Other

43-4199 Information and Record Clerks, All Other

All information and record clerks not listed separately. **Examples:** Student Admissions Clerk; Suggestion Clerk; Vault Custodian.

43-5000 Material Recording, Scheduling, Dispatching, and Distributing Workers

43-5010 Cargo and Freight Agents

This broad occupation is the same as the detailed occupation:
43-5011 Cargo and Freight Agents

43-5011 Cargo and Freight Agents

Expedite and route movement of incoming and outgoing cargo and freight shipments, in airline, train, and trucking terminals and in shipping docks. Take orders from customers; arrange pickup of freight and cargo for delivery to loading platform. Prepare and examine bills of lading to determine shipping charges and tariffs. **Examples:** Routing Agent; Shipping Agent.

43-5020 Couriers and Messengers

This broad occupation is the same as the detailed occupation:
43-5021 Couriers and Messengers

43-5021 Couriers and Messengers

Pick up and carry messages, documents, packages, and other items between offices or departments within an establishment or to other business concerns. Travel by foot, bicycle, motorcycle, automobile, or public conveyance. Excludes "Truck Drivers, Light or Delivery Services" (53-3033). **Examples:** Message Delivery Clerk; Telegraph Messenger.

43-5030 Dispatchers

This broad occupation includes the following two detailed occupations:
43-5031 Police, Fire, and Ambulance Dispatchers
43-5032 Dispatchers, Except Police, Fire, and Ambulance

43-5031 Police, Fire, and Ambulance Dispatchers

Receive complaints from the public, concerning crimes and police emergencies. Broadcast orders to police patrol units in vicinity of complaint to investigate. Operate radio, telephone, or computer equipment to receive reports of fires and medical emergencies and to relay information or orders to proper officials. **Examples:** 911 Operator; Emergency Operator; Public Safety Dispatcher.

43-5032 Dispatchers, Except Police, Fire, and Ambulance

Schedule and dispatch workers, work crews, equipment, or service vehicles for conveyance of materials, freight, or passengers or for normal installation, service, or emergency repairs rendered outside the place of business. Use radio, telephone, or computer to transmit assignments. Compile statistics and reports on work progress. **Examples:** Security Dispatcher; Repair Service Dispatcher; Taxicab Dispatcher.

43-5040 Meter Readers, Utilities

This broad occupation is the same as the detailed occupation:
43-5041 Meter Readers, Utilities

43-0000 Office and Administrative Support Occupations

43-5041 Meter Readers, Utilities

Read meter; record consumption of electricity, gas, water, or steam. **Examples:** Electric Meter Reader; Meter Record Clerk; Water Meter Reader.

43-5050 Postal Service Workers

This broad occupation includes the following three detailed occupations:
43-5051 Postal Service Clerks
43-5052 Postal Service Mail Carriers
43-5053 Postal Service Mail Sorters, Processors, and Processing Machine Operators

43-5051 Postal Service Clerks

Perform tasks in a post office. Receive letters and parcels; sell postage stamps, revenue stamps, postal cards, and stamped envelopes; fill out and sell money orders; place mail in pigeonholes of mail rack or in bags according to state, address, or other scheme; examine mail for correct postage. **Examples:** Parcel Post Clerk; Special Delivery Clerk; Stamp Clerk.

43-5052 Postal Service Mail Carriers

Sort mail for delivery. Deliver mail on established route, by vehicle or on foot. **Examples:** Letter Carrier; Mail Deliverer; Route Carrier.

43-5053 Postal Service Mail Sorters, Processors, and Processing Machine Operators

Prepare incoming and outgoing mail for distribution. Examine, sort, and route mail by state, type of mail, or other scheme. Load, operate, and occasionally adjust and repair mail processing, sorting, and canceling machinery. Keep records of shipments, pouches, and sacks; perform other duties related to mail handling within the postal service. Complete required competitive exam. Excludes "Postal Service Clerks" (43-5051) and "Postal Service Mail Carriers" (43-5052). **Examples:** Mail Weigher; Mail Handler Sorting Mail.

43-5060 Production, Planning, and Expediting Clerks

This broad occupation is the same as the detailed occupation:
43-5061 Production, Planning, and Expediting Clerks

43-5061 Production, Planning, and Expediting Clerks

Coordinate and expedite the flow of work and materials within or between departments of an establishment, according to production schedule. Review and distribute production, work, and shipment schedules. Confer with department supervisors to determine progress of work and completion dates. Compile reports on progress of work, inventory levels, costs, and production problems. Excludes

"Weighers, Measurers, Checkers, and Samplers, Recordkeeping" (43-5111).
Examples: Assignment Agent; Production Dispatcher; Expediter.

43-5070 Shipping, Receiving, and Traffic Clerks

This broad occupation is the same as the detailed occupation:
43-5071 Shipping, Receiving, and Traffic Clerks

43-5071 Shipping, Receiving, and Traffic Clerks

Verify and keep records on incoming and outgoing shipments. Prepare items for shipment. Assemble, address, stamp, and ship merchandise or material. Receive, unpack, verify, and record incoming merchandise or material. Arrange for the transportation of products. Excludes "Stock Clerks and Order Fillers" (43-5081) and "Weighers, Measurers, Checkers, and Samplers, Recordkeeping" (43-5111).
Examples: Receiver; Garment Sorter; Freight Separator.

43-5080 Stock Clerks and Order Fillers

This broad occupation is the same as the detailed occupation:
43-5081 Stock Clerks and Order Fillers

43-5081 Stock Clerks and Order Fillers

Receive, store, and issue sales-floor merchandise, materials, equipment, and other items from stockroom, warehouse, or storage yard, to fill shelves, racks, tables, or customers' orders. Mark prices on merchandise and set up sales displays. Excludes "Laborers and Freight, Stock, and Material Movers, Hand" (53-7062) and "Shipping, Receiving, and Traffic Clerks" (43-5071). **Examples:** Inventory Control Clerk; Tool-Crib Attendant; Warehouse Clerk.

43-5110 Weighers, Measurers, Checkers, and Samplers, Recordkeeping

This broad occupation is the same as the detailed occupation:
43-5111 Weighers, Measurers, Checkers, and Samplers, Recordkeeping

43-5111 Weighers, Measurers, Checkers, and Samplers, Recordkeeping

Weigh, measure, and check materials, supplies, and equipment, to keep relevant records. Perform clerical duties. Includes workers who collect and keep record of samples of products or materials. Excludes production "Inspectors, Testers, Sorters, Samplers, and Weighers" (51-9061). **Examples:** Counter; Inventory Checker; Scale Attendant.

43-0000
Office and
Administra-
tive Support
Occupations

43-6000 Secretaries and Administrative Assistants

43-6010 Secretaries and Administrative Assistants

This broad occupation includes the following four detailed occupations:
43-6011 Executive Secretaries and Administrative Assistants
43-6012 Legal Secretaries
43-6013 Medical Secretaries
43-6014 Secretaries, Except Legal, Medical, and Executive

43-6011 Executive Secretaries and Administrative Assistants

Provide high-level administrative support. Conduct research; prepare statistical reports; handle information requests; perform clerical functions such as preparing correspondence, receiving visitors, arranging conference calls, and scheduling meetings. Train and supervise lower-level clerical staff. Excludes "Secretaries" (43-6012 through 43-6014). **Example:** Administrative Aide.

43-6012 Legal Secretaries

Perform secretarial duties, using legal terminology, procedures, and documents. Prepare legal papers and correspondence, such as summonses, complaints, motions, and subpoenas. Assist with legal research.

43-6013 Medical Secretaries

Perform secretarial duties, using specific knowledge of medical terminology and of hospital, clinic, or laboratory procedures. Schedule appointments; bill patients; compile and record medical charts, reports, and correspondence. **Examples:** Psychiatric Secretary; Dental Secretary.

43-6014 Secretaries, Except Legal, Medical, and Executive

Perform routine clerical and administrative functions such as drafting correspondence, scheduling appointments, organizing and maintaining paper and electronic files, or providing information to callers. Excludes legal, medical, or executive secretaries and administrative assistants (43-6011 through 43-6013). **Examples:** Personal Secretary; Office Secretary; Receptionist Secretary.

43-9000 Other Office and Administrative Support Workers

43-9010 Computer Operators

This broad occupation is the same as the detailed occupation:
43-9011 Computer Operators

43-9011 Computer Operators

Monitor and control electronic computer and peripheral electronic data-processing equipment, to process business, scientific, engineering, and other data according to operating instructions. Enter commands at a computer terminal; set controls on computer and peripheral devices. Monitor and respond to operating and error messages. Excludes "Data Entry Keyers" (43-9021). **Examples:** Console Operator; Data Processing Clerk; Peripheral Equipment Operator.

43-9020 Data Entry and Information Processing Workers

This broad occupation includes the following two detailed occupations:
43-9021 Data Entry Keyers
43-9022 Word Processors and Typists

43-9021 Data Entry Keyers

Operate data entry device such as keyboard or photo-composing perforator. Verify data and prepare materials for printing. Excludes "Word Processors and Typists" (43-9022). **Examples:** Keypunch Operator; Data Typist.

43-9022 Word Processors and Typists

Use word processor, computer, or typewriter, to type letters, reports, forms, or other material, from rough draft, from corrected copy, or from voice recording. Perform other clerical duties as assigned. Includes composing data keyers. Excludes "Data Entry Keyers" (43-9021), "Secretaries and Administrative Assistants" (43-6011 through 43-6014), "Court Reporters" (23-2091), and "Medical Transcriptionists" (31-9094). **Examples:** Clerk Typist; Dictaphone Typist.

43-9030 Desktop Publishers

This broad occupation is the same as the detailed occupation:
43-9031 Desktop Publishers

43-9031 Desktop Publishers

Format typescript and graphic elements using computer software, to produce publication-ready material. **Examples:** Computer Compositor; Electronic Pagination System Operator; Page Makeup System Operator.

43-9040 Insurance Claims and Policy Processing Clerks

This broad occupation is the same as the detailed occupation:
43-9041 Insurance Claims and Policy Processing Clerks

43-9041 Insurance Claims and Policy Processing Clerks

Process new insurance policies, modifications to existing policies, and claims forms. Obtain information from policyholders to verify the accuracy and

43-0000 Office and Administrative Support Occupations

completeness of information on claims forms, on applications and related documents, and on company records. Update existing policies and company records, to reflect changes requested by policyholders and insurance company representatives. Excludes "Claims Adjusters, Examiners, and Investigators" (13-1031). **Examples:** Claim Taker; Policy Issue Clerk; Underwriting Clerk.

43-9050 Mail Clerks and Mail Machine Operators, Except Postal Service

This broad occupation is the same as the detailed occupation:
43-9051 Mail Clerks and Mail Machine Operators, Except Postal Service

43-9051 Mail Clerks and Mail Machine Operators, Except Postal Service

Prepare incoming and outgoing mail for distribution. Use hand or mail handling machines to time stamp, open, read, sort, and route incoming mail. Address, seal, stamp, fold, stuff, and affix postage to outgoing mail or packages. Keep necessary records and complete forms. **Examples:** Addressing Machine Operator; Mail Distributor; Mail Opener.

43-9060 Office Clerks, General

This broad occupation is the same as the detailed occupation:
43-9061 Office Clerks, General

43-9061 Office Clerks, General

Perform duties too varied and diverse to be classified in any specific office clerical occupation, requiring limited knowledge of office management systems and procedures. Perform clerical duties as assigned, in accordance with the office procedures of individual establishments. Answer telephones, do bookkeeping, type or do word processing, do stenography, operate office machines, and file. **Examples:** Administrative Clerk; Office Assistant; Real Estate Clerk.

43-9070 Office Machine Operators, Except Computer

This broad occupation is the same as the detailed occupation:
43-9071 Office Machine Operators, Except Computer

43-9071 Office Machine Operators, Except Computer

Operate one or more of a variety of office machines such as photocopying, photographic, and duplicating machines. Excludes "Computer Operators" (43-9011), "Mail Clerks and Mail Machine Operators" (43-9051), and "Billing and Posting Clerks and Machine Operators" (43-3021). **Examples:** Check Embosser; Coin Wrapping Machine Operator; Copy Machine Operator.

43-9080 Proofreaders and Copy Markers

This broad occupation is the same as the detailed occupation:
43-9081 Proofreaders and Copy Markers

43-9081 Proofreaders and Copy Markers

Read transcript or proof type setup to detect and mark for correction any grammatical, typographical, or compositional errors. Excludes workers whose primary duty is editing copy. Includes proofreaders of Braille. **Examples:** Braille Proofreader; Copy Reader.

43-9110 Statistical Assistants

This broad occupation is the same as the detailed occupation:
43-9111 Statistical Assistants

43-9111 Statistical Assistants

Compile and compute data, according to statistical formulas for use in statistical studies. Perform actuarial computations; compile charts and graphs for use by actuaries. Includes actuarial clerks. **Examples:** Tabulating Clerk; Compiler; Data Technician.

43-9190 Miscellaneous Office and Administrative Support Workers

This broad occupation is the same as the detailed occupation:
43-9199 Office and Administrative Support Workers, All Other

43-9199 Office and Administrative Support Workers, All Other

All office and administrative support workers not listed separately. **Examples:** Notary Public; Envelope Stuffer.

43-0000
Office and
Administrative Support
Occupations

45-0000 FARMING, FISHING, AND FORESTRY OCCUPATIONS

45-1000 Supervisors, Farming, Fishing, and Forestry Workers

45-1010 First-Line Supervisors/Managers of Farming, Fishing, and Forestry Workers

This broad occupation includes the following two detailed occupations:
45-1011 First-Line Supervisors/Managers of Farming, Fishing, and Forestry Workers
45-1012 Farm Labor Contractors

45-1011 First-Line Supervisors/Managers of Farming, Fishing, and Forestry Workers

Directly supervise and coordinate the activities of agricultural, forestry, aquacultural, and related workers. Excludes "First-Line Supervisors/Managers of Landscaping, Lawn Service, and Groundskeeping Workers" (37-1012). **Examples:** Christmas Tree Farm Manager; Harvest Crew Supervisor; Fish Hatchery Supervisor.

45-1012 Farm Labor Contractors

Recruit, hire, furnish, and supervise seasonal or temporary agricultural laborers for a fee. Transport, house, and provide meals for workers. **Example:** Harvesting Contractor.

45-2000 Agricultural Workers

45-2010 Agricultural Inspectors

This broad occupation is the same as the detailed occupation:
45-2011 Agricultural Inspectors

45-2011 Agricultural Inspectors

Inspect agricultural commodities, processing equipment and facilities, and fish and logging operations, to ensure compliance with regulations and laws governing health, quality, and safety. **Examples:** Cattle Examiner; Meat Grader; Grain Sampler.

45-2020 Animal Breeders

This broad occupation is the same as the detailed occupation:
45-2021 Animal Breeders

Standard Occupational Classification Manual

© JIST Works

45-2021 Animal Breeders

Breed animals, including cattle, goats, horses, sheep, swine, poultry, dogs, cats, or pet birds. Select and breed animals according to their genealogy, characteristics, and offspring. Have knowledge of artificial insemination techniques and equipment use. Keep records on heats, birth intervals, or pedigree. Excludes "Nonfarm Animal Caretakers" (39-2021) who may occasionally breed animals as part of their other caretaking duties. Excludes "Animal Scientists" (19-1011) whose primary function is research. **Examples:** Artificial Inseminator; Chicken Fancier; Horse Breeder.

45-2040 Graders and Sorters, Agricultural Products

This broad occupation is the same as the detailed occupation:
45-2041 Graders and Sorters, Agricultural Products

45-2041 Graders and Sorters, Agricultural Products

Grade, sort, or classify unprocessed food and other agricultural products by size, weight, color, or condition. Excludes "Agricultural Inspectors" (45-2011). **Examples:** Chicken Grader; Cotton Classer; Fruit Sorter.

45-2090 Miscellaneous Agricultural Workers

This broad occupation includes the following four detailed occupations:
45-2091 Agricultural Equipment Operators
45-2092 Farmworkers and Laborers, Crop, Nursery, and Greenhouse
45-2093 Farmworkers, Farm and Ranch Animals
45-2099 Agricultural Workers, All Other

45-2091 Agricultural Equipment Operators

Drive and control farm equipment to till soil and to plant, cultivate, and harvest crops. Perform tasks such as crop baling or hay bucking. Operate stationary equipment to perform post-harvest tasks such as husking, shelling, threshing, and ginning. **Examples:** Baler; Combine Operator; Tractor Driver.

45-2092 Farmworkers and Laborers, Crop, Nursery, and Greenhouse

Manually plant, cultivate, and harvest vegetables, fruits, nuts, horticultural specialties, and field crops. Use hand tools such as shovels, trowels, hoes, tampers, pruning hooks, shears, and knives. Till soil and apply fertilizers. Transplant, weed, thin, or prune crops. Apply pesticides. Clean, grade, sort, pack, and load harvested products. Construct trellises, repair fences and farm buildings, or participate in irrigation activities. Excludes "Graders and Sorters, Agricultural Products" (45-2041). Excludes "Forest, Conservation, and Logging Workers" (45-4011 through 45-4029). **Examples:** Apple Picker; Tobacco Cutter; Vegetable Loader.

45-0000
Farming,
Fishing, and
Forestry
Occupations

45-2093 Farmworkers, Farm and Ranch Animals

Attend to live farm, ranch, or aquacultural animals, including cattle, sheep, swine, goats, horses and other equines, poultry, finfish, shellfish, and bees. Attend to animals produced for animal products such as meat, fur, skins, feathers, eggs, milk, and honey. Feed, water, herd, graze, castrate, brand, debeak, weigh, catch, and load animals. Maintain records on animals; examine animals to detect diseases and injuries; assist in birth deliveries. Administer medications, vaccinations, or insecticides as appropriate. Clean and maintain animal housing areas. Includes workers who shear wool from sheep and who collect eggs in hatcheries. **Examples:** Horse Groomer; Beekeeper; Livestock Feeder.

45-2099 Agricultural Workers, All Other

All agricultural workers not listed separately. **Examples:** Irrigation Worker; Livestock Showman.

45-3000 Fishing and Hunting Workers

45-3010 Fishers and Related Fishing Workers

This broad occupation is the same as the detailed occupation:
45-3011 Fishers and Related Fishing Workers

45-3011 Fishers and Related Fishing Workers

Use nets, fishing rods, traps, or other equipment to catch and gather fish or other aquatic animals from rivers, lakes, or oceans, for human consumption or other uses. Haul game onto ship. Include aquacultural laborers who work on fish farms with "Agricultural Workers, All Other" (45-2099). **Examples:** Fishing Boat Captain; Crabber; Seaweed Harvester.

45-3020 Hunters and Trappers

This broad occupation is the same as the detailed occupation:
45-3021 Hunters and Trappers

45-3021 Hunters and Trappers

Hunt and trap wild animals for human consumption, fur, feed, bait, or other purposes. **Examples:** Predatory Animal Exterminator; Bird Trapper.

45-4000 Forest, Conservation, and Logging Workers

45-4010 Forest and Conservation Workers

This broad occupation is the same as the detailed occupation:
45-4011 Forest and Conservation Workers

45-4011 Forest and Conservation Workers

Under supervision, perform manual labor necessary to develop, maintain, or protect forest, forested areas, and woodlands, by raising and transporting tree seedlings, by combating insects, pests, and diseases harmful to trees, and by building erosion and water control structures and leaching of forest soil. Includes forester aides, seedling pullers, and tree planters. **Examples:** Christmas Tree Farm Worker; Seedling Puller; Forestry Laborer.

45-4020 Logging Workers

This broad occupation includes the following four detailed occupations:
45-4021 Fallers
45-4022 Logging Equipment Operators
45-4023 Log Graders and Scalers
45-4029 Logging Workers, All Other

45-4021 Fallers

Use axes or chainsaws to fell trees, using knowledge of tree characteristics and cutting techniques to control direction of fall and minimize tree damage. **Examples:** Cross Cut Sawyer; Lumberjack; Timber Cutter.

45-4022 Logging Equipment Operators

Drive logging tractor or wheeled vehicle equipped with one or more accessories such as bulldozer blade, frontal shear, grapple, logging arch, cable winches, hoisting rack, or crane boom. Drive and operate such vehicles to fell trees, to skid, load, unload, or stack logs, or to pull stumps or clear brush. **Examples:** Log Hauler; Logging Tractor Operator; Skidder Driver.

45-4023 Log Graders and Scalers

Grade logs or estimate the marketable content or value of logs or pulpwood, in sorting yards, millpond, log deck, or similar locations. Inspect logs for defects; measure logs to determine volume. Excludes "Purchasing Agents and Buyers, Farm Products" (13-1021). **Examples:** Timber Estimator; Landing Scaler.

45-4029 Logging Workers, All Other

All logging workers not listed separately. **Examples:** Barker; Cable Hooker; Rigging Slinger.

45-0000
Farming,
Fishing, and
Forestry
Occupations

47-0000 CONSTRUCTION AND EXTRACTION OCCUPATIONS

47-1000 Supervisors, Construction and Extraction Workers

47-1010 First-Line Supervisors/Managers of Construction Trades and Extraction Workers

This broad occupation is the same as the detailed occupation:
47-1011 First-Line Supervisors/Managers of Construction Trades and Extraction Workers

47-1011 First-Line Supervisors/Managers of Construction Trades and Extraction Workers

Directly supervise and coordinate activities of construction or extraction workers. **Examples:** Cement Contractor; Quarry Boss.

47-2000 Construction Trades Workers

47-2010 Boilermakers

This broad occupation is the same as the detailed occupation:
47-2011 Boilermakers

47-2011 Boilermakers

Construct, assemble, maintain, and repair stationary steam boilers and boiler house auxiliaries. Align structures or plate sections to assemble boiler frame tanks or vats, following blueprints. Use hand and power tools, plumb bobs, levels, wedges, dogs, or turnbuckles. Assist in testing assembled vessels. Direct cleaning of boilers and boiler furnaces. Inspect and repair boiler fittings such as safety valves, regulators, automatic-control mechanisms, water columns, and auxiliary machines. **Examples:** Boiler Installer; Boiler Mechanic; Pressure Tester.

47-2020 Brickmasons, Blockmasons, and Stonemasons

This broad occupation includes the following two detailed occupations:
47-2021 Brickmasons and Blockmasons
47-2022 Stonemasons

47-2021 Brickmasons and Blockmasons

Lay and bind building materials, such as brick, structural tile, concrete block, cinder block, glass block, and terra-cotta block, with mortar and other substances, to construct or repair walls, partitions, arches, sewers, and other structures. Excludes "Stonemasons" (47-2022). Excludes installers of mortarless segmental concrete masonry wall units, as they are classified as "Landscaping and Groundskeeping Workers" (37-3011). **Examples:** Adobe Layer; Chimney Builder; Furnace Liner.

47-2022 Stonemasons

Build stone structures such as piers, walls, and abutments. Lay walks, curbstones, or special types of masonry for vats, tanks, and floors. **Examples:** Granite Setter; Monument Installer; Rock Mason.

47-2030 Carpenters

This broad occupation is the same as the detailed occupation:
47-2031 Carpenters

47-2031 Carpenters

Construct, erect, install, or repair structures and fixtures made of wood—concrete forms; building frameworks, including partitions, joists, studding, and rafters; wood stairways; window and door frames; and hardwood floors. Install cabinets, siding, drywall, and batt or roll insulation. Includes brattice builders who build doors or brattices (ventilation walls or partitions) in underground passageways, to control the proper circulation of air through the passageways and to the working places. **Examples:** Shipwright; Cabinetmaker; Wood Floor Layer.

47-2040 Carpet, Floor, and Tile Installers and Finishers

This broad occupation includes the following four detailed occupations:
47-2041 Carpet Installers
47-2042 Floor Layers, Except Carpet, Wood, and Hard Tiles
47-2043 Floor Sanders and Finishers
47-2044 Tile and Marble Setters

47-2041 Carpet Installers

Lay and install carpet from rolls or blocks on floors. Install padding and trim flooring materials. Excludes "Floor Layers, Except Carpet, Wood, and Hard Tiles" (47-2042). **Examples:** Floor Coverer; Rug Layer.

47-2042 Floor Layers, Except Carpet, Wood, and Hard Tiles

Apply blocks, strips, or sheets of shock-absorbing, sound-deadening, or decorative coverings to floors. **Examples:** Composition Floor Setter; Linoleum Layer; Soft Tile Setter.

47-2043 Floor Sanders and Finishers

Scrape and sand wooden floors to smooth surfaces, using floor scraper and floor sanding machine. Apply coats of finish. **Examples:** Floor Sanding Machine Operator; Floor Surfacer; Hardwood Finisher.

47-2044 Tile and Marble Setters

Apply hard tile, marble, and wood tile to walls, floors, ceilings, and roof decks. **Examples:** Ceramic Tile Installer; Hard Tile Setter; Marble Installer.

47-2050 Cement Masons, Concrete Finishers, and Terrazzo Workers

This broad occupation includes the following two detailed occupations:
47-2051 Cement Masons and Concrete Finishers
47-2053 Terrazzo Workers and Finishers

47-2051 Cement Masons and Concrete Finishers

Smooth and finish surfaces of poured concrete, such as floors, walks, sidewalks, roads, or curbs using a variety of hand and power tools. Align forms for sidewalks, curbs, or gutters; patch voids; use saws to cut expansion joints. Excludes installers of mortarless segmental concrete masonry wall units, as they are classified as "Landscaping and Groundskeeping Workers" (37-3011). **Examples:** Curb Builder; Concrete Floor Installer.

47-2053 Terrazzo Workers and Finishers

Apply a mixture of cement, sand, pigment, or marble chips to floors, stairways, and cabinet fixtures, to fashion durable and decorative surfaces. **Example:** Artificial Marble Worker.

47-2060 Construction Laborers

This broad occupation is the same as the detailed occupation:
47-2061 Construction Laborers

47-2061 Construction Laborers

Perform tasks involving physical labor, at building, highway, and heavy construction projects, at tunnel and shaft excavations, and at demolition sites. Operate hand and power tools such as air hammers, earth tampers, cement mixers, small mechanical hoists, and surveying and measuring equipment. Clean and prepare sites; dig trenches; set braces to support the sides of excavations; erect scaffolding; clean up rubble and debris; remove asbestos, lead, and other hazardous waste materials. Assist other craft workers. Excludes construction laborers who primarily assist a particular craft worker, as they are classified as "Helpers, Construction Trades" (47-3011 through 47-3016). **Examples:** Air Hammer Operator; Asphalt Patcher; Construction Craft Laborer.

47-2070 Construction Equipment Operators

This broad occupation includes the following three detailed occupations:
47-2071 Paving, Surfacing, and Tamping Equipment Operators
47-2072 Pile-Drive Operators
47-2073 Operating Engineers and Other Construction Equipment Operators

47-2071 Paving, Surfacing, and Tamping Equipment Operators

Operate equipment used for applying concrete, asphalt, or other materials to road beds, parking lots, or airport runways and taxiways. Operate equipment used for tamping gravel, dirt, or other materials. Includes concrete and asphalt paving machine operators, form tampers, tamping machine operators, and stone spreader operators. **Examples:** Asphalt Spreader Operator; Black Top Machine Operator; Road Grader.

47-2072 Pile-Driver Operators

Operate pile drivers mounted on skids, barges, crawler treads, or locomotive cranes, to drive pilings for retaining walls, bulkheads, and foundations of structures such as buildings, bridges, and piers. **Examples:** Nozzle Operator; Pile Driver Engineer.

47-2073 Operating Engineers and Other Construction Equipment Operators

Operate one or several types of power construction equipment, such as motor graders, bulldozers, scrapers, compressors, pumps, derricks, shovels, tractors, or front-end loaders, to excavate, move, and grade earth, to erect structures, or to pour concrete or other hard surface pavement. Repair and maintain equipment. Excludes "Crane and Tower Operators" (53-7021) and equipment operators who work in extraction or other nonconstruction industries. **Examples:** Bulldozer Operator; Power Grader Operator; Steam Shovel Operator.

47-2080 Drywall Installers, Ceiling Tile Installers, and Tapers

This broad occupation includes the following two detailed occupations:
47-2081 Drywall and Ceiling Tile Installers
47-2082 Tapers

47-2081 Drywall and Ceiling Tile Installers

Apply plasterboard or other wallboard to ceilings or interior walls of buildings. Apply or mount acoustical tiles or blocks, strips, or sheets of shock-absorbing materials, to ceilings and walls of buildings, to reduce or reflect sound. Apply or mount decorative materials. Includes lathers who fasten wooden, metal, or rockboard lath to walls, ceilings, or partitions of buildings to provide support base for plaster, fire-proofing, or acoustical material. Excludes "Carpet Installers" (47-2041), "Carpenters" (47-2031), and "Tile and Marble Setters" (47-2044). **Examples:** Acoustical Carpenter; Lather; Sheet Rock Hanger.

47-2082 Tapers

Seal joints between plasterboard or other wallboard to prepare wall surface for painting or papering. **Examples:** Sheet Rock Taper; Wall Taper.

47-2110 Electricians

This broad occupation is the same as the detailed occupation:
47-2111 Electricians

47-2111 Electricians

Install, maintain, and repair electrical wiring, equipment, and fixtures. Ensure that work is in accordance with relevant codes. Install or service street lights, intercom systems, or electrical control systems. Excludes "Security and Fire Alarm Systems Installers" (49-2098). **Examples:** Electrical Sign Servicer; House Wirer; Chief Electrician.

47-2120 Glaziers

This broad occupation is the same as the detailed occupation:
47-2121 Glaziers

47-2121 Glaziers

Install glass in windows, skylights, store fronts, and display cases, or on surfaces such as building fronts, interior walls, ceilings, and tabletops. **Examples:** Window Glass Installer; Plate Glass Installer; Stained Glass Glazier.

47-2130 Insulation Workers

This broad occupation includes the following two detailed occupations:
47-2131 Insulation Workers, Floor, Ceiling, and Wall
47-2132 Insulation Workers, Mechanical

47-2131 Insulation Workers, Floor, Ceiling, and Wall

Line and cover structures with insulating materials. Work with batt, roll, or blown insulation materials. **Examples:** Composition Weatherboard Installer; Fiberglass Insulation Installer; Insulation Blower.

47-2132 Insulation Workers, Mechanical

Apply insulating materials to pipes or ductwork or to other mechanical systems, to help control and maintain temperature. **Examples:** Boiler Coverer; Pipe Coverer.

47-2140 Painters and Paperhangers

This broad occupation includes the following two detailed occupations:
47-2141 Painters, Construction and Maintenance
47-2142 Paperhangers

47-2141 Painters, Construction and Maintenance

Paint walls, equipment, buildings, bridges, and other structural surfaces, using brushes, rollers, and spray guns. Remove old paint to prepare surface prior to painting. Mix colors or oils to obtain desired color or consistency. Excludes "Paperhangers" (47-2142). **Examples:** Bridge Painter; Traffic Line Painter; House Painter.

47-2142 Paperhangers

Cover interior walls and ceilings of rooms with decorative wallpaper or fabric. Attach advertising posters on surfaces such as walls and billboards. Remove old materials from surface to be papered. **Examples:** Billboard Poster; Wallpaperer.

47-2150 Pipelayers, Plumbers, Pipefitters, and Steamfitters

This broad occupation includes the following two detailed occupations:
47-2151 Pipelayers
47-2152 Plumbers, Pipefitters, and Steamfitters

47-2151 Pipelayers

Lay pipe for storm or sanitation sewers, drains, and water mains. Grade trenches or culverts; position pipe; seal joints. Excludes "Welders, Cutters, Solderers, and Brazers" (51-4121). **Examples:** Trench Pipe Layer; Pipe Liner; Sewer Connector.

47-2152 Plumbers, Pipefitters, and Steamfitters

Assemble, install, alter, and repair pipelines or pipe systems that carry water, steam, air, or other liquids or gases. Install heating and cooling equipment and mechanical-control systems. **Examples:** Gas Line Installer; Hot Water Heater Installer; Sprinkling System Installer.

47-2160 Plasterers and Stucco Masons

This broad occupation is the same as the detailed occupation:
47-2161 Plasterers and Stucco Masons

47-2161 Plasterers and Stucco Masons

Apply interior or exterior plaster, cement, stucco, or similar materials. Set ornamental plaster. **Examples:** Dry Plasterer; Stucco Worker; Ornamental Plasterer.

47-2170 Reinforcing Iron and Rebar Workers

This broad occupation is the same as the detailed occupation:
47-2171 Reinforcing Iron and Rebar Workers

47-2171 Reinforcing Iron and Rebar Workers

Position and secure steel bars or mesh in concrete forms to reinforce concrete. Use a variety of fasteners, rod-bending machines, blowtorches, and hand tools. Includes rod busters. **Examples:** Reinforcing Rod Layer; Rod Buster; Steel Tier.

47-2180 Roofers

This broad occupation is the same as the detailed occupation:
47-2181 Roofers

47-2181 Roofers

Cover roofs of structures with shingles, slate, asphalt, aluminum, wood, and related materials. Spray roofs, sidings, and walls with material to bind, seal, insulate, or soundproof sections of structures. **Examples:** Slater; Hot Tar Roofer; Terra Cotta Roofer.

47-2210 Sheet Metal Workers

This broad occupation is the same as the detailed occupation:
47-2211 Sheet Metal Workers

47-2211 Sheet Metal Workers

Fabricate, assemble, install, and repair sheet metal products and equipment, such as ducts, control boxes, drainpipes, and furnace casings. Set up and operate fabricating machines, to cut, bend, and straighten sheet metal. Shape metal over anvils, blocks, or forms, using hammer. Operate soldering and welding equipment to join sheet metal parts. Inspect, assemble, and smooth seams and joints of burred surfaces. Includes sheet metal duct installers who install prefabricated sheet metal ducts used for heating, air conditioning, or other purposes. **Examples:** Duct Installer, Metal Work; Tinsmith.

47-2220 Structural Iron and Steel Workers

This broad occupation is the same as the detailed occupation:
47-2221 Structural Iron and Steel Workers

47-2221 Structural Iron and Steel Workers

Raise, place, and unite iron or steel girders, columns, and other structural members to form completed structures or structural frameworks. Erect metal storage tanks; assemble prefabricated metal buildings. Excludes "Reinforcing Iron and

Rebar Workers" (47-2171). **Examples:** Bolter; Guard Rail Installer; Construction Ironworker.

47-3000 Helpers, Construction Trades

47-3010 Helpers, Construction Trades

This broad occupation includes the following seven detailed occupations:
47-3011 Helpers—Brickmasons, Blockmasons, Stonemasons, and Tile and Marble Setters
47-3012 Helpers—Carpenters
47-3013 Helpers—Electrician
47-3014 Helpers—Painters, Paperhangers, Plasterers, and Stucco Masons
47-3015 Helpers—Pipelayers, Plumbers, Pipefitters, and Steamfitters
47-3016 Helpers—Roofers
47-3019 Helpers, Construction Trades, All Other

47-3011 Helpers—Brickmasons, Blockmasons, Stonemasons, and Tile and Marble Setters

Help brickmasons, blockmasons, stonemasons, or tile and marble setters by performing duties of lesser skill. Use, supply, or hold materials or tools; clean work area and equipment. Excludes apprentice workers, as they are to be reported with the appropriate skilled construction trade occupation (47-2011 through 47-2221). Excludes construction laborers who do not primarily assist brickmasons, blockmasons, and stonemasons or tile and marble setters, as they are classified as "Construction Laborers" (47-2061). **Examples:** Brick Carrier; Brick Washer; Tile Layers Helper.

47-3012 Helpers—Carpenters

Help carpenters by performing duties of lesser skill. Use, supply or holding materials or tools; clean work area and equipment. Excludes apprentice workers, as they are to be reported with the appropriate skilled construction trade occupation (47-2011 through 47-2221). Excludes construction laborers who do not primarily assist carpenters, as they are classified as "Construction Laborers" (47-2061). **Examples:** Carpenter's Mate; Joiner's Helper; Cabinetmakers Helper.

47-3013 Helpers—Electricians

Help electricians by performing duties of lesser skill. Use, supply, or hold materials or tools; clean work area and equipment. Excludes apprentice workers, as they are to be reported with the appropriate skilled construction trade occupation (47-2011 through 47-2221). Excludes construction laborers who do not primarily assist electricians, as they are classified as "Construction Laborers" (47-2061). **Examples:** Utilities Ground Worker; Electrician's Assistant.

47-3014 Helpers—Painters, Paperhangers, Plasterers, and Stucco Masons

Help painters, paperhangers, plasterers, or stucco masons by performing duties of lesser skill. Use, supply, or hold materials or tools; clean work area and equipment. Excludes apprentice workers, as they are to be reported with the appropriate skilled construction trade occupation (47-2011 through 47-2221). Excludes construction laborers who do not primarily assist painters, paperhangers, plasterers, or stucco masons, as they are classified as "Construction Laborers" (47-2061). **Example:** Plaster Tender.

47-3015 Helpers—Pipelayers, Plumbers, Pipefitters, and Steamfitters

Help plumbers, pipefitters, steamfitters, or pipelayers by performing duties of lesser skill. Use, supply, or hold materials or tools; clean work area and equipment. Excludes apprentice workers, as they are to be reported with the appropriate skilled construction trade occupation (47-2011 through 47-2221). Excludes construction laborers who do not primarily assist plumbers, pipefitters, steamfitters, or pipelayers, as they are classified as "Construction Laborers" (47-2061). **Examples:** Pipe Cutter; Plumbers Assistant; Water Main Installers Helper.

47-3016 Helpers—Roofers

Help roofers by performing duties of lesser skill. Use, supply, or hold materials or tools; clean work area and equipment. Excludes apprentice workers, as they are to be reported with the appropriate skilled construction trade occupation (47-2011 through 47-2221). Excludes construction laborers who do not primarily assist roofers, as they are classified as "Construction Laborers" (47-2061). **Example:** Roofer's Assistant.

47-3019 Helpers, Construction Trades, All Other

All construction trades helpers not listed separately. **Examples:** Cement Mixer; Glazier's Helper; Surveyor Helper.

47-4000 Other Construction and Related Workers

47-4010 Construction and Building Inspectors

This broad occupation is the same as the detailed occupation:
47-4011 Construction and Building Inspectors

47-4011 Construction and Building Inspectors

Inspect structures, using engineering skills to determine structural soundness and compliance with specifications, building codes, and other regulations. Conduct inspections which are general in nature or which are limited to a specific area such as electrical systems or plumbing. **Examples:** Highway Inspector; Electrical Inspector; Architectural Inspector.

47-4020 Elevator Installers and Repairers

This broad occupation is the same as the detailed occupation:
47-4021 Elevator Installers and Repairers

47-4021 Elevator Installers and Repairers

Assemble, install, repair, or maintain electric or hydraulic freight or passenger elevators, escalators, or dumbwaiters. **Examples:** Escalator Installer; Elevator Mechanic; Hydraulic Elevator Constructor.

47-4030 Fence Erectors

This broad occupation is the same as the detailed occupation:
47-4031 Fence Erectors

47-4031 Fence Erectors

Erect and repair metal and wooden fences and fence gates around highways, industrial establishments, residences, or farms, using hand and power tools. **Examples:** Wire Fence Builder; Wood Fence Installer.

47-4040 Hazardous Materials Removal Workers

This broad occupation is the same as the detailed occupation:
47-4041 Hazardous Materials Removal Workers

47-4041 Hazardous Materials Removal Workers

Identify, remove, pack, transport, or dispose of hazardous materials, including asbestos, lead-based paint, waste oil, fuel, transmission fluid, radioactive materials, and contaminated soil. Obtain required specialized training and certification in hazardous materials handling. Obtain required confined-entry permit. Operate earth-moving equipment or trucks. **Examples:** Asbestos Remover; Irradiated Fuel Handler; Hazardous Waste Remover.

47-4050 Highway Maintenance Workers

This broad occupation is the same as the detailed occupation:
47-4051 Highway Maintenance Workers

47-4051 Highway Maintenance Workers

Maintain highways, municipal and rural roads, airport runways, and rights-of-way. Patch broken or eroded pavement; repair guard rails, highway markers, and snow fences. Mow or clear brush from along road; plow snow from roadway. Excludes "Tree Trimmers and Pruners" (37-3013). **Examples:** Snow Plow Operator; Road Patcher; Road Sign Installer.

47-4060 Rail-Track Laying and Maintenance Equipment Operators

This broad occupation is the same as the detailed occupation:
47-4061 Rail-Track Laying and Maintenance Equipment Operators

47-4061 Rail-Track Laying and Maintenance Equipment Operators

Lay, repair, and maintain track for standard or narrow-gauge railroad equipment used in regular railroad service or in plant yards, quarries, sand and gravel pits, and mines. Includes ballast cleaning machine operators and road bed tamping machine operators. **Examples:** Ballast Cleaning Machine Operator; Track Surfacing Machine Operator; Track Dresser.

47-4070 Septic Tank Servicers and Sewer Pipe Cleaners

This broad occupation is the same as the detailed occupation:
47-4071 Septic Tank Servicers and Sewer Pipe Cleaners

47-4071 Septic Tank Servicers and Sewer Pipe Cleaners

Clean and repair septic tanks, sewer lines, or drains. Patch walls and partitions of tank; replace damaged drain tile; repair breaks in underground piping. **Examples:** Sewage Screen Operator; Septic Tank Cleaner; Electric Sewer Cleaning Machine Operator.

47-4090 Miscellaneous Construction and Related Workers

This broad occupation includes the following two detailed occupations:
47-4091 Segmental Pavers
47-4099 Construction and Related Workers, All Other

47-4091 Segmental Pavers

Lay out, cut, and paste segmental paving units. Includes installers of bedding and restraining materials for the paving units. **Examples:** Concrete Paver Installer; Interlocking Concrete Pavement Installer.

47-4099 Construction and Related Workers, All Other

All construction and related workers not listed separately. **Examples:** Aluminum Pool Installer; Building Wrecker; Waterproofer.

47-5000 Extraction Workers

47-5010 Derrick, Rotary Drill, and Service Unit Operators, Oil, Gas, and Mining

This broad occupation includes the following three detailed occupations:
47-5011 Derrick Operators, Oil and Gas
47-5012 Rotary Drill Operators, Oil and Gas
47-5013 Service Unit Operators, Oil, Gas, and Mining

47-5011 Derrick Operators, Oil and Gas

Rig derrick equipment and operate pumps to circulate mud through drill hole. **Examples:** Rotary Derrick Operator; Well Service Derrick Worker.

47-5012 Rotary Drill Operators, Oil and Gas

Set up or operate a variety of drills, to remove petroleum products from the earth and to find and remove core samples for testing during oil and gas exploration. **Examples:** Cable Tool Operator; Core Driller; Well Driller.

47-5013 Service Unit Operators, Oil, Gas, and Mining

Operate equipment to increase oil flow from producing wells or to remove stuck pipe, casing, tools, or other obstructions from drilling wells. Perform similar services in mining exploration operations. Includes fishing-tool technicians. **Examples:** Fishing Tool Operator; Well Cleaner.

47-5020 Earth Drillers, Except Oil and Gas

This broad occupation is the same as the detailed occupation:
47-5021 Earth Drillers, Except Oil and Gas

47-5021 Earth Drillers, Except Oil and Gas

Operate a variety of drills, such as rotary, churn, and pneumatic drills, to tap subsurface water and salt deposits, to remove core samples during mineral exploration or soil testing, and to facilitate the use of explosives in mining or construction. Use explosives. Includes horizontal and earth boring machine operators. **Examples:** Auger Operator; Earth Boring Machine Operator; Tunneling Machine Operator.

47-5030 Explosives Workers, Ordnance Handling Experts, and Blasters

This broad occupation is the same as the detailed occupation:
47-5031 Explosives Workers, Ordnance Handling Experts, and Blasters

47-5031 Explosives Workers, Ordnance Handling Experts, and Blasters

Place and detonate explosives, to demolish structures or to loosen, remove, or displace earth, rock, or other materials. Perform specialized handling, storage, and accounting procedures. Includes seismograph shooters. Excludes "Earth Drillers, Except Oil and Gas" (47-5021) who may also work with explosives. **Examples:** Dynamiter; Explosives Expert; Blast Setter.

47-5040 Mining Machine Operators

This broad occupation includes the following three detailed occupations:
47-5041 Continuous Mining Machine Operators
47-5042 Mine Cutting and Channeling Machine Operators
47-5049 Mining Machine Operators, All Other

47-5041 Continuous Mining Machine Operators

Operate self-propelled mining machines that rip coal, metal and nonmetal ores, rock, stone, or sand from the face and load it onto conveyors or into shuttle cars in a continuous operation.

47-5042 Mine Cutting and Channeling Machine Operators

Operate machinery such as longwall shears, plows, and cutting machines, to cut or channel along the face or seams of coal mines, stone quarries, or other mining surfaces, to facilitate blasting, separating, or removing minerals or materials from mines or from the earth's surface. Includes shale planers. **Examples:** Coal Cutter; Long Wall Mining Machine Tender; Shale Planer Operator.

47-5049 Mining Machine Operators, All Other

All mining machine operators not listed separately. **Examples:** Extraction Machine Operator; Hydraulic Operator; Rock Duster.

47-5050 Rock Splitters, Quarry

This broad occupation is the same as the detailed occupation:
47-5051 Rock Splitters, Quarry

47-5051 Rock Splitters, Quarry

Separate blocks of rough-dimension stone from quarry mass, using jackhammer and wedges. **Examples:** Quarry Plug and Feather Driller; Rock Breaker.

47-5060 Roof Bolters, Mining

This broad occupation is the same as the detailed occupation:
47-5061 Roof Bolters, Mining

47-5061 Roof Bolters, Mining

Operate machinery to install roof support bolts in underground mine.

47-5070 Roustabouts, Oil and Gas

This broad occupation is the same as the detailed occupation:
47-5071 Roustabouts, Oil and Gas

47-5071 Roustabouts, Oil and Gas

Assemble or repair oil field equipment using hand and power tools. Perform other tasks as needed. **Examples:** Connection Worker; Oil Field Laborer.

47-5080 Helpers—Extraction Workers

This broad occupation is the same as the detailed occupation:
47-5081 Helpers—Extraction Workers

47-5081 Helpers—Extraction Workers

Help extraction craft workers, such as earth drillers, blasters and explosives workers, derrick operators, and mining machine operators, by performing duties of lesser skill. Supply equipment; clean work area. Excludes apprentice workers, as they are to be reported with the appropriate extraction trade occupation (47-5011 through 47-5099). **Examples:** Blasters Helper; Tunnel Mucker; Mining Helper.

47-5090 Miscellaneous Extraction Workers

This broad occupation is the same as the detailed occupation:
47-5099 Extraction Workers, All Other

47-5099 Extraction Workers, All Other

All extraction workers not listed separately. **Examples:** Chute Operator; Coal Digger; Sandfill Operator.

49-0000 INSTALLATION, MAINTENANCE, AND REPAIR OCCUPATIONS

49-1000 Supervisors of Installation, Maintenance, and Repair Workers

49-1010 First-Line Supervisors/Managers of Mechanics, Installers, and Repairers

This broad occupation is the same as the detailed occupation:
49-1011 First-Line Supervisors/Managers of Mechanics, Installers, and Repairers

49-1011 First-Line Supervisors/Managers of Mechanics, Installers, and Repairers

Supervise and coordinate the activities of mechanics, installers, and repairers. Excludes team or work leaders. **Examples:** Marine Service Manager; Ground Crew Chief; Engine Repair Supervisor.

49-2000 Electrical and Electronic Equipment Mechanics, Installers, and Repairers

49-2010 Computer, Automated Teller, and Office Machine Repairers

This broad occupation is the same as the detailed occupation:
49-2011 Computer, Automated Teller, and Office Machine Repairers

49-2011 Computer, Automated Teller, and Office Machine Repairers

Repair, maintain, or install computers, word processing systems, automated teller machines, and electronic office machines such as duplicating and fax machines. **Examples:** ATM Specialist; Cash Register Servicer; Computer Installer.

49-2020 Radio and Telecommunications Equipment Installers and Repairers

This broad occupation includes the following two detailed occupations:
49-2021 Radio Mechanics
49-2022 Telecommunications Equipment Installers and Repairers, Except Line Installers

49-2021 Radio Mechanics

Test or repair mobile or stationary radio transmitting and receiving equipment and two-way radio communications systems used in ship-to-shore communications and found in service and emergency vehicles. **Examples:** Radio Electrician; Radio Rigger.

49-2022 Telecommunications Equipment Installers and Repairers, Except Line Installers

Set up, rearrange, or remove switching and dialing equipment used in central offices. Service or repair telephones and other communication equipment on customer's property. Install equipment in new locations or install wiring and telephone jacks in buildings under construction. **Examples:** Central Office Equipment Installer; Electronics Installer; Exchange Mechanic.

49-2090 Miscellaneous Electrical and Electronic Equipment Mechanics, Installers, and Repairers

This broad occupation includes the following eight detailed occupations:
49-2091 Avionics Technicians
49-2092 Electric Motor, Power Tool, and Related Repairers
49-2093 Electrical and Electronics Installers and Repairers, Transportation Equipment
49-2094 Electrical and Electronics Repairers, Commercial and Industrial Equipment
49-2095 Electrical and Electronics Repairers, Powerhouse, Substation, and Relay
49-2096 Electronic Equipment Installers and Repairers, Motor Vehicles
49-2097 Electronic Home Entertainment Equipment Installers and Repairers
49-2098 Security and Fire Alarm Systems Installers

49-2091 Avionics Technicians

Install, inspect, test, adjust, or repair avionics equipment, such as radar, radio, navigation, and missile control systems in aircraft or space vehicles. **Examples:** Aircraft Electrician; Automatic Pilot Mechanic; Missile Facilities Repairer.

49-2092 Electric Motor, Power Tool, and Related Repairers

Repair, maintain, or install electric motors, wiring, or switches. **Examples:** Armature Winder; Generator Mechanic; Electric Golf Cart Repairer.

49-2093 Electrical and Electronics Installers and Repairers, Transportation Equipment

Install, adjust, or maintain mobile electronics communication equipment, including sound, sonar, security, navigation, and surveillance systems on trains, watercraft, or other mobile equipment. Excludes "Avionics Technicians" (49-2091) and

"Electronic Equipment Installers and Repairers, Motor Vehicles" (49-2096). **Example:** Locomotive Electrician.

49-2094 Electrical and Electronics Repairers, Commercial and Industrial Equipment

Repair, test, adjust, or install electronic equipment such as industrial controls, transmitters, and antennas. Excludes "Avionics Technicians" (49-2091), "Electronic Equipment Installers and Repairers, Motor Vehicles" (49-2096), and "Electrical and Electronics Installers and Repairers, Transportation Equipment" (49-2093). **Examples:** Missile Pad Mechanic; Radar Technician; Amplifier Mechanic.

49-2095 Electrical and Electronics Repairers, Powerhouse, Substation, and Relay

Inspect, test, repair, or maintain electrical equipment in generating stations, substations, and in-service relays. **Examples:** Powerhouse Electrician; Relay Technician; Power Transformer Repairer.

49-2096 Electronic Equipment Installers and Repairers, Motor Vehicles

Install, diagnose, or repair communications, sound, security, or navigation equipment in motor vehicles. **Examples:** Auto Phone Installer; Automotive Electrician.

49-2097 Electronic Home Entertainment Equipment Installers and Repairers

Repair, adjust, or install audio or television receivers, stereo systems, camcorders, video systems, or other electronic home entertainment equipment. **Examples:** Electric Organ Technician; Television Mechanic; Satellite Dish Installer.

49-2098 Security and Fire Alarm Systems Installers

Install, program, maintain, and repair security and fire alarm wiring and equipment. Ensure that work is done in accordance with relevant codes. Excludes "Electricians" (47-2111) who do a broad range of electrical wiring. **Examples:** Fire Alarm Installer; Burglar Alarm Mechanic.

49-3000 Vehicle and Mobile Equipment Mechanics, Installers, and Repairers

49-3010 Aircraft Mechanics and Service Technicians

This broad occupation is the same as the detailed occupation:
49-3011 Aircraft Mechanics and Service Technicians

49-3011 Aircraft Mechanics and Service Technicians

Diagnose, adjust, repair, or overhaul aircraft engines and assemblies, such as hydraulic and pneumatic systems. Includes helicopter and aircraft engine specialists. Excludes "Avionics Technician" (49-2091). **Examples:** Aircraft Engine Specialist; Flight Test Mechanic; Airframe Mechanic.

49-3020 Automotive Technicians and Repairers

This broad occupation includes the following three detailed occupations:
49-3021 Automotive Body and Related Repairers
49-3022 Automotive Glass Installers and Repairers
49-3023 Automotive Service Technicians and Mechanics

49-3021 Automotive Body and Related Repairers

Repair and refinish automotive vehicle bodies; straighten vehicle frames. Excludes "Painters, Transportation Equipment" (51-9122) and "Automotive Glass Installers and Repairers" (49-3022). **Examples:** Auto Body Customizer; Collision Mechanic; Frame Straightener.

49-3022 Automotive Glass Installers and Repairers

Replace or repair broken windshields and window glass in motor vehicles. **Examples:** Auto Glass Mechanic; Windshield Installer; Auto Glass Fitter.

49-3023 Automotive Service Technicians and Mechanics

Diagnose, adjust, repair, or overhaul automotive vehicles. Excludes "Automotive Body and Related Repairers" (49-3021), "Bus and Truck Mechanics and Diesel Engine Specialists" (49-3031), and "Electronic Equipment Installers and Repairers, Motor Vehicles" (49-2096). **Examples:** Auto Brake Mechanic; Fuel Injection Servicer; Auto Transmission Specialist.

49-3030 Bus and Truck Mechanics and Diesel Engine Specialists

This broad occupation is the same as the detailed occupation:
49-3031 Bus and Truck Mechanics and Diesel Engine Specialists

49-3031 Bus and Truck Mechanics and Diesel Engine Specialists

Diagnose, adjust, repair, or overhaul trucks, buses, and all types of diesel engines. Includes mechanics working primarily with automobile diesel engines. **Examples:** Tractor Trailer Mechanic; Diesel Mechanic; Farm Equipment Engine Mechanic.

49-3040 Heavy Vehicle and Mobile Equipment Service Technicians and Mechanics

This broad occupation includes the following three detailed occupations:
49-3041 Farm Equipment Mechanics

49-3042 Mobile Heavy Equipment Mechanics, Except Engines
49-3043 Rail Car Repairers

49-3041 Farm Equipment Mechanics

Diagnose, adjust, repair, or overhaul farm machinery and vehicles such as tractors, harvesters, dairy equipment, and irrigation systems. Excludes "Bus and Truck Mechanics and Diesel Engine Specialists" (49-3031). **Examples:** Irrigation Equipment Mechanic; Dairy Equipment Installer.

49-3042 Mobile Heavy Equipment Mechanics, Except Engines

Diagnose, adjust, repair, or overhaul mobile mechanical, hydraulic, and pneumatic equipment such as cranes, bulldozers, graders, and conveyors used in construction, logging, and surface mining. Excludes "Rail Car Repairers" (49-3043) and "Bus and Truck Mechanics and Diesel Engine Specialists" (49-3031). **Examples:** Construction Equipment Mechanic; Fork Lift Mechanic; Bulldozer Mechanic.

49-3043 Rail Car Repairers

Diagnose, adjust, repair, or overhaul railroad rolling stock, mine cars, or mass transit rail cars. Excludes "Bus and Truck Mechanics and Diesel Engine Specialists" (49-3031). **Examples:** Streetcar Repairer; Mine Car Mechanic.

49-3050 Small Engine Mechanics

This broad occupation includes the following three detailed occupations:
49-3051 Motorboat Mechanics
49-3052 Motorcycle Mechanics
49-3053 Outdoor Power Equipment and Other Small Engine Mechanics

49-3051 Motorboat Mechanics

Repair and adjust electrical and mechanical equipment of gasoline or diesel powered inboard or inboard-outboard boat engines. Excludes "Diesel Engine Specialists" (49-3031). **Example:** Outboard Motor Mechanic.

49-3052 Motorcycle Mechanics

Diagnose, adjust, repair, or overhaul motorcycles, scooters, mopeds, dirt bikes, or similar motorized vehicles. **Examples:** Motor Scooter Mechanic; Motorcycle Repairer.

49-3053 Outdoor Power Equipment and Other Small Engine Mechanics

Diagnose, adjust, repair, or overhaul small engines used to power lawn mowers, chain saws, and related equipment. **Examples:** Chainsaw Mechanic; Lawn Mower Repairer; Snowmobile Mechanic.

49-3090 Miscellaneous Vehicle and Mobile Equipment Mechanics, Installers, and Repairers

This broad occupation includes the following three detailed occupations:
49-3091 Bicycle Repairers
49-3092 Recreational Vehicle Service Technicians
49-3093 Tire Repairers and Changers

49-3091 Bicycle Repairers

Repair and service bicycles. **Example:** Bicycle Mechanic.

49-3092 Recreational Vehicle Service Technicians

Diagnose, inspect, adjust, repair, or overhaul recreational vehicles, including travel trailers. Specialize in maintaining gas, electrical, hydraulic, plumbing, or chassis/towing systems as well as repairing generators, appliances, and interior components. Includes workers who perform customized van conversions. Excludes "Automotive Service Technicians and Mechanics" (49-3023) and "Bus and Truck Mechanics and Diesel Engine Specialists" (49-3031) who also work on recreation vehicles. **Example:** RV Mechanic.

49-3093 Tire Repairers and Changers

Repair and replace tires. **Examples:** Tire Balancer; Tire Fixer.

49-9000 Other Installation, Maintenance, and Repair Occupations

49-9010 Control and Valve Installers and Repairers

This broad occupation includes the following two detailed occupations:
49-9011 Mechanical Door Repairers
49-9012 Control and Valve Installers and Repairers, Except Mechanical Door

49-9011 Mechanical Door Repairers

Install, service, or repair opening and closing mechanisms of automatic doors and hydraulic door closers. Includes garage door mechanics. **Example:** Automatic Door Mechanic.

49-9012 Control and Valve Installers and Repairers, Except Mechanical Door

Install, repair, and maintain mechanical regulating and controlling devices such as electric meters, gas regulators, thermostats, safety and flow valves, and other mechanical governors. **Examples:** Electric Meter Installer; Gas Meter Prover; Thermostat Repairer.

49-9020 Heating, Air Conditioning, and Refrigeration Mechanics and Installers

This broad occupation is the same as the detailed occupation:
49-9021 Heating, Air Conditioning, and Refrigeration Mechanics and Installers

49-9021 Heating, Air Conditioning, and Refrigeration Mechanics and Installers

Install or repair heating, central air conditioning, or refrigeration systems, including oil burners, hot-air furnaces, and heating stoves. **Examples:** Furnace Converter; Gas Furnace Installer; Oil Burner Repairer.

49-9030 Home Appliance Repairers

This broad occupation is the same as the detailed occupation:
49-9031 Home Appliance Repairers

49-9031 Home Appliance Repairers

Repair, adjust, or install all types of electric or gas household appliances, such as refrigerators, washers, dryers, and ovens. **Examples:** Window Air Conditioner Mechanic; Vacuum Cleaner Repairer; Washing Machine Installer.

49-9040 Industrial Machinery Installation, Repair, and Maintenance Workers

This broad occupation includes the following five detailed occupations:
49-9041 Industrial Machinery Mechanics
49-9042 Maintenance and Repair Workers, General
49-9043 Maintenance Workers, Machinery
49-9044 Millwrights
49-9045 Refractory Materials Repairers, Except Brickmasons

49-9041 Industrial Machinery Mechanics

Repair, install, adjust, or maintain industrial production and processing machinery or refinery and pipeline distribution systems. Excludes "Millwrights" (49-9044), "Mobile Heavy Equipment Mechanics, Except Engines" (49-3042), and "Maintenance Workers, Machinery" (49-9043) who perform only routine tasks. **Examples:** Conveyor Belt Installer; Turbine Mechanic; Hydroelectric Machinery Mechanic.

49-9042 Maintenance and Repair Workers, General

Perform work involving the skills of two or more maintenance or craft occupations to keep machines, mechanical equipment, or the structure of an establishment in repair. Participate in pipe fitting; boiler making; insulating; welding; machining; carpentry; repairing electrical or mechanical equipment, installing, aligning, and balancing new equipment; and repairing buildings, floors, or stairs. Excludes "Maintenance Workers, Machinery" (49-9043). **Examples:** Building Maintenance Repairer; Trouble Shooting Mechanic; Mechanical Adjuster.

49-9043 Maintenance Workers, Machinery

Lubricate machinery, change parts, or perform other routine machinery maintenance. Excludes "Maintenance and Repair Workers, General" (49-9042). **Examples:** Belt Repairer; Grease Packer; Machine Oiler.

49-9044 Millwrights

Install, dismantle, or move machinery and heavy equipment according to layout plans, blueprints, or other drawings. **Examples:** Machine Erector; Machine Rigger; Machinery Dismantler.

49-9045 Refractory Materials Repairers, Except Brickmasons

Build or repair furnaces, kilns, cupolas, boilers, converters, ladles, soaking pits, or ovens, using refractory materials. **Examples:** Bondactor Machine Operator; Kiln Door Repairer.

49-9050 Line Installers and Repairers

This broad occupation includes the following two detailed occupations:
49-9051 Electrical Power-Line Installers and Repairers
49-9052 Telecommunications Line Installers and Repairers

49-9051 Electrical Power-Line Installers and Repairers

Install or repair cables or wires used in electrical power or distribution systems. Erect poles and light- or heavy-duty transmission towers. Excludes "Electrical and Electronics Repairers, Powerhouse, Substation, and Relay" (49-2095). **Examples:** Pole Climber; High Tension Tester; Electric Utility Wire Stretcher.

49-9052 Telecommunications Line Installers and Repairers

String and repair telephone and television cable, including fiber optics and other equipment for transmitting messages or television programming. **Examples:** Telecommunications Cable Splicer; Telecommunications Wire Stretcher; Cable Television Installer.

49-9060 Precision Instrument and Equipment Repairers

This broad occupation includes the following five detailed occupations:
49-9061 Camera and Photographic Equipment Repairers

49-9062 Medical Equipment Repairers
49-9063 Musical Instrument Repairers and Tuners
49-9064 Watch Repairers
49-9069 Precision Instrument and Equipment Repairers, All Other

49-9061 Camera and Photographic Equipment Repairers

Repair and adjust cameras and photographic equipment, including commercial video and motion picture camera equipment. **Examples:** Camera Machinist; Photographic Equipment Technician.

49-9062 Medical Equipment Repairers

Test, adjust, or repair biomedical or electromedical equipment. **Examples:** Biomedical Equipment Technician; Hearing Aid Mechanic; Surgical Instrument Mechanic.

49-9063 Musical Instrument Repairers and Tuners

Repair percussion, stringed, reed, or wind instruments. Specialize in one area, such as piano tuning. Excludes "Electronic Home Entertainment Equipment Installers and Repairers" (49-2097) who repair electrical and electronic musical instruments. **Examples:** Piano Tuner; Violin Repairer; Tone Regulator.

49-9064 Watch Repairers

Repair, clean, and adjust mechanisms of timing instruments such as watches and clocks. Includes watchmakers. **Examples:** Watch and Clock Crowner; Horologist; Watchmaker.

49-9069 Precision Instrument and Equipment Repairers, All Other

All precision instrument and equipment repairers not listed separately. **Examples:** Laboratory Equipment Installer; Gyro Mechanic; Meteorological Equipment Repairer.

49-9090 Miscellaneous Installation, Maintenance, and Repair Workers

This broad occupation includes the following nine detailed occupations:
49-9091 Coin, Vending, and Amusement Machine Servicers and Repairers
49-9092 Commercial Divers
49-9093 Fabric Menders, Except Garment
49-9094 Locksmiths and Safe Repairers
49-9095 Manufactured Building and Mobile Home Installers
49-9096 Riggers
49-9097 Signal and Track Switch Repairers
49-9098 Helpers—Installation, Maintenance, and Repair Workers
49-9099 Installation, Maintenance, and Repair Workers, All Other

49-9091 Coin, Vending, and Amusement Machine Servicers and Repairers

Install, service, adjust, or repair coin, vending, or amusement machines, including video games, juke boxes, pinball machines, or slot machines. **Examples:** Cigarette Machine Mechanic; Slot Machine Mechanic; Video Game Mechanic.

49-9092 Commercial Divers

Work below surface of water, using scuba gear to inspect, repair, remove, or install equipment and structures. Use various power and hand tools such as drills, sledge-hammers, torches, and welding equipment. Conduct tests or experiments, rig explosives, or photograph structures or marine life. Excludes "Fishers and Related Fishing Workers" (45-3011), "Athletes and Sports Competitors" (27-2021), and "Police and Sheriff's Patrol Officers" (33-3051). **Examples:** Marine Diver; Scuba Diver; Skin Diver.

49-9093 Fabric Menders, Except Garment

Repair tears, holes, and other defects in fabrics such as draperies, linens, para-chutes, and tents. **Examples:** Canvas Repairer; Bag Repairer; Seat Mender.

49-9094 Locksmiths and Safe Repairers

Repair and open locks; make keys; change locks and safe combinations; and install and repair safes. **Examples:** Key Maker; Vault Service Mechanic; Lock Expert.

49-9095 Manufactured Building and Mobile Home Installers

Move or install mobile homes or prefabricated buildings. **Examples:** Mobile Home Mechanic; Housetrailer Servicer.

49-9096 Riggers

Set up or repair rigging for construction projects, manufacturing plants, logging yards, ships, and shipyards. Set up or repair rigging for the entertainment indus-try. **Examples:** Acrobatic Rigger; Rigging Slinger; Yard Rigger.

49-9097 Signal and Track Switch Repairers

Install, inspect, test, maintain, or repair electric gate crossings, signals, signal equipment, track switches, section lines, or intercommunications systems within a railroad system. **Examples:** Signal Mechanic; Signal Maintainer; Third Rail Installer.

49-9098 Helpers—Installation, Maintenance, and Repair Workers

Help installation, maintenance, and repair workers in maintenance, parts replace-ment, and repair of vehicles, industrial machinery, and electrical and electronic equipment. Furnish tools, materials, and supplies to other workers; clean work

area, machines, and tools; and hold materials or tools for other workers.
Examples: Mechanic's Helper; Diver's Helper; Blacksmith's Helper.

49-9099 Installation, Maintenance, and Repair Workers, All Other

All mechanical, installation, and repair workers and helpers not listed separately.
Examples: Blacksmith; Cooper; Gunsmith.

51-0000 PRODUCTION OCCUPATIONS

51-1000 Supervisors, Production Workers

51-1010 First-Line Supervisors/Managers of Production and Operating Workers

This broad occupation is the same as the detailed occupation:
51-1011 First-Line Supervisors/Managers of Production and Operating Workers

51-1011 First-Line Supervisors/Managers of Production and Operating Workers

Supervise and coordinate the activities of production and operating workers, such as inspectors, precision workers, machine setters and operators, assemblers, fabricators, and plant and system operators. Excludes team or work leaders. **Examples:** Laundromat Manager; Station Chief; Assembly Line Supervisor.

51-2000 Assemblers and Fabricators

51-2010 Aircraft Structure, Surfaces, Rigging, and Systems Assemblers

This broad occupation is the same as the detailed occupation:
51-2011 Aircraft Structure, Surfaces, Rigging, and Systems Assemblers

51-2011 Aircraft Structure, Surfaces, Rigging, and Systems Assemblers

Assemble, fit, fasten, and install parts of airplanes, space vehicles, or missiles, such as tails, wings, fuselage, bulkheads, stabilizers, landing gear, rigging and control equipment, or heating and ventilating systems. **Examples:** Aircraft Riveter; Fuselage Framer; Skin Installer.

51-2020 Electrical, Electronics, and Electromechanical Assemblers

This broad occupation includes the following three detailed occupations:
51-2021 Coil Winders, Tapers, and Finishers
51-2022 Electrical and Electronic Equipment Assemblers
51-2023 Electromechanical Equipment Assemblers

51-2021 Coil Winders, Tapers, and Finishers

Wind wire coils used in electrical components, such as resistors and transformers, and in electrical equipment and instruments, such as field cores, bobbins, armature cores, electrical motors, generators, and control equipment. **Examples:** Coil Builder; Motor Winder; Wire Coiler.

51-2022 Electrical and Electronic Equipment Assemblers

Assemble or modify electrical or electronic equipment, such as computers, test equipment telemetering systems, electric motors, and batteries. **Examples:** Anode Builder; Battery Builder; Industrial Equipment Wirer.

51-2023 Electromechanical Equipment Assemblers

Assemble or modify electromechanical equipment or devices, such as servomechanisms, gyros, dynamometers, magnetic drums, tape drives, brakes, control linkage, actuators, and appliances. **Examples:** Appliance Assembler; Vending Machine Assembler.

51-2030 Engine and Other Machine Assemblers

This broad occupation is the same as the detailed occupation:
51-2031 Engine and Other Machine Assemblers

51-2031 Engine and Other Machine Assemblers

Construct, assemble, or rebuild machines, such as engines, turbines, and similar equipment used in such industries as construction, extraction, textiles, and paper manufacturing. **Examples:** Machine Builder; Motor Installer; Turbine Assembler.

51-2040 Structural Metal Fabricators and Fitters

This broad occupation is the same as the detailed occupation:
51-2041 Structural Metal Fabricators and Fitters

51-2041 Structural Metal Fabricators and Fitters

Fabricate, lay out, position, align, and fit parts of structural metal products. **Examples:** Manufacturing Ornamental Metal Worker; Metal Box Maker; Protector Plate Attacher.

51-2090 Miscellaneous Assemblers and Fabricators

This broad occupation includes the following four detailed occupations:
51-2091 Fiberglass Laminators and Fabricators
51-2092 Team Assemblers
51-2093 Timing Device Assemblers, Adjusters, and Calibrators
51-2099 Assemblers and Fabricators, All Other

51-2091 Fiberglass Laminators and Fabricators

Laminate layers of fiberglass on molds, to form boat decks and hulls, bodies for golf carts, automobiles, or other products. **Examples:** Fiberglass Ski Maker; Fiberglass Boat Builder; Golf Cart Maker.

51-2092 Team Assemblers

Work as part of a team having responsibility for assembling an entire product or a component of a product. Perform all tasks conducted by the team in the assembly process; rotate through all or most of the tasks, rather than being assigned to a specific task on a permanent basis. Participate in making management decisions affecting the work. Includes team leaders who work as part of the team. Excludes assemblers (51-2011 through 51-2099) who continuously perform the same task.

51-2093 Timing Device Assemblers, Adjusters, and Calibrators

Perform precision assembling or adjusting, within narrow tolerances, of timing devices such as watches, clocks, or chronometers. Excludes "Watch Repairers" (49-9064). **Examples:** Chronometer Assembler; Hair Spring Truer; Escapement Matcher.

51-2099 Assemblers and Fabricators, All Other

All assemblers and fabricators not listed separately. **Examples:** Barrel Raiser; Automobile Assembler, except engines; Doll Maker.

51-3000 Food Processing Workers

51-3010 Bakers

This broad occupation is the same as the detailed occupation:
51-3011 Bakers

51-3011 Bakers

Mix and bake ingredients according to recipes, to produce breads, rolls, cookies, cakes, pies, pastries, or other baked goods. Include pastry chefs in restaurants and hotels with "Chefs and Head Cooks" (35-1011). **Examples:** Cake Maker; Head Baker; Pastry Finisher.

51-3020 Butchers and Other Meat, Poultry, and Fish Processing Workers

This broad occupation includes the following three detailed occupations:
51-3021 Butchers and Meat Cutters
51-3022 Meat, Poultry, and Fish Cutters and Trimmers
51-3023 Slaughterers and Meat Packers

51-3021 Butchers and Meat Cutters

Cut, trim, or prepare consumer-sized portions of meat for use or sale in retail establishments. **Examples:** Carver; Meat Department Manager; Cleaver.

51-3022 Meat, Poultry, and Fish Cutters and Trimmers

Use hand tools to perform routine cutting and trimming of meat, poultry, and fish. **Examples:** Calf Skinner; Eviscerator; Filleter.

51-3023 Slaughterers and Meat Packers

Work in slaughtering, meat packing, or wholesale establishments, performing precision functions involving the preparation of meat. Perform specialized slaughtering tasks, cutting standard or premium cuts of meat for marketing, making sausage, or wrapping meats. Excludes "Meat, Poultry, and Fish Cutters and Trimmers" (51-3022) who perform routine, lower-skilled meat cutting. **Examples:** Hog Sticker; Shactor; Beef Splitter.

51-3090 Miscellaneous Food Processing Workers

This broad occupation includes the following three detailed occupations:
51-3091 Food and Tobacco Roasting, Baking, and Drying Machine Operators and Tenders
51-3092 Food Batchmakers
51-3093 Food Cooking Machine Operators and Tenders

51-3091 Food and Tobacco Roasting, Baking, and Drying Machine Operators and Tenders

Operate or tend food or tobacco roasting, baking, or drying equipment, including hearth ovens, kiln driers, roasters, char kilns, and vacuum drying equipment. **Examples:** Coffee Roaster; Smokehouse Worker; Curing Room Worker.

51-3092 Food Batchmakers

Set up and operate equipment that mixes or blends ingredients used in the manufacturing of food products. Includes candy makers and cheese makers. **Examples:** Candy Maker; Honey Blender; Peanut Butter Maker.

51-3093 Food Cooking Machine Operators and Tenders

Operate or tend cooking equipment such as steam cooking vats, deep fry cookers, pressure cookers, kettles, and boilers, to prepare food products. Excludes "Food and Tobacco Roasting, Baking, and Drying Machine Operators and Tenders" (51-3091). **Examples:** Doughnut Maker; Sausage Cooker; Potato Chip Fryer.

51-4000 Metal Workers and Plastic Workers

51-4010 Computer Control Programmers and Operators

This broad occupation includes the following two detailed occupations:
51-4011 Computer-Controlled Machine Tool Operators, Metal and Plastic
51-4012 Numerical Tool and Process Control Programmers

51-4011 Computer-Controlled Machine Tool Operators, Metal and Plastic

Operate computer-controlled machines or robots to perform one or more machine functions on metal or plastic work pieces. **Examples:** Numerical Control Machine Operator; Robot Operator.

51-4012 Numerical Tool and Process Control Programmers

Develop programs to control machining or processing of parts by automatic machine tools, equipment, or systems. **Examples:** Tool Programmer; NC Programmer.

51-4020 Forming Machine Setters, Operators, and Tenders, Metal and Plastic

This broad occupation includes the following three detailed occupations:
51-4021 Extruding and Drawing Machine Setters, Operators, and Tenders, Metal and Plastic
51-4022 Forging Machine Setters, Operators, and Tenders, Metal and Plastic
51-4023 Rolling Machine Setters, Operators, and Tenders, Metal and Plastic

51-4021 Extruding and Drawing Machine Setters, Operators, and Tenders, Metal and Plastic

Set up, operate, or tend machines to extrude or draw thermoplastic or metal materials into tubes, rods, hoses, wire, bars, or structural shapes. **Examples:** Draw Bench Operator; Tube Drawer; Wire Drawing Setter.

51-4022 Forging Machine Setters, Operators, and Tenders, Metal and Plastic

Set up, operate, or tend forging machines to taper, shape, or form metal or plastic parts. **Examples:** Cold Header Operator; Swager Operator; Drop Hammer Operator.

51-0000
Production
Occupations

51-4023 Rolling Machine Setters, Operators, and Tenders, Metal and Plastic

Set up, operate, or tend machines, to roll steel or plastic forming bends, beads, knurls, rolls, or plate or to flatten, temper, or reduce gauge of material. **Examples:** Forming Roll Operator; Rolling Mill Operator; Tubing Machine Operator.

51-4030 Machine Tool Cutting Setters, Operators, and Tenders, Metal and Plastic

This broad occupation includes the following five detailed occupations:
51-4031 Cutting, Punching, and Press Machine Setters, Operators, and Tenders, Metal and Plastic
51-4032 Drilling and Boring Machine Tool Setters, Operators, and Tenders, Metal and Plastic
51-4033 Grinding, Lapping, Polishing, and Buffing Machine Tool Setters, Operators, and Tenders, Metal and Plastic
51-4034 Lathe and Turning Machine Tool Setters, Operators, and Tenders, Metal and Plastic
51-4035 Milling and Planing Machine Setters, Operators, and Tenders, Metal and Plastic

51-4031 Cutting, Punching, and Press Machine Setters, Operators, and Tenders, Metal and Plastic

Set up, operate, or tend machines, to saw, cut, shear, slit, punch, crimp, notch, bend, or straighten metal or plastic material. **Examples:** Perforator Operator; Crimping Machine Operator; Four Slide Machine Setter.

51-4032 Drilling and Boring Machine Tool Setters, Operators, and Tenders, Metal and Plastic

Set up, operate, or tend drilling machines, to drill, bore, ream, mill, or countersink metal or plastic work pieces. **Examples:** Drill Press Operator; Jewel Cupping Machine Operator; Reaming Press Operator.

51-4033 Grinding, Lapping, Polishing, and Buffing Machine Tool Setters, Operators, and Tenders, Metal and Plastic

Set up, operate, or tend grinding and related tools to remove excess material or burrs from surfaces, to sharpen edges or corners, or to buff, hone, or polish metal or plastic work pieces. **Examples:** Barrel Polisher; Jewel Bearing Facer; Metal Filer.

51-4034 Lathe and Turning Machine Tool Setters, Operators, and Tenders, Metal and Plastic

Set up, operate, or tend lathe and turning machines, to turn, bore, thread, form, or face metal or plastic materials such as wire, rod, or bar stock. **Examples:** Gear Cutter; Screw Machine Operator; Threading Machine Setter.

51-4035 Milling and Planing Machine Setters, Operators, and Tenders, Metal and Plastic

Set up, operate, or tend milling or planing machines, to mill, plane, shape, groove, or profile metal or plastic work pieces. **Examples:** Broaching Machine Operator; Profiler Operator; Scribing Machine Operator.

51-4040 Machinists

This broad occupation is the same as the detailed occupation:
51-4041 Machinists

51-4041 Machinists

Set up and operate a variety of machine tools, to produce precision parts and instruments. Fabricate and modify parts, to make or repair machine tools or to maintain industrial machines, applying knowledge of mechanics, shop mathematics, metal properties, layout, and machining procedures. Includes precision instrument makers who fabricate, modify, or repair mechanical instruments. **Examples:** Electrical Instrument Maker; Machine Fitter.

51-4050 Metal Furnace and Kiln Operators and Tenders

This broad occupation includes the following two detailed occupations:
51-4051 Metal-Refining Furnace Operators and Tenders
51-4052 Pourers and Casters, Metal

51-4051 Metal-Refining Furnace Operators and Tenders

Operate or tend furnaces, such as gas, oil, coal, electric-arc or electric induction, open-hearth, or oxygen furnaces, to melt and refine metal before casting or to produce specified types of steel. Excludes "Heat Treating Equipment Setters, Operators, and Tenders, Metal and Plastic" (51-4191). **Examples:** Blast Furnace Blower; Bessemer Regulator; Smelter.

51-4052 Pourers and Casters, Metal

Operate hand-controlled mechanisms, to pour and regulate the flow of molten metal into molds, to produce castings or ingots. **Examples:** Ingot Header; Ladle Operator; Steel Pourer.

51-4060 Model Makers and Patternmakers, Metal and Plastic

This broad occupation includes the following two detailed occupations:
51-4061 Model Makers, Metal and Plastic
51-4062 Patternmakers, Metal and Plastic

51-4061 Model Makers, Metal and Plastic

Set up and operate machines such as lathes, milling and engraving machines, and jig borers, to make working models of metal or plastic objects. Includes template makers. **Examples:** Jig and Fixture Builder; Mandrel Maker; Mock Up Maker.

51-4062 Patternmakers, Metal and Plastic

Lay out, machine, fit, and assemble castings and parts to metal or plastic foundry patterns, core boxes, or match plates. **Examples:** Pattern Fitter; Stencil Cutter.

51-4070 Molders and Molding Machine Setters, Operators, and Tenders, Metal and Plastic

This broad occupation includes the following two detailed occupations:
51-4071 Foundry Mold and Coremakers
51-4072 Molding, Coremaking, and Casting Machine Setters, Operators, and Tenders, Metal and Plastic

51-4071 Foundry Mold and Coremakers

Make or form wax or sand cores or molds used in the production of metal castings in foundries. **Examples:** Core Setter; Mold Closer; Dry Sand Molder.

51-4072 Molding, Coremaking, and Casting Machine Setters, Operators, and Tenders, Metal and Plastic

Set up, operate, or tend metal or plastic molding, casting, or coremaking machines, to mold or cast metal or thermoplastic parts or products. **Examples:** Centrifugal Casting Machine Operator; Injection Molding Machine Setter; Core Mounter.

51-4080 Multiple Machine Tool Setters, Operators, and Tenders, Metal and Plastic

This broad occupation is the same as the detailed occupation:
51-4081 Multiple Machine Tool Setters, Operators, and Tenders, Metal and Plastic

51-4081 Multiple Machine Tool Setters, Operators, and Tenders, Metal and Plastic

Set up, operate, or tend more than one type of cutting or forming machine tool or robot. **Examples:** Machine Tool Operator; Combination Machine Tool Setter; Metal and Plastic Transfer Machine Operator.

51-4110 Tool and Die Makers

This broad occupation is the same as the detailed occupation:
51-4111 Tool and Die Makers

51-4111 Tool and Die Makers

Analyze specifications; lay out metal stock; set up and operate machine tools; fit and assemble parts, to make and repair dies, cutting tools, jigs, fixtures, gauges, and machinists' hand tools. **Examples:** Die Sinker; Die Finisher; Sawsmith.

51-4120 Welding, Soldering, and Brazing Workers

This broad occupation includes the following two detailed occupations:
51-4121 Welders, Cutters, Solderers, and Brazers
51-4122 Welding, Soldering, and Brazing Machine Setters, Operators, and Tenders

51-4121 Welders, Cutters, Solderers, and Brazers

Use hand welding, flame cutting, hand soldering, or brazing equipment, to weld or join metal components or to fill holes, indentations, or seams of fabricated metal products. **Examples:** Acetylene Burner; Arc Welder; Blow Torch Operator.

51-4122 Welding, Soldering, and Brazing Machine Setters, Operators, and Tenders

Set up, operate, or tend welding, soldering, or brazing machines or robots that weld, braze, solder, or heat-treat metal products, components, or assemblies. Includes workers who operate laser cutters or laser-beam machines. **Examples:** Electron Beam Welder Setter; Laser-Beam Machine Operator; Ultrasonic Welding Machine Operator.

51-4190 Miscellaneous Metalworkers and Plastic Workers

This broad occupation includes the following five detailed occupations:
51-4191 Heat Treating Equipment Setters, Operators, and Tenders, Metal and Plastic
51-4192 Lay-Out Workers, Metal and Plastic
51-4193 Plating and Coating Machine Setters, Operators, and Tenders, Metal and Plastic
51-4194 Tool Grinders, Filers, and Sharpeners
51-4199 Metalworkers and Plastic Workers, All Other

51-4191 Heat Treating Equipment Setters, Operators, and Tenders, Metal and Plastic

Set up, operate, or tend heating equipment such as heat-treating furnaces, flame-hardening machines, induction machines, soaking pits, or vacuum equipment, to temper, harden, anneal, or heat-treat metal or plastic objects. **Examples:** Metal & Plastic Annealer; Metal & Plastic Temperer; Induction Machine Setter.

51-4192 Lay-Out Workers, Metal and Plastic

Lay out reference points and dimensions on metal or plastic stock or workpieces, such as sheets, plates, tubes, structural shapes, castings, or machine parts, for further processing. Includes shipfitters. **Examples:** Pattern Setter; Location and Measurement Technician; Shipfitter.

51-4193 Plating and Coating Machine Setters, Operators, and Tenders, Metal and Plastic

Set up, operate, or tend plating or coating machines, to coat metal or plastic products with chromium, zinc, copper, cadmium, nickel, or other metal, to protect or decorate surfaces. Includes electrolytic processes. **Examples:** Anodizer; Electroplater; Galvanizer.

51-4194 Tool Grinders, Filers, and Sharpeners

Perform precision smoothing, sharpening, polishing, or grinding of metal objects. **Examples:** Die Polisher; Precision Honer; Tool Maintenance Worker.

51-4199 Metal Workers and Plastic Workers, All Other

All metal workers and plastic workers not listed separately. **Examples:** Balancing Machine Operator; Film Casting Operator; Nail Making Machine Setter.

51-5000 Printing Workers

51-5010 Bookbinders and Bindery Workers

This broad occupation includes the following two detailed occupations:
51-5011 Bindery Workers
51-5012 Bookbinders

51-5011 Bindery Workers

Set up or operate binding machines that produce books and other printed materials. Includes hand bindery workers. Excludes "Bookbinders" (51-5012). **Examples:** Book Coverer; Stitching Machine Operator; Bookbinding Machine Operator.

51-5012 Bookbinders

Perform highly skilled hand-finishing operations such as grooving and lettering, to bind books. **Examples:** Book Finisher; Book Mender.

51-5020 Printers

This broad occupation includes the following three detailed occupations:
51-5021 Job Printers
51-5022 Prepress Technicians and Workers
51-5023 Printing Machine Operators

51-5021 Job Printers

Set type according to copy; operate press to print job order; read proof for errors and clarity of impression; correct imperfections. Work in small establishments where work combines several job skills. **Examples:** Job Press Operator; Apprentice Job Printer.

51-5022 Prepress Technicians and Workers

Set up and prepare material for printing presses. Perform prepress functions such as compositing, typesetting, layout, paste-up, camera operating, scanning, film stripping, and photoengraving. **Examples:** Compositor; Lithographer; Photoengraving Etcher.

51-5023 Printing Machine Operators

Set up or operate various types of printing machines, such as offset, letterset, intaglio, or gravure presses or screen printers, to produce print on paper or other materials. **Examples:** Bag Printer; Offset Press Operator; Lithoplate Maker.

51-6000 Textile, Apparel, and Furnishings Workers

51-6010 Laundry and Dry-Cleaning Workers

This broad occupation is the same as the detailed occupation:
51-6011 Laundry and Dry-Cleaning Workers

51-6011 Laundry and Dry-Cleaning Workers

Operate or tend washing or dry-cleaning machines, to wash or dry-clean industrial or household articles such as cloth garments, suede, leather, furs, blankets, draperies, fine linens, rugs, and carpets. Includes spotters and dyers of these articles. **Examples:** Laundry Carpet Cleaner; Silk Spotter; Washing Machine Operator.

51-0000
Production
Occupations

51-6020 Pressers, Textile, Garment, and Related Materials

This broad occupation is the same as the detailed occupation:
51-6021 Pressers, Textile, Garment, and Related Materials

51-6021 Pressers, Textile, Garment, and Related Materials

Press or shape articles by hand or machine. **Examples:** Clothes Ironer; Garment Steamer; Steam Operator.

51-6030 Sewing Machine Operators

This broad occupation is the same as the detailed occupation:
51-6031 Sewing Machine Operators

51-6031 Sewing Machine Operators

Operate or tend sewing machines, to join, reinforce, or decorate material or to perform related sewing operations in the manufacture of garment or nongarment products. **Examples:** Blind Stitch Machine Operator; Loop Tacker; Hemmer.

51-6040 Shoe and Leather Workers

This broad occupation includes the following two detailed occupations:
51-6041 Shoe and Leather Workers and Repairers
51-6042 Shoe Machine Operators and Tenders

51-6041 Shoe and Leather Workers and Repairers

Construct, decorate, or repair leather and leather-like products such as luggage, shoes, and saddles. **Examples:** Upper Cutter; Cobbler; Saddle Maker.

51-6042 Shoe Machine Operators and Tenders

Operate or tend a variety of machines, to join, decorate, reinforce, or finish shoes and shoe parts. **Examples:** Counter Maker; Lasting Machine Operator; Shoe Archer.

51-6050 Tailors, Dressmakers, and Sewers

This broad occupation includes the following two detailed occupations:
51-6051 Sewers, Hand
51-6052 Tailors, Dressmakers, and Custom Sewers

51-6051 Sewers, Hand

Sew, join, reinforce, or finish, usually with needle and thread, a variety of manufactured items. Includes weavers and stitchers. Excludes "Fabric Menders, Except Garment" (49-9093). **Examples:** Hand Stitcher; Hand Weaver; Hosiery Mender.

51-6052 Tailors, Dressmakers, and Custom Sewers

Design, make, alter, repair, or fit garments. **Examples:** Coat Maker; Hand Finisher, Except Toys; Shop Tailor.

51-6060 Textile Machine Setters, Operators, and Tenders

This broad occupation includes the following four detailed occupations:
51-6061 Textile Bleaching and Dyeing Machine Operators and Tenders
51-6062 Textile Cutting Machine Setters, Operators, and Tenders
51-6063 Textile Knitting and Weaving Machine Setters, Operators, and Tenders
51-6064 Textile Winding, Twisting, and Drawing Out Machine Setters, Operators, and Tenders

51-6061 Textile Bleaching and Dyeing Machine Operators and Tenders

Operate or tend machines to bleach, shrink, wash, dye, or finish textiles or synthetic or glass fibers. **Examples:** Bleach Range Operator; Rug Dyer; Skein Yarn Dyer.

51-6062 Textile Cutting Machine Setters, Operators, and Tenders

Set up, operate, or tend machines that cut textiles. **Examples:** Canvas Cutter; Rag Shredder; Welt Trimming Machine Operator.

51-6063 Textile Knitting and Weaving Machine Setters, Operators, and Tenders

Set up, operate, or tend machines that knit, loop, weave, or draw in textiles. Excludes "Sewing Machine Operators" (51-6031). **Examples:** Crochet Machine Operator; Ribbing Machine Operator; Looping Machine Operator.

51-6064 Textile Winding, Twisting, and Drawing Out Machine Setters, Operators, and Tenders

Set up, operate, or tend machines that wind or twist textiles or that draw out and combine sliver such as wool, hemp, or synthetic fibers. Includes slubber machine and drawing frame operators. **Examples:** Beamer Operator; Bobbin Doffer; Frame Tender.

51-6090 Miscellaneous Textile, Apparel, and Furnishings Workers

This broad occupation includes the following four detailed occupations:
51-6091 Extruding and Forming Machine Setters, Operators, and Tenders, Synthetic and Glass Fibers
51-6092 Fabric and Apparel Patternmakers
51-6093 Upholsterers
51-6099 Textile, Apparel, and Furnishings Workers, All Other

51-6091 Extruding and Forming Machine Setters, Operators, and Tenders, Synthetic and Glass Fibers

Set up, operate, or tend machines that extrude and form continuous filaments from synthetic materials such as liquid polymer, rayon, and fiberglass. **Examples:** Fiber Machine Tender; Box Spinner; Synthetic Filament Spinner.

51-6092 Fabric and Apparel Patternmakers

Draw and construct sets of precision master fabric patterns or layouts. Mark and cut fabrics and apparel. **Examples:** Pattern Grader; Shoe Patternmaker.

51-6093 Upholsterers

Make, repair, or replace upholstery for household furniture or transportation vehicles. **Examples:** Car Seat Maker; Casket Coverer; Auto Top Mechanic.

51-6099 Textile, Apparel, and Furnishings Workers, All Other

All textile, apparel, and furnishings workers not listed separately. **Examples:** Napper; Carding Machine Operator; Mercerizer.

51-7000 Woodworkers

51-7010 Cabinetmakers and Bench Carpenters

This broad occupation is the same as the detailed occupation:
51-7011 Cabinetmakers and Bench Carpenters

51-7011 Cabinetmakers and Bench Carpenters

Cut, shape, and assemble wooden articles. Set up and operate a variety of woodworking machines such as power saws, jointers, and mortisers, to surface, cut, or shape lumber or to fabricate parts for wood products. Excludes "Woodworking Machine Setters, Operators, and Tenders" (51-7041 through 51-7042) who specialize in one or a limited number of machine phases. **Examples:** Marquetry Worker; Antique Furniture Repairer; Wood Machinist.

51-7020 Furniture Finishers

This broad occupation is the same as the detailed occupation:
51-7021 Furniture Finishers

51-7021 Furniture Finishers

Shape, finish, and refinish damaged, worn, or used furniture or new high-grade furniture to specified color or finish. **Examples:** Furniture Polisher; Refinisher; Wood Grainer.

51-7030 Model Makers and Patternmakers, Wood

This broad occupation includes the following two detailed occupations:
51-7031 Model Makers, Wood
51-7032 Patternmakers, Wood

51-7031 Model Makers, Wood

Construct full-size and scale wooden precision models of products. Includes wood jig builders and loft workers. **Examples:** Wood Jig Builder; Loft Worker.

51-7032 Patternmakers, Wood

Plan, lay out, and construct wooden unit or sectional patterns used in forming sand molds for castings. **Examples:** Experimental Wood Mechanic; Wood Die Maker.

51-7040 Woodworking Machine Setters, Operators, and Tenders

This broad occupation includes the following two detailed occupations:
51-7041 Sawing Machine Setters, Operators, and Tenders, Wood
51-7042 Woodworking Machine Setters, Operators, and Tenders, Except Sawing

51-7041 Sawing Machine Setters, Operators, and Tenders, Wood

Set up, operate, or tend wood sawing machines. Includes head sawyers. **Examples:** Crozer Operator; Sawyer; Wood Cutter.

51-7042 Woodworking Machine Setters, Operators, and Tenders, Except Sawing

Set up, operate, or tend woodworking machines such as drill presses, lathes, shapers, routers, sanders, planers, and wood nailing machines. **Examples:** Frazer; Molding Sander.

51-7090 Miscellaneous Woodworkers

This broad occupation is the same as the detailed occupation:
51-7099 Woodworkers, All Other

51-7099 Woodworkers, All Other

All woodworkers not listed separately. **Examples:** Wood Carver; Pole Framer; Veneer Taper.

51-8000 Plant and System Operators

51-8010 Power Plant Operators, Distributors, and Dispatchers

This broad occupation includes the following three detailed occupations:
51-8011 Nuclear Power Reactor Operators
51-8012 Power Distributors and Dispatchers
51-8013 Power Plant Operators

51-8011 Nuclear Power Reactor Operators

Control nuclear reactors. **Examples:** Nuclear Reactor Operator; Power Reactor Operator.

51-8012 Power Distributors and Dispatchers

Coordinate, regulate, or distribute electricity or steam. **Examples:** Feeder Switchboard Operator; Electric and Gas Load Dispatcher; Substation Operator.

51-8013 Power Plant Operators

Control, operate, or maintain machinery to generate electric power. Includes auxiliary equipment operators. Excludes "Nuclear Power Reactor Operators" (51-8011). **Examples:** Hydroelectric Operator; Generator Operator; Power House Operator.

51-8020 Stationary Engineers and Boiler Operators

This broad occupation is the same as the detailed occupation:
51-8021 Stationary Engineers and Boiler Operators

51-8021 Stationary Engineers and Boiler Operators

Operate or maintain stationary engines, boilers, or other mechanical equipment, to provide utilities for buildings or industrial processes. Operate equipment such as steam engines, generators, motors, turbines, and steam boilers. **Examples:** Cooling System Operator; Low Pressure Firer; Steam Engineer.

51-8030 Water and Liquid Waste Treatment Plant and System Operators

This broad occupation is the same as the detailed occupation:
51-8031 Water and Liquid Waste Treatment Plant and System Operators

51-8031 Water and Liquid Waste Treatment Plant and System Operators

Operate or control an entire process or system of machines, often through the use of control boards, to transfer or treat water or liquid waste. **Examples:** Disposal Operator; Filtration Plant Operator; Sewage Plant Operator.

51-8090 Miscellaneous Plant and System Operators

This broad occupation includes the following four detailed occupations:
51-8091 Chemical Plant and System Operators
51-8092 Gas Plant Operators
51-8093 Petroleum Pump System Operators, Refinery Operators, and Gaugers
51-8099 Plant and System Operators, All Other

51-8091 Chemical Plant and System Operators

Control or operate an entire chemical process or system of machines. **Examples:** Denitrator; Nitrogen Operator; Wash Operator.

51-8092 Gas Plant Operators

Distribute or process gas for utility companies and others by controlling compressors to maintain specified pressures on main pipelines. **Examples:** Liquefaction Plant Operator; Pressure Dispatcher.

51-8093 Petroleum Pump System Operators, Refinery Operators, and Gaugers

Control the operation of petroleum refining or processing units. Specialize in controlling manifold and pumping systems, gauging or testing oil in storage tanks, or regulating the flow of oil into pipelines. **Examples:** Absorption Plant Operator; Gasoline Plant Operator; Oil Refiner.

51-8099 Plant and System Operators, All Other

All plant and system operators not listed separately. **Examples:** Asphalt Plant Operator; Lime Filter Operator; Incinerator Operator.

51-9000 Other Production Occupations

51-9010 Chemical Processing Machine Setters, Operators, and Tenders

This broad occupation includes the following two detailed occupations:
51-9011 Chemical Equipment Operators and Tenders
51-9012 Separating, Filtering, Clarifying, Precipitating, and Still Machine Setters, Operators, and Tenders

51-9011 Chemical Equipment Operators and Tenders

Operate or tend equipment to control chemical changes or reactions in the processing of industrial or consumer products. Use devulcanizers, steam-jacketed kettles, and reactor vessels. Excludes "Chemical Plant and System Operators"

51-0000
Production
Occupations

(51-8091). **Examples:** Acetylene Plant Operator; Acid Purifier; Caustic Purification Operator.

51-9012 Separating, Filtering, Clarifying, Precipitating, and Still Machine Setters, Operators, and Tenders

Set up, operate, or tend continuous flow or vat-type equipment; filter presses; shaker screens; centrifuges; condenser tubes; precipitating, fermenting, or evaporating tanks; scrubbing towers; or batch stills. Use this equipment to extract, sort, or separate liquids, gases, or solids from other materials, to recover a refined product. Includes dairy processing equipment operators. Excludes "Chemical Equipment Operators and Tenders" (51-9011). **Examples:** Brewmaster; Dairy Processing Equipment Operator; Distiller.

51-9020 Crushing, Grinding, Polishing, Mixing, and Blending Workers

This broad occupation includes the following three detailed occupations:
51-9021 Crushing, Grinding, and Polishing Machine Setters, Operators, and Tenders
51-9022 Grinding and Polishing Workers, Hand
51-9023 Mixing and Blending Machine Setters, Operators, and Tenders

51-9021 Crushing, Grinding, and Polishing Machine Setters, Operators, and Tenders

Set up, operate, or tend machines to crush, grind, or polish materials such as coal, glass, grain, stone, food, or rubber. **Examples:** Beveling and Edging Machine Operator; Pulverizer Operator; Sand Blast Operator, Except Construction.

51-9022 Grinding and Polishing Workers, Hand

Grind, sand, or polish a variety of metal, wood, stone, clay, plastic, or glass objects, using hand tools or hand-held power tools. Includes chippers, buffers, and finishers. **Examples:** Metal Sander; Gun Barrel Finisher; Hand Buffer.

51-9023 Mixing and Blending Machine Setters, Operators, and Tenders

Set up, operate, or tend machines to mix or blend materials such as chemicals, tobacco, liquids, color pigments, or explosive ingredients. Excludes "Food Batchmakers" (51-3092). **Examples:** Batch Maker; Clay Mixer; Tumbler Tender.

51-9030 Cutting Workers

This broad occupation includes the following two detailed occupations:
51-9031 Cutters and Trimmers, Hand
51-9032 Cutting and Slicing Machine Setters, Operators, and Tenders

51-9031 Cutters and Trimmers, Hand

Use hand tools or hand-held power tools to cut and trim a variety of manufactured items such as carpet, fabric, stone, glass, or rubber. **Examples:** Buttonhole Maker; Fur Trimmer; Thread Clipper.

51-9032 Cutting and Slicing Machine Setters, Operators, and Tenders

Set up, operate, or tend machines that cut or slice materials such as glass, stone, cork, rubber, tobacco, food, paper, or insulating material. Excludes "Woodworking Machine Setters, Operators, and Tenders" (51-7041 through 51-7042), "Cutting, Punching, and Press Machine Setters, Operators, and Tenders, Metal and Plastic" (51-4031), and "Textile Cutting Machine Setters, Operators, and Tenders" (51-6062). **Examples:** Bias Machine Operator; Shear Operator; Slate Trimmer.

51-9040 Extruding, Forming, Pressing, and Compacting Machine Setters, Operators, and Tenders

This broad occupation is the same as the detailed occupation:
51-9041 Extruding, Forming, Pressing, and Compacting Machine Setters, Operators, and Tenders

51-9041 Extruding, Forming, Pressing, and Compacting Machine Setters, Operators, and Tenders

Set up, operate, or tend machines, such as glass forming machines, plodder machines, and tuber machines, to shape and form products such as glassware, food, rubber, soap, brick, tile, clay, wax, tobacco, or cosmetics. Excludes "Paper Goods Machine Setters, Operators, and Tenders" (51-9196) and "Shoe Machine Operators and Tenders" (51-6042). **Examples:** Briquette Maker; Cigarette Machine Operator; Rubber Laminating Machine Operator.

51-9050 Furnace, Kiln, Oven, Drier, and Kettle Operators and Tenders

This broad occupation is the same as the detailed occupation:
51-9051 Furnace, Kiln, Oven, Drier, and Kettle Operators and Tenders

51-9051 Furnace, Kiln, Oven, Drier, and Kettle Operators and Tenders

Operate or tend heating equipment other than basic metal, plastic, or food processing equipment. Participate in annealing glass, drying lumber, curing rubber, removing moisture from materials, or boiling soap. **Examples:** Brick Baker; Stoker; Tunnel Kiln Operator.

51-9060 Inspectors, Testers, Sorters, Samplers, and Weighers

This broad occupation is the same as the detailed occupation:
51-9061 Inspectors, Testers, Sorters, Samplers, and Weighers

51-9061 Inspectors, Testers, Sorters, Samplers, and Weighers

Inspect, test, sort, sample, or weigh nonagricultural raw materials or processed, machined, fabricated, or assembled parts or products for defects, wear, and deviations from specifications. Use precision measuring instruments and complex test equipment. **Examples:** Bearing Inspector; Quality Checker; Testing and Regulating Technician.

51-9070 Jewelers and Precious Stone and Metal Workers

This broad occupation is the same as the detailed occupation:
51-9071 Jewelers and Precious Stone and Metal Workers

51-9071 Jewelers and Precious Stone and Metal Workers

Design, fabricate, adjust, repair, or appraise jewelry, gold, silver, other precious metals, or gems. Includes diamond polishers and gem cutters and persons who perform precision casting and modeling of molds, casting metal in molds, or setting precious and semi-precious stones for jewelry and related products. **Examples:** Diamond Expert; Gemologist; Goldsmith.

51-9080 Medical, Dental, and Ophthalmic Laboratory Technicians

This broad occupation includes the following three detailed occupations:
51-9081 Dental Laboratory Technicians
51-9082 Medical Appliance Technicians
51-9083 Ophthalmic Laboratory Technicians

51-9081 Dental Laboratory Technicians

Construct and repair full or partial dentures or dental appliances. Excludes "Dental Assistants" (31-9091). **Examples:** Ceramist; Crown and Bridge Technician; Orthodontic Technician.

51-9082 Medical Appliance Technicians

Construct, fit, maintain, or repair medical supportive devices such as braces, artificial limbs, joints, arch supports, and other surgical and medical appliances. **Examples:** Brace Maker; Orthotics Technician; Prosthetics Technician.

51-9083 Ophthalmic Laboratory Technicians

Cut, grind, and polish eyeglasses, contact lenses, or other precision optical elements. Assemble and mount lenses into frames; process other optical elements.

Includes precision lens polishers or grinders, centerer-edgers, and lens mounters. Excludes "Opticians, Dispensing" (29-2081). **Examples:** Eyeglass Maker; Lens Grinder; Spectacle Truer.

51-9110 Packaging and Filling Machine Operators and Tenders

This broad occupation is the same as the detailed occupation:
51-9111 Packaging and Filling Machine Operators and Tenders

51-9111 Packaging and Filling Machine Operators and Tenders

Operate or tend machines to prepare industrial or consumer products for storage or shipment. Includes cannery workers who pack food products. **Examples:** Bottle Caser; Wrapper Layer; Strapping Machine Operator.

51-9120 Painting Workers

This broad occupation includes the following three detailed occupations:
51-9121 Coating, Painting, and Spraying Machine Setters, Operators, and Tenders
51-9122 Painters, Transportation Equipment
51-9123 Painting, Coating, and Decorating Workers

51-9121 Coating, Painting, and Spraying Machine Setters, Operators, and Tenders

Set up, operate, or tend machines to coat or paint any of a wide variety of products including food, glassware, cloth, ceramics, metal, plastic, paper, or wood. Coat or paint these items with lacquer, silver, copper, rubber, varnish, glaze, enamel, oil, or rust-proofing materials. Excludes "Plating and Coating Machine Setters, Operators, and Tenders, Metal and Plastic" (51-4193) and "Painters, Transportation Equipment" (51-9122). **Examples:** Electrostatic Paint Operator; Silvering Applicator; Supercalender Operator.

51-9122 Painters, Transportation Equipment

Operate or tend painting machines, to paint surfaces of transportation equipment such as automobiles, buses, trucks, trains, boats, and airplanes. Includes painters in auto body repair facilities. **Examples:** Auto Painter; Rust Proofer.

51-9123 Painting, Coating, and Decorating Workers

Paint, coat, or decorate articles such as furniture, glass, plateware, pottery, jewelry, cakes, toys, books, or leather. Excludes "Artists and Related Workers" (27-1011 through 27-1019), "Designers" (27-1021 through 27-1029), "Photographic Process Workers" (51-9131), and "Etchers and Engravers" (51-9194). **Examples:** Stenciler; Candy Dipper; Mirror Silverer.

51-9130 Photographic Process Workers and Processing Machine Operators

This broad occupation includes the following two detailed occupations:
51-9131 Photographic Process Workers
51-9132 Photographic Processing Machine Operators

51-9131 Photographic Process Workers

Perform precision work involved in photographic processing, such as editing photographic negatives and prints, using photo-mechanical, chemical, or computerized methods. **Examples:** Photographic Colorist; Darkroom Technician; Photo Finisher.

51-9132 Photographic Processing Machine Operators

Operate photographic processing machines such as photographic printing machines, film developing machines, and mounting presses. **Examples:** Film Printer; Film Processor; Reproduction Machine Loader.

51-9140 Semiconductor Processors

This broad occupation is the same as the detailed occupation:
51-9141 Semiconductor Processors

51-9141 Semiconductor Processors

Perform various functions in the manufacture of electronic semiconductors. Load semiconductor material into furnace; saw formed ingots into segments; load individual segment into crystal growing chamber and monitor controls; locate crystal axis in ingot using X-ray equipment; saw ingots into wafers; clean, polish, and load wafers into series of special purpose furnaces, chemical baths, and equipment used to form circuitry and change conductive properties. **Examples:** Circuit Recorder; Crystal Grower; Wafer Machine Operator.

51-9190 Miscellaneous Production Workers

This broad occupation includes the following nine detailed occupations:
51-9191 Cementing and Gluing Machine Operators and Tenders
51-9192 Cleaning, Washing, and Metal Pickling Equipment Operators and Tenders
51-9193 Cooling and Freezing Equipment Operators and Tenders
51-9194 Etchers and Engravers
51-9195 Molders, Shapers, and Casters, Except Metal and Plastic
51-9196 Paper Goods Machine Setters, Operators, and Tenders
51-9197 Tire Builders
51-9198 Helpers—Production Workers
51-9199 Production Workers, All Other

51-9191 Cementing and Gluing Machine Operators and Tenders

Operate or tend cementing and gluing machines, to join items for further processing or to form a completed product. Join veneer sheets into plywood; glue paper; join rubber and rubberized fabric parts; join plastic, simulated leather, or other materials. Excludes "Shoe Machine Operators and Tenders" (51-6042). **Examples:** Bonding Molder; Paper Sealer; Taper Operator.

51-9192 Cleaning, Washing, and Metal Pickling Equipment Operators and Tenders

Operate or tend machines to wash or clean products such as barrels or kegs, glass items, tin plate, food, pulp, coal, plastic, or rubber, to remove impurities. **Examples:** Acid Dipper; Degreaser Operator; Pulp Bleacher.

51-9193 Cooling and Freezing Equipment Operators and Tenders

Operate or tend equipment such as cooling and freezing units, refrigerators, batch freezers, and freezing tunnels, to cool or freeze products, food, blood plasma, and chemicals. **Examples:** Chiller Tender; Ice Maker; Refrigerating Machine Operator.

51-9194 Etchers and Engravers

Engrave or etch metal, wood, rubber, or other materials for identification or decorative purposes. Includes etcher-circuit processors, pantograph engravers, and silk screen etchers. Include photoengravers with "Prepress Technicians and Workers" (51-5022). **Examples:** Embosser; Letterer; Siderographer.

51-9195 Molders, Shapers, and Casters, Except Metal and Plastic

Mold, shape, form, cast, or carve products such as food products, figurines, tile, pipes, and candles consisting of clay, glass, plaster, concrete, stone, or combinations of materials. **Examples:** Cigar Roller; Glass Blower; Marble Finisher.

51-9196 Paper Goods Machine Setters, Operators, and Tenders

Set up, operate, or tend paper goods machines that perform a variety of functions such as converting, sawing, corrugating, banding, wrapping, boxing, stitching, forming, or sealing paper or paperboard sheets into products. **Examples:** Bag Machine Operator; Box Fabricator; Carton Forming Machine Operator.

51-9197 Tire Builders

Operate machines to build tires from rubber components. **Examples:** Retreader; Tire Curer; Tube Builder.

51-9198 Helpers—Production Workers

Help production workers by performing duties of lesser skill. Supply or hold materials or tools; clean work area and equipment. Excludes apprentice workers, as they are to be reported with the appropriate production occupation (51-1011 through 51-9199). **Examples:** Welder's Assistant; Tailor's Aide; Millwright's Helper.

51-9199 Production Workers, All Other

All production workers not listed separately. **Examples:** Barrel Header; Mop Maker.

Standard Occupational Classification Manual   © *JIST Works*

53-0000 TRANSPORTATION AND MATERIAL MOVING OCCUPATIONS

53-1000 Supervisors, Transportation and Material Moving Workers

53-1010 Aircraft Cargo Handling Supervisors

This broad occupation is the same as the detailed occupation:
53-1011 Aircraft Cargo Handling Supervisors

53-1011 Aircraft Cargo Handling Supervisors

Direct ground crew in the loading, unloading, securing, and staging of aircraft cargo or baggage. Determine the quantity and orientation of cargo and compute aircraft center of gravity. Accompany aircraft as member of flight crew; monitor and handle cargo in flight; assist and brief passengers on safety and emergency procedures. Includes loadmasters. **Examples:** Loadmaster; Ramp Boss; Ground Crew Supervisor.

53-1020 First-Line Supervisors/Managers of Helpers, Laborers, and Material Movers, Hand

This broad occupation is the same as the detailed occupation:
53-1021 First-Line Supervisors/Managers of Helpers, Laborers, and Material Movers, Hand

53-1021 First-Line Supervisors/Managers of Helpers, Laborers, and Material Movers, Hand

Supervise and coordinate the activities of helpers, laborers, or material movers. **Examples:** Cargo Supervisor; Yard Supervisor; Warehouse Supervisor.

53-1030 First-Line Supervisors/Managers of Transportation and Material-Moving Machine and Vehicle Operators

This broad occupation is the same as the detailed occupation:
53-1031 First-Line Supervisors/Managers of Transportation and Material-Moving Machine and Vehicle Operators

53-1031 First-Line Supervisors/Managers of Transportation and Material-Moving Machine and Vehicle Operators

Directly supervise and coordinate activities of transportation and material-moving machine and vehicle operators and helpers. **Examples:** Dockmaster; Gas Station Manager; Roadmaster.

53-2000 Air Transportation Workers

53-2010 Aircraft Pilots and Flight Engineers

This broad occupation includes the following two detailed occupations:
53-2011 Airline Pilots, Copilots, and Flight Engineers
53-2012 Commercial Pilots

53-2011 Airline Pilots, Copilots, and Flight Engineers

Pilot and navigate the flight of multiengine aircraft in regularly scheduled service, for the transport of passengers and cargo. Hold required Federal Air Transport rating and certification in specific aircraft type used. Includes aircraft instructors with similar certification. **Examples:** Airline Captain; First Officer; Flight Navigator.

53-2012 Commercial Pilots

Pilot and navigate the flight of small fixed or rotary winged aircraft, primarily for the transport of cargo and passengers. Hold required Commercial Rating. Includes aircraft instructors with similar certification. **Examples:** Crop Duster; Helicopter Pilot; Test Pilot.

53-2020 Air Traffic Controllers and Airfield Operations Specialists

This broad occupation includes the following two detailed occupations:
53-2021 Air Traffic Controllers
53-2022 Airfield Operations Specialists

53-2021 Air Traffic Controllers

Control air traffic on and within vicinity of airport. Control movement of air traffic between altitude sectors and control centers, according to established procedures and policies. Authorize, regulate, and control commercial airline flights according to government or company regulations, to expedite and ensure flight safety. **Examples:** Control Tower Operator; Flight Control Specialist; Flight Dispatcher.

53-2022 Airfield Operations Specialists

Ensure the safe takeoff and landing of commercial and military aircraft. Coordinate activity between air-traffic control and maintenance personnel; dispatch aircraft; use airfield landing and navigational aids; implement airfield safety procedures; monitor and maintain flight records; apply knowledge of weather information. **Examples:** Airfield Manager; Flight Director; Flight Operations Coordinator.

53-3000 Motor Vehicle Operators

53-3010 Ambulance Drivers and Attendants, Except Emergency Medical Technicians

This broad occupation is the same as the detailed occupation:
53-3011 Ambulance Drivers and Attendants, Except Emergency Medical Technicians

53-3011 Ambulance Drivers and Attendants, Except Emergency Medical Technicians

Drive ambulance or assist ambulance driver in transporting sick, injured, or convalescent persons. Assist in lifting patients. **Example:** Patient Carrier.

53-3020 Bus Drivers

This broad occupation includes the following two detailed occupations:
53-3021 Bus Drivers, Transit and Intercity
53-3022 Bus Drivers, School

53-3021 Bus Drivers, Transit and Intercity

Drive bus or motor coach, including regular route operations, charters, and private carriage. Assist passengers with baggage. Collect fares or tickets. **Examples:** Motor Coach Operator; Jitney Driver.

53-3022 Bus Drivers, School

Transport students or special clients, such as the elderly or persons with disabilities. Ensure adherence to safety rules. Assist passengers in boarding or exiting.

53-3030 Driver/Sales Workers and Truck Drivers

This broad occupation includes the following three detailed occupations:
53-3031 Driver/Sales Workers
53-3032 Truck Drivers, Heavy and Tractor-Trailer
53-3033 Truck Drivers, Light or Delivery Services

53-3031 Driver/Sales Workers

Drive truck or other vehicle over established routes or within an established territory; sell goods such as food products, including restaurant take-out items; pick up and deliver items such as laundry. Take orders and collect payments. Includes newspaper delivery drivers. Excludes "Truck Drivers, Light or Delivery Services" (53-3033) and "Coin, Vending, and Amusement Machine Servicers and Repairers" (49-9091). **Examples:** Bakery Delivery Person; Milk Delivery Person; Bread Distributor.

53-0000 Transportation and Material Moving Occupations

53-3032 Truck Drivers, Heavy and Tractor-Trailer

Drive a tractor-trailer combination or a truck with a capacity of at least 26,000 GVW, to transport and deliver goods, livestock, or materials in liquid, loose, or packaged form. Unload truck as required. Use automated routing equipment. Obtain required commercial drivers' license. **Examples:** Auto Carrier Driver; Cement Truck Driver; Moving Van Driver.

53-3033 Truck Drivers, Light or Delivery Services

Drive a truck or van with a capacity of under 26,000 GVW, primarily to deliver or pick up merchandise or to deliver packages within a specified area. Use automatic routing or location software. Load and unload truck. Excludes "Couriers and Messengers" (43-5021). **Example:** Parcel Post Truck Driver.

53-3040 Taxi Drivers and Chauffeurs

This broad occupation is the same as the detailed occupation:
53-3041 Taxi Drivers and Chauffeurs

53-3041 Taxi Drivers and Chauffeurs

Drive automobiles, vans, or limousines to transport passengers. Carry cargo. Includes hearse drivers. Excludes "Ambulance Drivers and Attendants, Except Emergency Medical Technicians" (53-3011) and "Bus Drivers" (53-3021 through 53-3022). **Examples:** Cab Driver; Courtesy Van Driver; Limousine Driver.

53-3090 Miscellaneous Motor Vehicle Operators

This broad occupation is the same as the detailed occupation:
53-3099 Motor Vehicle Operators, All Other

53-3099 Motor Vehicle Operators, All Other

All motor vehicle operators not listed separately. **Examples:** Motorcycle Delivery Driver; Assembly Line Driver; Street Cleaning Equipment Operator.

53-4000 Rail Transportation Workers

53-4010 Locomotive Engineers and Operators

This broad occupation includes the following three detailed occupations:
53-4011 Locomotive Engineers
53-4012 Locomotive Firers
53-4013 Rail Yard Engineers, Dinkey Operators, and Hostlers

53-4011 Locomotive Engineers

Drive electric, diesel-electric, steam, or gas-turbine-electric locomotives to transport passengers or freight. Interpret train orders, electronic or manual signals, and railroad rules and regulations. **Examples:** Diesel Engineer; Narrow Gauge Operator; Rail Car Operator.

53-4012 Locomotive Firers

Monitor locomotive instruments and watch for dragging equipment, obstacles on rights-of-way, and train signals during run. Watch for and relay traffic signals from yard workers to yard engineer in railroad yard. **Examples:** Assistant Engineer; Railroad Firer.

53-4013 Rail Yard Engineers, Dinkey Operators, and Hostlers

Drive switching or other locomotive or dinkey engines within railroad yard, industrial plant, quarry, construction project, or similar location. **Examples:** Car Mover; Larry Car Operator; Coal Tram Driver.

53-4020 Railroad Brake, Signal, and Switch Operators

This broad occupation is the same as the detailed occupation:
53-4021 Railroad Brake, Signal, and Switch Operators

53-4021 Railroad Brake, Signal, and Switch Operators

Operate railroad track switches. Couple or uncouple rolling stock to make up or break up trains. Signal engineers by hand or flagging. Inspect couplings, air hoses, journal boxes, and hand brakes. **Examples:** Car Hopper; Coupler; Switch Tender.

53-4030 Railroad Conductors and Yardmasters

This broad occupation is the same as the detailed occupation:
53-4031 Railroad Conductors and Yardmasters

53-4031 Railroad Conductors and Yardmasters

Conductors coordinate activities of train crew on passenger or freight train. Coordinate activities of switch-engine crew within yard of railroad, industrial plant, or similar location. Coordinate activities of workers engaged in railroad traffic operations such as the makeup or breakup of trains and yard switching; review train schedules and switching orders. **Examples:** Car Dispatcher; Roadmaster; Yard Pilot.

53-4040 Subway and Streetcar Operators

This broad occupation is the same as the detailed occupation:
53-4041 Subway and Streetcar Operators

53-4041 Subway and Streetcar Operators

Operate subway or elevated suburban train with no separate locomotive. Operate electric-powered streetcar to transport passengers. Handle fares. **Examples:** Monorail Operator; Tram Operator; Trolley Operator.

53-4090 Miscellaneous Rail Transportation Workers

This broad occupation is the same as the detailed occupation:
53-4099 Rail Transportation Workers, All Other

53-4099 Rail Transportation Workers, All Other

All rail transportation workers not listed separately. **Examples:** Car Retarder Operator; Ballast Regulator Operator.

53-5000 Water Transportation Workers

53-5010 Sailors and Marine Oilers

This broad occupation is the same as the detailed occupation:
53-5011 Sailors and Marine Oilers

53-5011 Sailors and Marine Oilers

Watch for obstructions in path of vessel; measure water depth; turn wheel on bridge; use emergency equipment as directed by captain, mate, or pilot. Break out, rig, overhaul, and store cargo-handling gear, stationary rigging, and running gear. Perform a variety of maintenance tasks to preserve the painted surface of the ship and to maintain line and ship equipment. Hold government-issued certification and tankerman certification when working aboard liquid-carrying vessels. Includes able seamen and ordinary seamen. **Examples:** Able Seaman; Deckhand.

53-5020 Ship and Boat Captains and Operators

This broad occupation includes the following two detailed occupations:
53-5021 Captains, Mates, and Pilots of Water Vessels
53-5022 Motorboat Operators

53-5021 Captains, Mates, and Pilots of Water Vessels

Command or supervise operations of ships and water vessels such as tugboats and ferryboats that travel into and out of harbors, estuaries, straits, and sounds and on rivers, lakes, bays, and oceans. Hold required license issued by U.S. Coast Guard. Excludes "Motorboat Operators" (53-5022). **Examples:** Barge Captain; Deck Officer; Tugboat Operator.

53-5022 Motorboat Operators

Operate small motor-driven boats to carry passengers and freight between ships, or ship to shore. Patrol harbors and beach areas. Assist in navigational activities. **Examples:** Launch Operator; Speedboat Operator.

53-5030 Ship Engineers

This broad occupation is the same as the detailed occupation:
53-5031 Ship Engineers

53-5031 Ship Engineers

Supervise and coordinate activities of crew engaged in operating and maintaining engines, boilers, deck machinery, and electrical, sanitary, and refrigeration equipment aboard ship. **Examples:** Deck Engineer; Marine Engine Mechanic.

53-6000 Other Transportation Workers

53-6010 Bridge and Lock Tenders

This broad occupation is the same as the detailed occupation:
53-6011 Bridge and Lock Tenders

53-6011 Bridge and Lock Tenders

Operate and tend bridges, canal locks, and lighthouses to permit marine passage on inland waterways, near shores, and at danger points in waterway passages. Supervise such operations. Includes drawbridge operators, lock tenders and operators, and slip bridge operators. **Examples:** Drawbridge Operator; Lighthouse Keeper; Lock Master.

53-6020 Parking Lot Attendants

This broad occupation is the same as the detailed occupation:
53-6021 Parking Lot Attendants

53-6021 Parking Lot Attendants

Park automobiles or issue tickets for customers in a parking lot or garage. Collect fee. **Examples:** Car Hop; Car Runner; Valet Parker.

53-6030 Service Station Attendants

This broad occupation is the same as the detailed occupation:
53-6031 Service Station Attendants

53-6031 Service Station Attendants

Service automobiles, buses, trucks, boats, and other automotive or marine vehicles with fuel, lubricants, and accessories. Collect payment for services and supplies. Lubricate vehicle; change motor oil; install antifreeze; replace lights or other accessories such as windshield wiper blades or fan belts. Repair or replace tires. **Examples:** Filling Station Attendant; Gas and Oil Servicer; Pump Attendant.

53-6040 Traffic Technicians

This broad occupation is the same as the detailed occupation:
53-6041 Traffic Technicians

53-6041 Traffic Technicians

Conduct field studies to determine traffic volume, speed, effectiveness of signals, adequacy of lighting, and other factors influencing traffic conditions, under direction of traffic engineer. **Example:** Traffic Analyst.

53-6050 Transportation Inspectors

This broad occupation is the same as the detailed occupation:
53-6051 Transportation Inspectors

53-6051 Transportation Inspectors

Inspect equipment or goods in connection with the safe transport of cargo or people. Includes rail transport inspectors such as freight inspectors, car inspectors, rail inspectors, and other nonprecision inspectors of other types of transportation vehicles. **Examples:** Airplane Inspector; Motor Vehicle Examiner; Safety Agent.

53-6090 Miscellaneous Transportation Workers

This broad occupation is the same as the detailed occupation:
53-6099 Transportation Workers, All Other

53-6099 Transportation Workers, All Other

All transportation workers not listed separately. **Example:** Rickshaw Driver.

53-7000 Material Moving Workers

53-7010 Conveyor Operators and Tenders

This broad occupation is the same as the detailed occupation:
53-7011 Conveyor Operators and Tenders

53-7011 Conveyor Operators and Tenders

Control or tend conveyors or conveyor systems that move materials or products to and from stockpiles, processing stations, departments, or vehicles. Control speed and routing of materials or products. **Examples:** Belt Tender; Grain Elevator Operator.

53-7020 Crane and Tower Operators

This broad occupation is the same as the detailed occupation:
53-7021 Crane and Tower Operators

53-7021 Crane and Tower Operators

Operate mechanical boom and cable or tower and cable equipment to lift and move materials, machines, or products in many directions. Excludes "Excavating and Loading Machine and Dragline Operators" (53-7032). **Examples:** Boomswing Operator; Cherry Picker Operator; Scrap Drop Operator.

53-7030 Dredge, Excavating, and Loading Machine Operators

This broad occupation includes the following three detailed occupations:
53-7031 Dredge Operators
53-7032 Excavating and Loading Machine and Dragline Operators
53-7033 Loading Machine Operators, Underground Mining

53-7031 Dredge Operators

Operate dredge, to remove sand, gravel, or other materials from lakes, rivers, or streams and to excavate and maintain navigable channels in waterways. **Example:** Dredger.

53-7032 Excavating and Loading Machine and Dragline Operators

Operate or tend machinery equipped with scoops, shovels, or buckets, to excavate and load loose materials. Excludes "Dredge Operators" (53-7031). **Examples:** Back Hoe Operator; Payloader Operator; Shovel Operator.

53-7033 Loading Machine Operators, Underground Mining

Operate underground loading machine to load coal, ore, or rock into shuttle or mine car or onto conveyors. Operate loading equipment such as power shovels, hoisting engines equipped with cable-drawn scraper or scoop, or machines equipped with gathering arms and conveyor. **Example:** Coke Loader.

53-7040 Hoist and Winch Operators

This broad occupation is the same as the detailed occupation:
53-7041 Hoist and Winch Operators

53-7041 Hoist and Winch Operators

Operate or tend hoists or winches, to lift and pull loads using power-operated cable equipment. Excludes "Crane and Tower Operators" (53-7021). **Examples:** Derrick Operator; Hydraulic Boom Operator; Well Puller.

53-7050 Industrial Truck and Tractor Operators

This broad occupation is the same as the detailed occupation:
53-7051 Industrial Truck and Tractor Operators

53-7051 Industrial Truck and Tractor Operators

Operate industrial trucks or tractors equipped to move materials around a warehouse, storage yard, factory, construction site, or similar location. Excludes "Logging Equipment Operators" (45-4022). **Examples:** Fork Lift Driver; Skidder Operator; Stacker Operator.

53-7060 Laborers and Material Movers, Hand

This broad occupation includes the following four detailed occupations:
53-7061 Cleaners of Vehicles and Equipment
53-7062 Laborers and Freight, Stock, and Material Movers, Hand
53-7063 Machine Feeders and Offbearers
53-7064 Packers and Packagers, Hand

53-7061 Cleaners of Vehicles and Equipment

Wash or otherwise clean vehicles, machinery, and other equipment. Use materials such as water, cleaning agents, brushes, cloths, and hoses. Excludes "Janitors and Cleaners, Except Maids and Housekeeping Cleaners" (37-2011). **Examples:** Barrel Washer; Auto Detailer; Machine Cleaner.

53-7062 Laborers and Freight, Stock, and Material Movers, Hand

Manually move freight, stock, or other materials; perform other unskilled general labor. Includes all unskilled manual laborers not elsewhere classified. Excludes "Material Moving Workers" (53-7011 through 53-7199) who use power equipment. Excludes "Construction Laborers" (47-2061) and "Construction Trades Helpers" (47-3011 through 47-3019). **Examples:** Cargo Handler; Stevedore; Truck Loader and Unloader.

53-7063 Machine Feeders and Offbearers

Feed materials into, or remove materials from, machines or equipment that is automatic or tended by other workers. **Examples:** Hopper Filler; Board Catcher; Doffer.

53-7064 Packers and Packagers, Hand

Pack or package by hand a wide variety of products and materials. **Examples:** Bagger; Boxer; Gift Wrapper.

53-7070 Pumping Station Operators

This broad occupation includes the following three detailed occupations:
53-7071 Gas Compressor and Gas Pumping Station Operators
53-7072 Pump Operators, Except Wellhead Pumpers
53-7073 Wellhead Pumpers

53-7071 Gas Compressor and Gas Pumping Station Operators

Operate steam, gas, electric motor, or internal combustion engine driven compressors. Transmit, compress, or recover gases such as butane, nitrogen, hydrogen, and natural gas. **Examples:** Gas Booster Engineer; Gas Transfer Operator.

53-7072 Pump Operators, Except Wellhead Pumpers

Tend, control, or operate power-driven, stationary, or portable pumps and manifold systems, to transfer gases, oil, other liquids, slurries, or powdered materials to and from various vessels and processes. **Examples:** Brewery Pumper; Main-Line Station Engineer; Oil Pumper.

53-7073 Wellhead Pumpers

Operate power pumps and auxiliary equipment to produce flow of oil or gas from wells in oil field. **Examples:** Oil Well Service Operator.

53-7080 Refuse and Recyclable Material Collectors

This broad occupation is the same as the detailed occupation:
53-7081 Refuse and Recyclable Material Collectors

53-7081 Refuse and Recyclable Material Collectors

Collect and dump refuse or recyclable materials from containers into truck. Drive truck. **Examples:** Garbage Collector; Scrap Metal Collector; Trash Collector.

53-7110 Shuttle Car Operators

This broad occupation is the same as the detailed occupation:
53-7111 Shuttle Car Operators

53-7111 Shuttle Car Operators

Operate diesel or electric-powered shuttle car in underground mine, to transport materials from working face to mine cars or conveyor. **Examples:** Car Dumper; Cart Driver; Shuttle Buggy Operator.

53-0000
Transportation and Material Moving Occupations

53-7120 Tank Car, Truck, and Ship Loaders

This broad occupation is the same as the detailed occupation:
53-7121 Tank Car, Truck, and Ship Loaders

53-7121 Tank Car, Truck, and Ship Loaders

Load and unload chemicals and bulk solids such as coal, sand, and grain into or from tank cars, trucks, or ships, using material-moving equipment. Perform a variety of other tasks relating to shipment of products. Gauge or sample shipping tanks; test them for leaks. **Examples:** Coal Dumping Equipment Operator; Loader Operator; Spout Tender.

53-7190 Miscellaneous Material Moving Workers

This broad occupation is the same as the detailed occupation:
53-7199 Material Moving Workers, All Other

53-7199 Material Moving Workers, All Other

All material moving workers not listed separately. **Examples:** Elevator Operator; Hand Trucker; Longshore Equipment Operator.

55-0000 MILITARY SPECIFIC OCCUPATIONS

55-1000 Military Officer Special and Tactical Operations Leaders/Managers

55-1010 Military Officer Special and Tactical Operations Leaders/Managers

This broad occupation includes the following eight detailed occupations:
55-1011 Air Crew Officers
55-1012 Aircraft Launch and Recovery Officers
55-1013 Armored Assault Vehicle Officers
55-1014 Artillery and Missile Officers
55-1015 Command and Control Center Officers
55-1016 Infantry Officers
55-1017 Special Forces Officers
55-1019 Military Officer Special and Tactical Operations Leaders/Managers, All Other

55-1011 Air Crew Officers

Perform and direct in-flight duties to ensure the successful completion of combat, reconnaissance, transport, and search and rescue missions. Operate aircraft communications and radar equipment, such as establishing satellite linkages and jamming enemy communications capabilities. Operate aircraft weapons and defensive systems. Conduct preflight, in-flight, and postflight inspections of onboard equipment. Directing cargo and personnel drops. **Examples:** Airborne Antisubmarine Warfare Tactical Coordinator; Airborne Warning and Control Systems Officer.

55-1012 Aircraft Launch and Recovery Officers

Plan and direct the operation and maintenance of catapults, arresting gear, and associated mechanical, hydraulic, and control systems involved primarily in aircraft carrier takeoff and landing operations. Supervise readiness and safety of arresting gear, launching equipment, barricades, and visual landing aid systems. Plan and coordinate the design, development, and testing of launch and recovery systems. Prepare specifications for catapult and arresting gear installations. Evaluate design proposals. Determine handling equipment needed for new aircraft. Prepare technical data and instructions for operation of landing aids. Train personnel in carrier takeoff and landing procedures. **Examples:** Landing Signal Officer; Catapult and Arresting Gear Officer.

55-0000
Military
Specific
Occupations

55-1013 Armored Assault Vehicle Officers

Direct the operation of tanks, light armor, and amphibious assault vehicle units, during combat situations on land or in aquatic environments. Direct crew members in the operation of targeting and firing systems. Coordinate the operation of advanced onboard communications and navigation equipment. Direct the transport of personnel and equipment during combat. Formulate and implement battle plans, including the tactical employment of armored vehicle units. Coordinate with infantry, artillery, and air support units. **Examples:** Armor Platoon Leader; Cavalry Officer; Assault Amphibious Vehicle Officer.

55-1014 Artillery and Missile Officers

Manage personnel and weapons operations to destroy enemy positions, aircraft, and vessels. Plan, target, and coordinate the tactical deployment of field artillery and air defense artillery missile systems units. Direct the establishment and operation of fire-control communications systems. Target and launch intercontinental ballistic missiles. Direct the storage and handling of nuclear munitions and components. Oversee security of weapons storage and launch facilities. Manage maintenance of weapons systems. **Examples:** Field Artillery Battery Commander; Naval Surface Fire Support Planner; Air Defense Control Officer.

55-1015 Command and Control Center Officers

Manage the operation of communications, detection, and weapons systems essential for controlling air, ground, and naval operations. Manage critical communication links between air, naval, and ground forces. Formulate and implement emergency plans for natural and wartime disasters. Coordinate emergency response teams and agencies. Evaluate command center information and the need for high-level military and government reporting. Manage the operation of surveillance and detection systems. Provide technical information and advice on capabilities and operational readiness. Direct operation of weapons targeting, firing, and launch computer systems. **Examples:** Combat Information Center Officer; Air Support Control Officer; Combat Control Officer.

55-1016 Infantry Officers

Direct, train, and lead infantry units in ground combat operations. Direct deployment of infantry weapons, vehicles, and equipment. Direct location, construction, and camouflage of infantry positions and equipment. Manage field communications operations. Coordinate with armor, artillery, and air support units. Perform strategic and tactical planning, including battle plan development. Lead basic reconnaissance operations. **Examples:** Infantry Unit Commander; Infantry Weapons Officer.

55-1017 Special Forces Officers

Lead elite teams that implement unconventional operations by air, land, or sea, during combat or peacetime, including offensive raids, demolitions, reconnaissance, search and rescue, and counterterrorism. Receive specialized training in swimming, diving, parachuting, survival, emergency medicine, and foreign languages. Direct advanced reconnaissance operations and evaluate intelligence information. Recruit, train, and equip friendly forces. Lead raids and invasions on enemy territories. Train personnel to implement individual missions and contingency plans. Perform strategic and tactical planning for politically sensitive missions. Operate sophisticated communications equipment. **Examples:** Special Forces Commander; Scuba Marine Officer; Sea-Air-Land Officer (SEAL).

55-1019 Military Officer Special and Tactical Operations Leaders/Managers, All Other

All military officer special and tactical operations leaders/managers not listed separately. **Examples:** Special Assignment Officer; Joint Specialty Officer; Liaison Officer.

55-2000 First-Line Enlisted Military Supervisor/Managers

55-2010 First-Line Enlisted Military Supervisors/Managers

This broad occupation includes the following three detailed occupations:
55-2011 First-Line Supervisors/Managers of Air Crew Members
55-2012 First-Line Supervisors/Managers of Weapons Specialists/Crew Members
55-2013 First-Line Supervisors/Managers of All Other Tactical Operations Specialists

55-2011 First-Line Supervisors/Managers of Air Crew Members

Supervise and coordinate the activities of air crew members. Perform the same activities as the workers they supervise. **Examples:** Airborne Missions Systems Superintendent; In-Flight Refueling Manager.

55-2012 First-Line Supervisors/Managers of Weapons Specialists/Crew Members

Supervise and coordinate the activities of weapons specialists/crew members. Perform the same activities as the workers they supervise. **Examples:** Armor Senior Sergeant; Infantry Unit Leader; Senior Chief Torpedoperson's Mate.

55-2013 First-Line Supervisors/Managers of All Other Tactical Operations Specialists

Supervise and coordinate the activities of all other tactical operations specialists not classified separately above. Perform the same activities as the workers they supervise. **Examples:** Tactical Air Command and Control Manager; Operations Sergeant; Platoon Sergeant.

55-3000 Military Enlisted Tactical Operations and Air/Weapons Specialists and Crew Members

55-3010 Military Enlisted Tactical Operations and Air/Weapons Specialists and Crew Members

This broad occupation includes the following nine detailed occupations:
55-3011 Air Crew Members
55-3012 Aircraft Launch and Recovery Specialists
55-3013 Armored Assault Vehicle Crew Members
55-3014 Artillery and Missile Crew Members
55-3015 Command and Control Center Specialists
55-3016 Infantry
55-3017 Radar and Sonar Technicians
55-3018 Special Forces
55-3019 Military Enlisted Tactical Operations and Air/Weapons Specialists and Crew Members, All Other

55-3011 Air Crew Members

Perform in-flight duties to ensure the successful completion of combat, reconnaissance, transport, and search and rescue missions. Operate aircraft communications and detection equipment, including establishing satellite linkages and jamming enemy communications capabilities. Conduct preflight, in-flight, and postflight inspections of onboard equipment. Operate and maintain aircraft weapons and defensive systems and in-flight refueling systems. Execute aircraft safety and emergency procedures. Compute and verify passenger, cargo, fuel, and emergency and special equipment weight and balance data. Conduct cargo and personnel drops. **Examples:** Aerial Ice Observer; Helicopter Utility Aircrewperson; Airborne Radar Systems Journeyperson.

55-3012 Aircraft Launch and Recovery Specialists

Operate and maintain catapults, arresting gear, and associated mechanical, hydraulic, and control systems involved primarily in aircraft carrier takeoff and landing operations. Install and maintain visual landing aids. Test and maintain launch and recovery equipment, using electric and mechanical test equipment and hand tools. Activate airfield arresting systems such as crash barriers and cables, during emergency landing situations. Direct aircraft launch and recovery operations using hand or light signals. Maintain logs of airplane launches, recoveries, and equipment maintenance. **Examples:** Aircraft Recovery Specialist; Catapult Operator; Arresting Gear Operator.

55-3013 Armored Assault Vehicle Crew Members

Operate tanks, light armor, and amphibious assault vehicles, during combat situations on land or in aquatic environments. Drive armored vehicles which require specialized training. Operate and maintain targeting and firing systems. Operate and maintain advanced onboard communications and navigation equipment. Transport personnel and equipment in a combat environment. Operate and maintain auxiliary weapons, including machine guns and grenade launchers. **Examples:** Tank Crewperson; Assault Amphibious Vehicle Crewperson; Infantry Fighting Vehicle Crewperson.

55-3014 Artillery and Missile Crew Members

Target, fire, and maintain weapons used to destroy enemy positions, aircraft, and vessels. Use predominantly guns, cannons, and howitzers in ground combat operations, as field artillery crew members. Use predominantly missiles and rockets, as air defense artillery crew members. Use predominantly torpedoes and missiles launched from a ship or submarine, as naval artillery crew members. Test, inspect, and store ammunition, missiles, and torpedoes. Conduct preventive and routine maintenance on weapons and related equipment. Establish and maintain radio and wire communications. Operate weapons targeting, firing, and launch computer systems. **Examples:** Field Artillery Cannoneer; Torpedoperson's Mate.

55-3015 Command and Control Center Specialists

Operate and monitor communications, detection, and weapons systems essential for controlling air, ground, and naval operations. Maintain and relay critical communications between air, naval, and ground forces. Implement emergency plans for natural and wartime disasters. Relay command center information to high-level military and government decision makers. Monitor surveillance and detection systems such as air defense. Interpret and evaluate tactical situations; make recommendations to superiors. Operate weapons targeting, firing, and launch computer systems. **Examples:** Tactical Air Defense Controller; Early Warning System Operator; Command and Control Journeyperson.

55-3016 Infantry

Operate weapons and equipment in ground combat operations. Operate and maintain weapons such as rifles, machine guns, mortars, and hand grenades.

Locate, construct, and camouflage infantry positions and equipment. Evaluate terrain; record topographical information. Operate and maintain field communications equipment. Assess need for and direct supporting fire. Place explosives and perform minesweeping activities on land. Participate in basic reconnaissance operations. **Examples:** Rifleperson; Machinegunner; Heavy Antiarmor Weapons Crewmember.

55-3017 Radar and Sonar Technicians

Operate equipment using radio or sound wave technology to identify, track, and analyze objects or natural phenomena of military interest. Perform minor maintenance. Includes airborne, shipboard, and terrestrial positions. **Examples:** Field Artillery Firefinder Radar Operator; Sonar Technician; Minehunting Sonar Set Operator.

55-3018 Special Forces

Implement unconventional operations by air, land, or sea, during combat or peacetime as members of elite teams, including offensive raids, demolitions, reconnaissance, search and rescue, and counterterrorism. Receive specialized training in swimming, diving, parachuting, survival, emergency medicine, and foreign languages. Conduct advanced reconnaissance operations; collect intelligence information. Recruit, train, and equip friendly forces. Conduct raids and invasions on enemy territories. Lay and detonate explosives for demolition targets. Locate, identify, defuse, and dispose of ordnance. Operate and maintain sophisticated communications equipment. **Examples:** Combatant Swimmer; Pararescue Journeyman; Special Forces Weapons Sergeant.

55-3019 Military Enlisted Tactical Operations and Air/Weapons Specialists and Crew Members, All Other

All military enlisted tactical operations and air/weapons specialists and crew members not listed separately. **Examples:** Sensor Operator; Weapons Instructor; Operations and Intelligence Specialist.

APPENDIX A

Frequently Asked Questions About the SOC

These questions and answers are derived from the SOC Web site at http://stats.bls. gov/soc/socguide.htm.

1. How do I classify workers?

The classification guidelines in this book's introduction give the rules that are followed to classify workers based on occupational definitions and work activity.

2. Where can I get information on the occupations in the SOC?

Depending on the type of information you are seeking, you may obtain information from several agencies.

The Occupational Employment Statistics (OES) program provides occupational employment and wage estimates by industry and across industries. For state and area data, contact the state employment security agency for the state or states needed. For national data and selected state data, see the OES Web site at http://stats.bls.gov/ oeshome.htm or call the information request line at (202) 691-6569.

The Census Bureau publishes data on detailed occupations from the decennial censuses. Census 2000 is using the SOC to classify occupations; initial publication will be in 2002. Standard and customized tabulations will be available through its American Fact Finder at http://www.census.gov. Only summary data will be published on paper.

Biennially, the Bureau of Labor Statistics' Office of Employment Projections (OEP) publishes the *Occupational Outlook Handbook, Career Guide to Industries,* and *Occupational Projections and Training Data.* In addition, OEP publishes the *Occupational Outlook Quarterly.* For more information about these publications, visit the OEP Web site at http://stats.bls.gov/emphome.htm or contact the Chief, Division of Occupational Outlook, Bureau of Labor Statistics, 2 Massachusetts Ave. NW., Room 2135, Washington, DC 20212.

The Department of Defense publishes data that cross-references military occupational codes of the Army, Navy, Air Force, Marine Corps, and Coast Guard with civilian equivalent occupations. The next update of this data will include linkages of military occupations to the SOC. Additional information on available data products can be obtained by writing to Director, Defense Manpower Data Center, 1600 Wilson Boulevard, Suite 400, Arlington, VA 22209-2593.

The National Science Foundation Division of Science and Resource Studies Web site contains SESTAT, a comprehensive and integrated system of information about the employment, educational, and demographic characteristics of scientists and engineers in the United States. The site is intended for both policy analysis and general research, with features for both the casual and more intensive data user. More information may be obtained from the National Science Foundation's site at http://www.nsf.gov/sbe/srs/stats.htm.

Career and job vacancy information may be obtained from the Department of Labor's Employment and Training Administration's One-Stop Web page at http://www.ttrc.doleta.gov/onestop.

3. Why does the SOC have different levels of detail?

There are four hierarchical levels in the SOC to enable users to choose a level of detail corresponding to their interest and ability to collect data on different occupations. Users using different levels of detail will still be able to compare data at the defined levels.

4. Why can't I find my job title in the SOC?

The SOC lists occupations that may have many different job titles. The associated titles database will be available to help users classify workers into SOC occupations. If your title is not listed, you may contact an occupation specialist at the Census Bureau (301) 457-3239 to suggest its inclusion.

5. Why are supervisors of most professional occupations not listed? Where should they be classified?

Supervisors of professional occupations are classified with the occupations they supervise because they often need the same type of training, education, and experience as the workers they supervise.

6. The SOC isn't detailed enough for my needs. How do I modify it?

Users who would like to collect or tabulate data in more detail should add a decimal point and additional digits after the six-digit SOC code. For more information, see Appendix B.

7. Who uses the SOC?

All government agencies that collect and publish occupational data use the SOC. These agencies include the following:

Department of Agriculture
Department of Commerce Bureau of the
  Census
Department of Defense
Department of Education
Department of Health and Human Services
Department of Labor:
  Bureau of Labor Statistics:
  Occupational Employment Statistics
  Occupational Health and Safety
    Statistics
  Office of Employment Projections
  Employment and Training
    Administration
Department of Transportation
Department of Veterans Affairs
Employment Standards Administration
Equal Employment Opportunity Commission
Food and Drug Administration
National Occupational Information
  Coordinating Committee
National Science Foundation
Office of Personnel Management

8. When is the next revision of the SOC scheduled?

To ensure that the successful efforts of the Standard Occupational Classification Revision Policy Committee (SOCRPC) continue and that the SOC remains appropriate to the world of work, the Office of Management and Budget (OMB) plans to establish a new standing committee, the Standard Occupational Classification Policy Committee (SOCPC). The SOCPC will consult periodically to ensure that the implementation of the SOC is comparable across federal agencies. This consultation will include regularly scheduled interagency communication to ensure a smooth transition to the SOC. The SOCPC will also perform SOC maintenance functions, such as recommending changes in the SOC occupational definitions and placement of new occupations. It is anticipated that the next major review and revision of the SOC will begin in 2005 in preparation for use in the 2010 decennial census.

9. Can the SOC be used for nonstatistical purposes?

The SOC was designed solely for statistical purposes. Although it is likely that the SOC will also be used for various nonstatistical purposes (such as for administrative, regulatory, or taxation functions), the requirements of government agencies that choose to use the SOC for nonstatistical purposes have played no role in its development, nor will OMB modify the classification to meet the requirements of any nonstatistical program.

Consequently, as was the case with the 1980 SOC (Statistical Policy Directive No. 10, Standard Occupational Classification), the SOC is not to be used in any administrative, regulatory, or tax program unless the head of the agency administering that program has first determined that the use of such occupational definitions is appropriate to the implementation of the program's objectives.

10. How will the SOC be implemented?

The Standard Occupational Classification Revision Policy Committee (SOCRPC) has prepared the *Standard Occupational Classification Manual.* Agencies with occupational classification systems are developing crosswalks from their existing systems to the SOC. The committee will consult periodically to ensure that the implementation of the SOC is comparable across federal agencies. This consultation will include regularly scheduled interagency communication to ensure that there is a smooth federal transition to the SOC.

All federal government agencies that collect occupational data are expected to adopt the SOC over the next few years.

The Bureau of Labor Statistics annual Occupational Employment Statistics survey first reflected the SOC in 1999. National, state, and metropolitan statistical area data are expected to be available in 2001. The Office of Employment Projections will reflect the SOC in the industry-occupation matrix covering the 2000–10 period, which is expected to be released in November 2001. Occupational descriptions and data completely based on the SOC will be incorporated in the *Occupational Outlook Handbook* for the first time in the 2004–05 edition, which is expected to be published in early 2004.

Data collected by the 2000 Census of Population will be coded to the SOC and published in 2002. Data from the Current

Population Survey will be based on the new classification for the first time in 2003.

Here is a more detailed schedule showing SOC implementation for Bureau of Labor Statistics programs.

SOC Implementation Schedule

BLS Program	Data in SOC Form	Data in SOC Form Published
Occupational Employment Statistics	1999	December 2000
Office of Employment Projections	2000–2010	November 2001
Current Population Survey	January 2003	February 2003
Employer Costs for Employee Compensation	March 2004	June 2004
Locality Wage Levels	Spring 2004	Spring 2004
National and Census Division Publications	2004	Spring 2005
Integrated Benefit Provision Products	2004	Spring 2005
Employment Cost Index	March 2004	April 2004
Occupational Safety and Health— Census of Fatal Occupational Injuries	2003	August 2004
Occupational Safety and Health— Survey of Occupational Injuries and Illnesses	2003	April 2005

APPENDIX B

Revising the SOC

This appendix is derived from U.S. Department of Labor's Report 929, "Revising the Standard Occupational Classification System."

Concerns about the quality of the U.S. workforce, skills training issues, and changes in occupational structures due to new technology, competitive economic pressures, and shifts to forms of "high performance" work organizations, have focused attention on the quality of occupational information and statistics. Current occupational data and their underlying classification structures were criticized as being fragmented, incompatible, outdated, and lacking information on skills. Many users and producers of occupational data believed that it was time to revise the U.S. Standard Occupational Classification (SOC) system to a unified classification structure.

In 1994, the Office of Management and Budget established a Standard Occupational Classification Revision Policy Committee (SOC Committee) to develop a unified classification structure that would meet the needs of the 21st century. The committee was chaired by the Bureau of Labor Statistics and the Bureau of the Census, with representatives from the Bureau of Labor Statistics, the Bureau of the Census, the Employment and Training Administration (Department of Labor), the Office of Personnel Management, the Defense Manpower Data Center, and ex officio the National Science Foundation, the National Occupational Information Coordinating Committee, and the Office of Management and Budget.

This report is based on an article that appeared in the May 1999 *Monthly Labor Review* written by Chester Levine, manager of occupational outlook studies in the Division of Occupational Outlook, Bureau of Labor Statistics, and chair of the Construction, Extraction, Agricultural, and Transportation Occupations Work Group of the SOC Committee; Laurie Salmon, an economist in the Division of Occupational and Administrative Statistics, Bureau of Labor Statistics, and a member of the SOC Committee Secretariat; and Daniel H. Weinberg, chief of the Division of Housing and Household Economic Statistics, Bureau of the Census, and chair of the SOC Committee.

Although occupational data has been collected in the United States since the 1850 Census of Population, the modern SOC system was not introduced until 1977. The SOC is intended to include all occupations for which work is performed for pay or profit. As with any new taxonomy, there were flaws and omissions in the original SOC, and the system was revised in 1980, in time to be used for tabulations from the 1980 decennial census.

Despite plans for frequent review, it was not until the mid-1990s that the validity and usefulness of the 1980 SOC for current needs was examined. To determine how accurately the 1980 SOC reflected the world of work 15 years later, the Office of Management and Budget (OMB) chartered the SOC Committee. This article provides a description of the SOC revision process. For background, it begins with a brief summary of the Standard Industrial Classification (SIC) revision process and the work of the Economic Classification Policy Committee (ECP Committee), much of which was emulated by the SOC Committee. The article then details why the SOC was revised and describes its key characteristics.

The SIC Revision Process

The ECP Committee was established by OMB in 1992 to reexamine the SIC system. At the time, the SIC had been in use for more than 50 years. So pervasive was the system throughout U.S. industry that virtually every business establishment in the nation knew its SIC code. Yet, many SIC-based statistics were out of step with the changes that have occurred in the U.S. economy in recent decades.

The SIC system had been introduced in the 1930s to help classify the growing number of new manufacturing industries that had developed since the early 1900s. By 1992, however, it was clear that a new classification system was needed to accommodate newly developed industries in such areas as information services, healthcare services, and high-tech manufacturing. Further, the initiation of the North American Free Trade Agreement in 1994 increased the need for comparable statistics from the United States, Canada, and

Mexico. The resultant system, the North American Industry Classification System (NAICS), is a complete restructuring of the SIC, organized to conform to the principle of grouping establishments by their production processes alone—that is, NAICS is a supply-based or production-oriented classification system. By contrast, the former system used a combination of supply and demand characteristics to classify industries. Another advantage of NAICS is that each participating country can individualize the new system to meet its own needs, as long as data can be aggregated to standard NAICS industries.[1]

The SOC Committee identified four key steps in the ECP Committee process that the members thought would be useful to emulate in the SOC revision process: (1) identification of issues (including commissioned issue papers), (2) designation of an organizing principle, (3) work by subgroups, and (4) adjudication of differences of opinion.

Occupational Classification History

Occupational classification is not a new topic of government interest. The published tabulations from the 1850 Census of Population constitute the first de facto classification. There were 322 occupations listed, including such interesting jobs as *daguerrotypists* (photographers) and *salaeratus* (baking soda) *makers*. In early classification systems, too much emphasis was placed on the industry in which one worked. While it is true that the work setting can influence the job, it is the hallmark of more recent classification systems that characteristics of the work performed comes first.

More frequent data collection began in 1942 with the monthly labor force survey. The U.S. Employment Service needed occupational statistics for its work and developed a Convertibility List of Occupations with

Conversion Tables to serve as a bridge between its statistics and information from the 1940 Census of Population. Continued revisions to the census classification scheme and publication of the third edition of the Department of Labor's *Dictionary of Occupational Titles* in 1965 encouraged the government to begin a thorough reexamination of occupational taxonomy.

Without a standard, initially comparable systems will tend to drift apart, reducing the ability of an analyst to compare similar data collected for different purposes. Occupational data from household surveys, for example, which provide demographic information, could not easily be compared with occupational data from industry-supplied or establishment-based surveys. Similarly, detailed job descriptions from the *Dictionary of Occupational Titles* could not easily be linked to survey data. The need to devise such a standard in order to link these different systems resulted in the 1977 SOC (revised and reissued in 1980).

Despite agreements to maintain and update the original SOC system, for various reasons—the need to maintain each program's historical continuity, a lack of federal funding, and the absence of a clear directive to enforce comparability—the original system was not revised after 1980. Consequently, many agencies set up data collection systems with occupational classification schemes that differed from the SOC. Observing this problem, BLS hosted an International Occupational Classification Conference to establish a context for a new SOC revision process.[2] Many new ideas and approaches were presented that influenced the SOC Committee. Similarly, the Employment and Training Administration's Advisory Panel for the *Dictionary of Occupational Titles* had just completed a

review of the dictionary and had recommended substantial changes.[3]

Persuaded that a reconciliation was in order, OMB subsequently invited all federal agencies with an occupation classification system to join together to revise the SOC. The SOC Committee included representatives from BLS, the Bureau of the Census, the Employment and Training Administration, the Defense Manpower Data Center, and the Office of Personnel Management. In addition, ex-officio members included the National Science Foundation, the National Occupational Information Coordinating Committee, and OMB. Other federal agencies, such as the Department of Education, the Department of Health and Human Services, and the Equal Employment Opportunity Commission, participated in several meetings of the SOC Committee as well, or as part of the Federal Consultation Group.

The SOC Revision Process

OMB chartered the SOC Committee in October 1994. Shortly afterward, the SOC Committee published a notice in the *Federal Register* calling for comments specifically on the following: (1) the uses of occupational data, (2) the purpose and scope of occupational classification, (3) the principles underlying the 1980 SOC, (4) conceptual options for the new SOC, and (5) the SOC revision process.[4]

The SOC Committee's main concern was identifying an organizing principle for the revised SOC, which required careful consideration of the conceptual options. Four options were identified in the notice for public comment. The first, and the basic concept behind the 1980 SOC, was the type of work performed. The second option was to model the new SOC after the International

Standard Classification of Occupations in recognition of the increasing international-ization of employment. The third option was to devise a "skills-based system," following the recommendations of the Advisory Panel for the *Dictionary of Occupational Titles*. The fourth option identified, an "economic-based system," echoed the choice of the ECP Committee in their revision of the SIC sys-tem.

After the public comment period, the SOC Committee established the following criteria to guide the revision process:

- The new classification system covers all occupa-tions in which work is performed for pay or profit, including work performed in family-operated enterprises by family members who are not direct-ly compensated. It excludes occupations unique to volunteers.

- The new system reflects the current occupational structure of the United States and has sufficient flexibility to assimilate new occupations.

- Occupations are classified on the basis of work per-formed, and required skills, education, training, or credentials.

- Each occupation is assigned to only one group at the lowest level of the classification.

- Supervisors of professional and technical workers usually have a background similar to the workers they supervise and are therefore classified with the workers they supervise. Likewise, team leaders, lead workers, and supervisors of production work-ers who spend at least 20 percent of their time per-forming work similar to the workers they supervise, are classified with the workers they supervise.

- Supervisors of production workers who spend less than 20 percent of their time performing the same work as the workers they supervise are classified separately.

- First-line supervisors/managers are generally found in smaller establishments where they per-form both supervisory and management functions, such as accounting, marketing, and personnel work.

- Apprentices and trainees should be classified with the occupations for which they are being trained, while helpers and aides should be classified sepa-rately.

- Some data-reporting agencies may collect and report data at a more aggregated level, such as broad occupation, minor group, or major group, when enough detail is not available to classify work-ers into a detailed occupation.

- If an occupation is not included as a distinct detailed occupation listed in the structure, it should be classified in the appropriate residual occupation. Residual occupations are all other occupations in a major, minor, or broad group that are not classified separately.

- When workers may be classified in more than one occupation, they should be classified in the occu-pation that requires the highest level of skill. If there is no measurable difference in skill require-ments, the worker is included in the occupation in which he or she spends the most time.

The SOC Committee opted for practical approaches to classification rather than for (perhaps more appealing) theoretical approaches. The key classification principle chosen for the new SOC was to continue the previous focus on work performed (with "skills-based considerations"). In the SOC Committee's judgment, the ability to identify and measure skills consistently had not advanced far enough.[5] The International Standard Classification of Occupations was not used because it was not flexible enough for U.S. needs.[6] Finally, the SOC Committee believed that an economic-based approach would not provide sufficient practical guid-ance to employers or employees.[7]

The SOC Committee also solicited public participation in the next part of the process, building the revised SOC. To develop the new system of occupations, the committee formed six work groups—five of which were based on skills groupings of Occupation

Employment Statistics (OES) occupations and one of which dealt with military occupations. The OES was used as a starting point partly because doing so would enable some historical comparability and partly because BLS was leading much of the work group efforts and thus using BLS survey data would speed the revision process. The following six work groups were formed: (1) management, administrative, and clerical; (2) natural science, law, health, education, and arts; (3) sales and service; (4) construction, extraction, agricultural, and transportation; (5) mechanical and production; and (6) military.

The work groups invited experts from many areas to testify and also requested written recommendations using the SOC revision guidelines. Their procedure was to develop a proposed structure plus a title, a definition, and a list of associated job titles. Each proposed occupation was reviewed by the SOC Committee.

Once most of the occupations were defined and accepted, another work group was formed to discuss and recommend a hierarchy, a key characteristic of the new SOC. Developing the hierarchy ultimately proved one of the more challenging aspects of the process. Perhaps more than any other part of the SOC revision, the hierarchy changed most from its preliminary stage to its final structure, as the committee struggled to make the SOC more transparent to its users.

In July 1997, the SOC Committee published the proposed new structure. After considering more than 200 comments, a revised structure was submitted to OMB and issued in August 1998.[8] Subsequently, additional comments were requested by OMB and minor further changes were made.

Purpose: A Standardized System

The new SOC was developed in response to a concern that the existing SOC did not meet the need for a universal occupational classification system to which all federal government agencies and—it was hoped—other collectors of occupational information would adhere. The following selected government agencies have collected and used occupational data based on unique occupational classification systems that suit their needs.

Bureau of Labor Statistics. The Occupational Employment Statistics (OES) program collects employment data annually on nearly 800 occupations by industry based on establishment surveys of wage and salary workers, who account for about 9 out of 10 workers in the nation. The OES survey classifies workers according to occupational definitions, a characteristic used for classification in the revised SOC.

Bureau of the Census. Both the decennial Census of Population and the monthly Current Population Survey (CPS) tabulate data for about 500 occupations for each of the three classes of workers—wage and salary workers, the self-employed, and unpaid family workers. In addition to employment, these programs collect data on a number of demographic characteristics—age, sex, race, and Hispanic origin—as well as a wide range of other characteristics, such as educational attainment, number of hours worked, number of job openings, and employment status. Both the decennial Census of Population and the CPS classify workers according to the job titles given by the survey respondents. Classifying workers according to associated job titles is another characteristic of the revised SOC.

Employment and Training Administration. The *Dictionary of Occupational Titles* identified and defined more than 12,000 jobs. This classification system has been replaced by the Occupational Information Network (O*NET), which adheres to the SOC.

Other agencies. The Department of Education collects data on teachers, the Bureau of Health Professions gathers information on health occupations, and the National Science Foundation surveys focus on scientists and engineers. The Office of Personnel Management publishes data on occupations in the federal government, and the Department of Defense maintains data on military personnel.

The existence of different occupational data collection systems in the federal government presents a major problem—data collected by one program often is not suitable for other uses. Comparisons across programs are limited to the effectiveness and accuracy of crosswalks between different occupational classification systems. For example, data on educational attainment collected through the CPS can only be used with data on employment from the OES program for occupations that are considered comparable from both surveys. Universal adherence to the revised SOC will aid analysis of educational, demographic, economic, and other factors that affect employment, wages, and other worker characteristics.

Key Characteristics

Structured for comparability. The SOC is composed of four hierarchical levels to enable data collectors to choose a level of detail corresponding to their interests and abilities to collect data on different occupations. The Bureau of Labor Statistics, through its establishment survey that classifies workers according to occupational definitions, is generally able to collect data on more detailed

occupations than is the Bureau of the Census, whose household surveys rely almost exclusively on job titles given by respondents to classify workers. The Bureau of Labor Statistics collects data on both Heavy and Light Truck Drivers, for example, while the Bureau of the Census cannot differentiate between the two.

The following list shows the 23 major occupational groups of the revised SOC:

Management Occupations
Business and Financial Operations
    Occupations
Computer and Mathematical Occupations
Architecture and Engineering Occupations
Life, Physical, and Social Science
    Occupations
Community and Social Services Occupations
Legal Occupations
Education, Training, and Library
    Occupations
Arts, Design, Entertainment, Sports, and
    Media Occupations
Healthcare Practitioners and Technical
    Occupations
Healthcare Support Occupations
Protective Service Occupations
Food Preparation and Serving Related
    Occupations
Building and Grounds Cleaning and
    Maintenance Occupations
Personal Care and Service Occupations
Sales and Related Occupations
Office and Administrative Support
    Occupations
Farming, Fishing, and Forestry Occupations
Construction and Extraction Occupations
Installation, Maintenance, and Repair
    Occupations

Production Occupations
Transportation and Material Moving
Occupations
Military Specific Occupations

These major groups include 96 minor groups, 449 broad occupations, and 821 detailed occupations.[9] Occupations with similar skills or work activities are grouped at each of the four levels of hierarchy to facilitate comparisons. For example, the major group, Life, Physical, and Social Science Occupations, is divided into four minor groups: Life Scientists, Physical Scientists, Social Scientists and Related Workers, and Life, Physical, and Social Science Technicians. Life Scientists contains broad occupations, such as Agriculture and Food Scientists, as well as Biological Scientists. The broad occupation, Biological Scientists, includes detailed occupations such as Biochemists and Biophysicists as well as Microbiologists. The following example shows the hierarchical structure of the revised SOC:

19–0000 Life, Physical, and Social Science Occupations *(major group)*
19–1000 Life Scientists *(minor group)*
19–1020 Biological Scientists
(broad occupation)
19–1021 Biochemists and Biophysicists
(detailed occupation)
19–1022 Microbiologists *(detailed occupation)*
19–1023 Zoologists and Wildlife Biologists *(detailed occupation)*
19–1029 Biological Scientists, All Other *(detailed occupation)*

Broad occupations often include several detailed occupations that are difficult to distinguish without further information. For example, people may report their occupation as Biologist or Psychologist without identifying a concentration. Broad occupations, such as Psychologists, include more detailed occupations, such as Industrial-Organizational Psychologists, for those requiring further detail. For cases in which there is little confusion about the content of a detailed occupation, the broad occupation is the same as the detailed occupation. For example, because it is relatively easy to identify lawyers, the broad occupation, Lawyers, is the same as the detailed occupation.

Reflects structure of current workforce. In addition to ensuring comparability among various surveys, the new SOC was designed to mirror the current occupational structure in the nation, and, in effect, serve as a bridge to occupational classification in the 21st century. The new system should lead to the collection of meaningful data about the workforce and benefit various users of occupational data. These users might include education and training planners; job seekers, students and others seeking career guidance; various government programs, including occupational safety and health, welfare-to-work, and equal employment opportunity; and private companies wishing to relocate or set salary scales.

Reflecting advances in factory and office automation and information technology, the shift to a services-oriented economy, and increasing concern for the environment, the new classification structure has more professional, technical, and service occupations and fewer production and administrative support occupations than earlier classification systems. Although the designation "professional" does not exist in the new SOC, the new classification system reflects expanded coverage of occupations classified as professional and technical in earlier classification systems. These occupations have been dispersed among a number of major occupational groups, such as Computer and Mathematical Occupations, Community and Social Services Occupations, Healthcare Practitioners and Technical Occupations, and Legal Occupations.

Designers, Systems Analysts, Drafters, Counselors, Dentists, Physicians, Artists, and Social Scientists are among the occupations that are covered in greater detail in the new SOC. For example, the SOC breaks out a number of designer specialties—Commercial and Industrial, Fashion, Floral, Graphic, Interior, and Set and Exhibit Designers. Similarly, the new classification breaks out additional social science specialties—Market and Survey Researchers, Sociologists, Anthropologists and Archeologists, Geographers, Historians, and Political Scientists. Examples of new occupations include Environmental Engineers; Environmental Engineering Technicians; Environmental Scientists and Specialists, Including Health; Environmental Science and Protection Technicians, Including Health; Computer Software Engineers; Multimedia Artists and Animators; and Forensic Science Technicians.

In the services groups, gaming occupations, such as Gaming and Sportsbook Writers and Runners, have been added as a result of growth among these occupations in several states. Other relatively new service occupations include Skin Care Specialists, Concierges, Massage Therapists, and Fitness Trainers and Aerobics Instructors.

Production occupations, on the other hand, have undergone significant consolidation. For example, various Printing Machine Operators have been combined into one occupation in the new SOC. Because many factories now employ one person to perform

the tasks of setting up and operating machines, both tasks have been combined into one occupation. In addition, many factories now employ teams in which each team member is able to perform all or most of the team assembly activities; these people are included in the occupation, Team Assemblers. The SOC also includes relatively new production occupations such as Semiconductor Processors and Fiberglass Laminators and Fabricators. Office and administrative support occupations—for example, Office Machine Operators—also have been consolidated. Relatively new office and administrative support occupations include Customer Service Representatives and Executive Secretaries and Administrative Assistants.

Greater flexibility. To accommodate the needs of different data collection agencies, the SOC enables data collection at more detailed or less detailed levels, while still allowing data comparability at certain levels of the hierarchy. Each occupation in the SOC is assigned a six-digit code. (The first two digits represent the major group, the third digit represents the minor group, the fourth and fifth digits represent the broad occupation, and the sixth digit represents the detailed occupation.) Data collection agencies wanting more detail to measure additional worker characteristics can split a defined occupation into more detailed occupations by adding a decimal point and more digits to the SOC code. Additional levels of detail also may be used to distinguish workers who have different training, demographic characteristics, or years of experience. For users wanting less detail, the SOC Committee suggests combining the 23 major groups into 11 or even 6 groups if needed for tabulation purposes.[10]

Comprehensive coverage. The Standard Occupational Classification covers all workers in the United States. In some cases, the worker will not exactly fit into a defined occupation and will be classified in a residual occupation at the most detailed level possible. These residual categories are placed throughout the structure as needed. Like other detailed occupations, residual occupations may be individually defined so that separate data can be collected. For example, the broad occupation, Biological Scientists, lists three types of Biological Scientists explicitly, but this list is not exhaustive. In order to include all workers in the appropriate classification, residual occupations are added for the workers not defined separately. Geneticists, for example, are included in the residual category, All Other Biological Scientists.

Associated job titles. To facilitate consistent classification by data collection agencies across surveys, the new SOC associates some 30,000 job titles with detailed occupations. For example, associated titles will ensure that a Podiatric Surgeon consistently will be classified as a podiatrist rather than as a surgeon. Because many of these job titles are industry-specific, the industries also are listed for many titles.

Occupational definitions. A universal occupational classification cannot rely on job title alone. To further facilitate consistent classification, each detailed occupation has a definition that uniquely defines the workers that are included. Definitions begin with tasks that all workers in the occupation are expected to perform. The qualifier "may" precedes duties that only some workers perform. Where a definition includes duties also performed by workers in another occupation, cross-references to the occupation are

provided. A sample of occupational definitions follows:

(15–1081) *Network Systems and Data Communications Analysts:* Analyze, design, test, and evaluate network systems, such as local area networks (LAN), wide area networks (WAN), Internet, intranet, and other data communications systems. Perform network modeling, analysis, and planning. Research and recommend network and data communications hardware and software. Supervise computer programmers. Include telecommunications specialists who deal with the interfacing of computer and communications equipment. Illustrative examples: Internet Developer; Systems Integrator; Webmaster.

Military occupations. The new SOC also covers military jobs. Workers in military occupations that are similar to nonmilitary occupations, such as Physicians, Cooks, or Secretaries, are classified with nonmilitary workers. Those in occupations specific to the military, such as infantry, are in a separate group. However, data on all military personnel—whether specific to the military or not—usually will be separate from data on the civilian labor force collected by the Bureau of Labor Statistics, the Bureau of the Census, and other government agencies.

Historical comparability. Comparability with older classification systems is important for analyzing long-term trends in employment and other characteristics of workers. While such comparability was not the primary consideration in development of the new SOC, researchers will retain the ability to make most historical comparisons.

Flexibility for change. The SOC Committee has proposed that a permanent review committee be established to keep the SOC up to date. This committee would consider proposals for new occupations, redefine occupations as job duties change, and amend the list of associated job titles accordingly. For example, some associated job titles in the new SOC might become detailed occupations in future versions of the SOC. The next major revision is expected to begin in 2005, in preparation for the 2010 Census of Population.

[1]For a recent summary of NAICS, see John B. Murphy, "Introducing the North American Industry Classification System," *Monthly Labor Review,* July 1998, pp. 43–47. [2]For more on the conference, see *Proceedings of the International Occupation Classification Conference,* Report 833 (Bureau of Labor Statistics, September 1993). [3]See *The New DOT: A Database of Occupational Titles for the Twenty-First Century,* final report of the Advisory Panel for the *Dictionary of Occupational Titles* (U.S. Department of Labor, Employment and Training Administration, May 1993). [4]See *Federal Register,* February 28, 1995, p. 10998. [5]The Bureau of the Census tested the feasibility of data collection to implement a skills-based approach on its 1995 National Content Survey test of questions for the 2000 Census of Population. The SOC Committee also commissioned work by the Joint Program in Survey Methodology on the collectibility of skills information. BLS also developed a prototype job family matrix (modeled on the Canadian system) that classified occupations by skill level. See "Prototype Skills-based Job Family Matrix," unpublished report (Bureau of Labor Statistics, April 1994). [6]An additional drawback of ISCO-88 was its inclusion of "female" occupations; the SOC Committee decided not to make any gender-based distinctions in the SOC. [7]See *Federal Register,* October 5, 1995, p. 52285. [8]See *Federal Register,* July 7, 1997, pp. 36338–36409; and August 5, 1998, pp. 41896–41923. OMB received comments on the final report as well. [9]In comparison, the 1980 SOC included 22 divisions (comparable to major groups in the new SOC), 60 major groups (comparable to minor groups in the new SOC), 223 minor groups (comparable to broad occupations in the new SOC), and 664 unit groups (comparable to detailed occupations in the new SOC). [10]*Federal Register,* August 5, 1998, pp. 41897–41898.

APPENDIX C
SOC-to-O*NET Cross-Reference Table

The following table helps you find the O*NET (for Occupational Information Network) codes and job titles that correspond to SOC codes and job titles. The O*NET is an occupational information database from the U.S. Department of Labor that includes descriptions and many details on about 1,000 occupations.

The O*NET database uses the basic six-digit numeric coding structure of the SOC as its framework, adding a two-digit extension (sequentially numbered beginning with .01) to differentiate unique O*NET occupations within the SOC system.

You can find more facts on O*NET occupations at http://online.onetcenter.org. A book titled the *O*NET Dictionary of Occupational Titles, Second Edition* (JIST Works, 2002) offers useful information about each O*NET job in print form for convenient reference by job seekers, career changers, students, counselors, educators, and others.

This list is derived from the O*NET 3.1 database.

SOC Code and Title		O*NET-SOC Code and Title	
11-1011	Chief Executives	11-1011.00	Chief Executives
11-1011	Chief Executives	11-1011.01	Government Service Executives
11-1011	Chief Executives	11-1011.02	Private Sector Executives
11-1021	General and Operations Managers	11-1021.00	General and Operations Managers
11-1031	Legislators	11-1031.00	Legislators
11-2011	Advertising and Promotions Managers	11-2011.00	Advertising and Promotions Managers
11-2021	Marketing Managers	11-2021.00	Marketing Managers
11-2022	Sales Managers	11-2022.00	Sales Managers
11-2031	Public Relations Managers	11-2031.00	Public Relations Managers
11-3011	Administrative Services Managers	11-3011.00	Administrative Services Managers
11-3021	Computer and Information Systems Managers	11-3021.00	Computer and Information Systems Managers
11-3031	Financial Managers	11-3031.00	Financial Managers
11-3031	Financial Managers	11-3031.01	Treasurers, Controllers, and Chief Financial Officers
11-3031	Financial Managers	11-3031.02	Financial Managers, Branch or Department

SOC Code and Title		O*NET-SOC Code and Title	
11-3040	Human Resources Managers	11-3040.00	Human Resources Managers
11-3041	Compensation and Benefits Managers	11-3041.00	Compensation and Benefits Managers
11-3042	Training and Development Managers	11-3042.00	Training and Development Managers
11-3049	Human Resources Managers, All Other	11-3049.99	Human Resources Managers, All Other
11-3051	Industrial Production Managers	11-3051.00	Industrial Production Managers
11-3061	Purchasing Managers	11-3061.00	Purchasing Managers
11-3071	Transportation, Storage, and Distribution Managers	11-3071.00	Transportation, Storage, and Distribution Manager
11-3071	Transportation, Storage, and Distribution Managers	11-3071.01	Transportation Managers
11-3071	Transportation, Storage, and Distribution Managers	11-3071.02	Storage and Distribution Managers
11-9011	Farm, Ranch, and Other Agricultural Managers	11-9011.00	Farm, Ranch, and Other Agricultural Managers
11-9011	Farm, Ranch, and Other Agricultural Managers	11-9011.01	Nursery and Greenhouse Managers
11-9011	Farm, Ranch, and Other Agricultural Managers	11-9011.02	Agricultural Crop Farm Managers
11-9011	Farm, Ranch, and Other Agricultural Managers	11-9011.03	Fish Hatchery Managers
11-9012	Farmers and Ranchers	11-9012.00	Farmers and Ranchers
11-9021	Construction Managers	11-9021.00	Construction Managers
11-9031	Education Administrators, Preschool and Child Care Center/Program	11-9031.00	Education Administrators, Preschool and Child Care Center/Program
11-9032	Education Administrators, Elementary and Secondary School	11-9032.00	Education Administrators, Elementary and Secondary School
11-9033	Education Administrators, Postsecondary	11-9033.00	Education Administrators, Postsecondary
11-9039	Education Administrators, All Other	11-9039.99	Education Administrators, All Other
11-9041	Engineering Managers	11-9041.00	Engineering Managers
11-9051	Food Service Managers	11-9051.00	Food Service Managers
11-9061	Funeral Directors	11-9061.00	Funeral Directors
11-9071	Gaming Managers	11-9071.00	Gaming Managers
11-9081	Lodging Managers	11-9081.00	Lodging Managers
11-9111	Medical and Health Services Managers	11-9111.00	Medical and Health Services Managers
11-9121	Natural Sciences Managers	11-9121.00	Natural Sciences Managers
11-9131	Postmasters and Mail Superintendents	11-9131.00	Postmasters and Mail Superintendents
11-9141	Property, Real Estate, and Community Association Managers	11-9141.00	Property, Real Estate, and Community Association Managers
11-9151	Social and Community Service Managers	11-9151.00	Social and Community Service Managers
11-9199	Managers, All Other	11-9199.99	Managers, All Other
13-1011	Agents and Business Managers of Artists, Performers, and Athletes	13-1011.00	Agents and Business Managers of Artists, Performers, and Athletes
13-1021	Purchasing Agents and Buyers, Farm Products	13-1021.00	Purchasing Agents and Buyers, Farm Products
13-1022	Wholesale and Retail Buyers, Except Farm Products	13-1022.00	Wholesale and Retail Buyers, Except Farm Products

SOC Code and Title		O*NET-SOC Code and Title	
13-1023	Purchasing Agents, Except Wholesale, Retail, and Farm Products	13-1023.00	Purchasing Agents, Except Wholesale, Retail, and Farm Products
13-1031	Claims Adjusters, Examiners, and Investigators	13-1031.00	Claims Adjusters, Examiners, and Investigators
13-1031	Claims Adjusters, Examiners, and Investigators	13-1031.01	Claims Examiners, Property and Casualty Insurance
13-1031	Claims Adjusters, Examiners, and Investigators	13-1031.02	Insurance Adjusters, Examiners, and Investigators
13-1032	Insurance Appraisers, Auto Damage	13-1032.00	Insurance Appraisers, Auto Damage
13-1041	Compliance Officers, Except Agriculture, Construction, Health and Safety, and Transportation	13-1041.00	Compliance Officers, Except Agriculture, Construction, Health and Safety, and Transportation
13-1041	Compliance Officers, Except Agriculture, Construction, Health and Safety, and Transportation	13-1041.01	Environmental Compliance Inspectors
13-1041	Compliance Officers, Except Agriculture, Construction, Health and Safety, and Transportation	13-1041.02	Licensing Examiners and Inspectors
13-1041	Compliance Officers, Except Agriculture, Construction, Health and Safety, and Transportation	13-1041.03	Equal Opportunity Representatives and Officers
13-1041	Compliance Officers, Except Agriculture, Construction, Health and Safety, and Transportation	13-1041.04	Government Property Inspectors and Investigators
13-1041	Compliance Officers, Except Agriculture, Construction, Health and Safety, and Transportation	13-1041.05	Pressure Vessel Inspectors
13-1041	Compliance Officers, Except Agriculture, Construction, Health and Safety, and Transportation	13-1041.06	Coroners
13-1051	Cost Estimators	13-1051.00	Cost Estimators
13-1061	Emergency Management Specialists	13-1061.00	Emergency Management Specialists
13-1071	Employment, Recruitment, and Placement Specialists	13-1071.00	Employment, Recruitment, and Placement Specialists
13-1071	Employment, Recruitment, and Placement Specialists	13-1071.01	Employment Interviewers, Privarte or Public Employment Service
13-1071	Employment, Recruitment, and Placement Specialists	13-1071.02	Personnel Recruiters
13-1072	Compensation, Benefits, and Job Analysis Specialists	13-1072.00	Compensation, Benefits, and Job Analysis Specialists
13-1073	Training and Development Specialists	13-1073.00	Training and Development Specialists
13-1079	Human Resources, Training, and Labor Relations Specialists, All Other	13-1079.99	Human Resources, Training, and Labor Relations Specialists, All Other
13-1081	Logisticians	13-1081.00	Logisticians
13-1111	Management Analysts	13-1111.00	Management Analysts
13-1121	Meeting and Convention Planners	13-1121.00	Meeting and Convention Planners
13-1199	Business Operations Specialists, All Other	13-1199.99	Business Operations Specialists, All Other
13-2011	Accountants and Auditors	13-2011.00	Accountants and Auditors
13-2011	Accountants and Auditors	13-2011.01	Accountants
13-2011	Accountants and Auditors	13-2011.02	Auditors
13-2021	Appraisers and Assessors of Real Estate	13-2021.00	Appraisers and Assessors of Real Estate
13-2021	Appraisers and Assessors of Real Estate	13-2021.01	Assessors

SOC Code and Title		O*NET-SOC Code and Title	
13-2021	Appraisers and Assessors of Real Estate	13-2021.02	Appraisers, Real Estate
13-2031	Budget Analysts	13-2031.00	Budget Analysts
13-2041	Credit Analysts	13-2041.00	Credit Analysts
13-2051	Financial Analysts	13-2051.00	Financial Analysts
13-2052	Personal Financial Advisors	13-2052.00	Personal Financial Advisors
13-2053	Insurance Underwriters	13-2053.00	Insurance Underwriters
13-2061	Financial Examiners	13-2061.00	Financial Examiners
13-2071	Loan Counselors	13-2071.00	Loan Counselors
13-2072	Loan Officers	13-2072.00	Loan Officers
13-2081	Tax Examiners, Collectors, and Revenue Agents	13-2081.00	Tax Examiners, Collectors, and Revenue Agents
13-2082	Tax Preparers	13-2082.00	Tax Preparers
13-2099	Financial Specialists, All Other	13-2099.99	Financial Specialists, All Other
15-1011	Computer and Information Scientists Research,	15-1011.00	Computer and Information Scientists, Research
15-1021	Computer Programmers	15-1021.00	Computer Programmers
15-1031	Computer Software Engineers, Applications	15-1031.00	Computer Software Engineers, Applications
15-1032	Computer Software Engineers, Systems Software	15-1032.00	Computer Software Engineers, Systems Software
15-1041	Computer Support Specialists	15-1041.00	Computer Support Specialists
15-1051	Computer Systems Analysts	15-1051.00	Computer Systems Analysts
15-1061	Database Administrators	15-1061.00	Database Administrators
15-1071	Network and Computer Systems Administrators	15-1071.00	Network and Computer Systems Administrators
15-1071	Network and Computer Systems Administrators	15-1071.01	Computer Security Specialists
15-1081	Network Systems and Data Communications Analysts	15-1081.00	Network Systems and Data Communications Analysts
15-1099	Computer Specialists, All Other	15-1099.99	Computer Specialists, All Other
15-2011	Actuaries	15-2011.00	Actuaries
15-2021	Mathematicians	15-2021.00	Mathematicians
15-2031	Operations Research Analysts	15-2031.00	Operations Research Analysts
15-2041	Statisticians	15-2041.00	Statisticians
15-2099	Mathematical Science Occupations, All Other	15-2099.99	Mathematical Science Occupations, All Other
15-3011	Mathematical Technicians	15-3011.00	Mathematical Technicians
17-1011	Architects, Except Landscape and Naval	17-1011.00	Architects, Except Landscape and Naval
17-1012	Landscape Architects	17-1012.00	Landscape Architects
17-1021	Cartographers and Photogrammetrists	17-1021.00	Cartographers and Photogrammetrists
17-1022	Surveyors	17-1022.00	Surveyors
17-2011	Aerospace Engineers	17-2011.00	Aerospace Engineers
17-2021	Agricultural Engineers	17-2021.00	Agricultural Engineers
17-2031	Biomedical Engineers	17-2031.00	Biomedical Engineers
17-2041	Chemical Engineers	17-2041.00	Chemical Engineers

SOC Code and Title		O*NET-SOC Code and Title	
17-2051	Civil Engineers	17-2051.00	Civil Engineers
17-2061	Computer Hardware Engineers	17-2061.00	Computer Hardware Engineers
17-2071	Electrical Engineers	17-2071.00	Electrical Engineers
17-2072	Electronics Engineers, Except Computer	17-2072.00	Electronics Engineers, Except Computer
17-2081	Environmental Engineers	17-2081.00	Environmental Engineers
17-2111	Health and Safety Engineers, Except Mining Safety Engineers and Inspectors	17-2111.00	Health and Safety Engineers, Except Mining Safety Engineers and Inspectors
17-2111	Health and Safety Engineers, Except Mining Safety Engineers and Inspectors	17-2111.01	Industrial Safety and Health Engineers
17-2111	Health and Safety Engineers, Except Mining Safety Engineers and Inspectors	17-2111.02	Fire-Prevention and Protection Engineers
17-2111	Health and Safety Engineers, Except Mining Safety Engineers and Inspectors	17-2111.03	Product Safety Engineers
17-2112	Industrial Engineers	17-2112.00	Industrial Engineers
17-2121	Marine Engineers and Naval Architects	17-2121.00	Marine Engineers and Naval Architects
17-2121	Marine Engineers and Naval Architects	17-2121.01	Marine Engineers
17-2121	Marine Engineers and Naval Architects	17-2121.02	Marine Architects
17-2131	Materials Engineers	17-2131.00	Materials Engineers
17-2141	Mechanical Engineers	17-2141.00	Mechanical Engineers
17-2151	Mining and Geological Engineers, Including Mining Safety Engineers	17-2151.00	Mining and Geological Engineers, Including Mining Safety Engineers
17-2161	Nuclear Engineers	17-2161.00	Nuclear Engineers
17-2171	Petroleum Engineers	17-2171.00	Petroleum Engineers
17-2199	Engineers, All Other	17-2199.99	Engineers, All Other
17-3011	Architectural and Civil Drafters	17-3011.00	Architectural and Civil Drafters
17-3011	Architectural and Civil Drafters	17-3011.01	Architectural Drafters
17-3011	Architectural and Civil Drafters	17-3011.02	Civil Drafters
17-3012	Electrical and Electronics Drafters	17-3012.00	Electrical and Electronics Drafters
17-3012	Electrical and Electronics Drafters	17-3012.01	Electronic Drafters
17-3012	Electrical and Electronics Drafters	17-3012.02	Electrical Drafters
17-3013	Mechanical Drafters	17-3013.00	Mechanical Drafters
17-3019	Drafters, All Other	17-3019.99	Drafters, All Other
17-3021	Aerospace Engineering and Operations Technicians	17-3021.00	Aerospace Engineering and Operations Technicians
17-3022	Civil Engineering Technicians	17-3022.00	Civil Engineering Technicians
17-3023	Electrical and Electronic Engineering Technicians	17-3023.00	Electrical and Electronic Engineering Technicians
17-3023	Electrical and Electronic EngineeringTechnicians	17-3023.01	Electronics Engineering Technicians
17-3023	Electrical and Electronic Engineering Technicians	17-3023.02	Calibration and Instrumentation Technicians
17-3023	Electrical and Electronic Engineering Technicians	17-3023.03	Electrical Engineering Technicians

SOC Code and Title		O*NET-SOC Code and Title	
17-3024	Electro-Mechanical Technicians	17-3024.00	Electro-Mechanical Technicians
17-3025	Environmental Engineering Technicians	17-3025.00	Environmental Engineering Technicians
17-3026	Industrial Engineering Technicians	17-3026.00	Industrial Engineering Technicians
17-3027	Mechanical Engineering Technicians	17-3027.00	Mechanical Engineering Technicians
17-3029	Engineering Technicians, Except Drafters, All Other	17-3029.99	Engineering Technicians, Except Drafters, All Other
17-3031	Surveying and Mapping Technicians	17-3031.00	Surveying and Mapping Technicians
17-3031	Surveying and Mapping Technicians	17-3031.01	Surveying Technicians
17-3031	Surveying and Mapping Technicians	17-3031.02	Mapping Technicians
19-1011	Animal Scientists	19-1011.00	Animal Scientists
19-1012	Food Scientists and Technologists	19-1012.00	Food Scientists and Technologists
19-1013	Soil and Plant Scientists	19-1013.00	Soil and Plant Scientists
19-1013	Soil and Plant Scientists	19-1013.01	Plant Scientists
19-1013	Soil and Plant Scientists	19-1013.02	Soil Scientists
19-1020	Biological Scientists	19-1020.01	Biologists
19-1021	Biochemists and Biophysicists	19-1021.00	Biochemists and Biophysicists
19-1021	Biochemists and Biophysicists	19-1021.01	Biochemists
19-1021	Biochemists and Biophysicists	19-1021.02	Biophysicists
19-1022	Microbiologists	19-1022.00	Microbiologists
19-1023	Zoologists and Wildlife Biologists	19-1023.00	Zoologists and Wildlife Biologists
19-1029	Biological Scientists, All Other	19-1029.99	Biological Scientists, All Other
19-1031	Conservation Scientists	19-1031.00	Conservation Scientists
19-1031	Conservation Scientists	19-1031.01	Soil Conservationists
19-1031	Conservation Scientists	19-1031.02	Range Managers
19-1031	Conservation Scientists	19-1031.03	Park Naturalists
19-1032	Foresters	19-1032.00	Foresters
19-1041	Epidemiologists	19-1041.00	Epidemiologists
19-1042	Medical Scientists, Except Epidemiologists	19-1042.00	Medical Scientists, Except Epidemiologists
19-1099	Life Scientists, All Other	19-1099.99	Life Scientists, All Other
19-2011	Astronomers	19-2011.00	Astronomers
19-2012	Physicists	19-2012.00	Physicists
19-2021	Atmospheric and Space Scientists	19-2021.00	Atmospheric and Space Scientists
19-2031	Chemists	19-2031.00	Chemists
19-2032	Materials Scientists	19-2032.00	Materials Scientists
19-2041	Environmental Scientists and Specialists, Including Health	19-2041.00	Environmental Scientists and Specialists, Including Health
19-2042	Geoscientists, Except Hydrologists and Geographers	19-2042.00	Geoscientists, Except Hydrologists and Geographers
19-2042	Geoscientists, Except Hydrologists and Geographers	19-2042.01	Geologists

SOC Code and Title		O*NET-SOC Code and Title	
19-2043	Hydrologists	19-2043.00	Hydrologists
19-2099	Physical Scientists, All Other	19-2099.99	Physical Scientists, All Other
19-3011	Economists	19-3011.00	Economists
19-3021	Market Research Analysts	19-3021.00	Market Research Analysts
19-3022	Survey Researchers	19-3022.00	Survey Researchers
19-3031	Clinical, Counseling, and School Psychologists	19-3031.00	Clinical, Counseling, and School Psychologists
19-3031	Clinical, Counseling, and School Psychologists	19-3031.01	Educational Psychologists
19-3031	Clinical, Counseling, and School Psychologists	19-3031.02	Clinical Psychologists
19-3031	Clinical, Counseling, and School Psychologists	19-3031.03	Counseling Psychologists
19-3032	Industrial-Organizational Psychologists	19-3032.00	Industrial-Organizational Psychologists
19-3039	Psychologists, All Other	19-3039.99	Psychologists, All Other
19-3041	Sociologists	19-3041.00	Sociologists
19-3051	Urban and Regional Planners	19-3051.00	Urban and Regional Planners
19-3091	Anthropologists and Archeologists	19-3091.00	Anthropologists and Archeologists
19-3091	Anthropologists and Archeologists	19-3091.01	Anthropologists
19-3091	Anthropologists and Archeologists	19-3091.02	Archeologists
19-3092	Geographers	19-3092.00	Geographers
19-3093	Historians	19-3093.00	Historians
19-3094	Political Scientists	19-3094.00	Political Scientists
19-3099	Social Scientists and Related Workers, All Other	19-3099.99	Social Scientists and Related Workers, All Other
19-4011	Agricultural and Food Science Technicians	19-4011.00	Agricultural and Food Science Technicians
19-4011	Agricultural and Food Science Technicians	19-4011.01	Agricultural Technicians
19-4011	Agricultural and Food Science Technicians	19-4011.02	Food Science Technicians
19-4021	Biological Technicians	19-4021.00	Biological Technicians
19-4031	Chemical Technicians	19-4031.00	Chemical Technicians
19-4041	Geological and Petroleum Technicians	19-4041.00	Geological and Petroleum Technicians
19-4041	Geological and Petroleum Technicians	19-4041.01	Geological Data Technicians
19-4041	Geological and Petroleum Technicians	19-4041.02	Geological Sample Test Technicians
19-4051	Nuclear Technicians	19-4051.00	Nuclear Technicians
19-4051	Nuclear Technicians	19-4051.01	Nuclear Equipment Operation Technicians
19-4051	Nuclear Technicians	19-4051.02	Nuclear Monitoring Technicians
19-4061	Social Science Research Assistants	19-4061.00	Social Science Research Assistants
19-4061	Social Science Research Assistants	19-4061.01	City Planning Aides
19-4091	Environmental Science and Protection Technicians, Including Health	19-4091.00	Environmental Science and Protection Technicians, Including Health
19-4092	Forensic Science Technicians	19-4092.00	Forensic Science Technicians
19-4093	Forest and Conservation Technicians	19-4093.00	Forest and Conservation Technicians

SOC Code and Title		O*NET-SOC Code and Title	
19-4099	Life, Physical, and Social Science Technicians, All Other	19-4099.99	Life, Physical, and Social Science Technicians, All Other
21-1011	Substance Abuse and Behavioral Disorder Counselors	21-1011.00	Substance Abuse and Behavioral Disorder Counselors
21-1012	Educational, Vocational, and School Counselors	21-1012.00	Educational, Vocational, and School Counselors
21-1013	Marriage and Family Therapists	21-1013.00	Marriage and Family Therapists
21-1014	Mental Health Counselors	21-1014.00	Mental Health Counselors
21-1015	Rehabilitation Counselors	21-1015.00	Rehabilitation Counselors
21-1019	Counselors, All Other	21-1019.99	Counselors, All Other
21-1021	Child, Family, and School Social Workers	21-1021.00	Child, Family, and School Social Workers
21-1022	Medical and Public Health Social Workers	21-1022.00	Medical and Public Health Social Workers
21-1023	Mental Health and Substance Abuse Social Workers	21-1023.00	Mental Health and Substance Abuse Social Workers
21-1029	Social Workers, All Other	21-1029.99	Social Workers, All Other
21-1091	Health Educators	21-1091.00	Health Educators
21-1092	Probation Officers and Correctional Treatment Specialists	21-1092.00	Probation Officers and Correctional Treatment Specialists
21-1093	Social and Human Service Assistants	21-1093.00	Social and Human Service Assistants
21-1099	Community and Social Service Specialists, All Other	21-1099.99	Community and Social Service Specialists, All Other
21-2011	Clergy	21-2011.00	Clergy
21-2021	Directors, Religious Activities and Education	21-2021.00	Directors, Religious Activities and Education
21-2099	Religious Workers, All Other	21-2099.99	Religious Workers, All Other
23-1011	Lawyers	23-1011.00	Lawyers
23-1021	Administrative Law Judges, Adjudicators, and Hearing Officers	23-1021.00	Administrative Law Judges, Adjudicators, and Hearing Officers
23-1022	Arbitrators, Mediators, and Conciliators	23-1022.00	Arbitrators, Mediators, and Conciliators
23-1023	Judges, Magistrate Judges, and Magistrates	23-1023.00	Judges, Magistrate Judges, and Magistrates
23-2011	Paralegals and Legal Assistants	23-2011.00	Paralegals and Legal Assistants
23-2091	Court Reporters	23-2091.00	Court Reporters
23-2092	Law Clerks	23-2092.00	Law Clerks
23-2093	Title Examiners, Abstractors, and Searchers	23-2093.00	Title Examiners, Abstractors, and Searchers
23-2093	Title Examiners, Abstractors, and Searchers	23-2093.01	Title Searchers
23-2093	Title Examiners, Abstractors, and Searchers	23-2093.02	Title Examiners and Abstractors
23-2099	Legal Support Workers, All Other	23-2099.99	Legal Support Workers, All Other
25-1011	Business Teachers, Postsecondary	25-1011.00	Business Teachers, Postsecondary
25-1021	Computer Science Teachers, Postsecondary	25-1021.00	Computer Science Teachers, Postsecondary
25-1022	Mathematical Science Teachers, Postsecondary	25-1022.00	Mathematical Science Teachers, Postsecondary
25-1031	Architecture Teachers, Postsecondary	25-1031.00	Architecture Teachers, Postsecondary
25-1032	Engineering Teachers, Postsecondary	25-1032.00	Engineering Teachers, Postsecondary
25-1041	Agricultural Sciences Teachers, Postsecondary	25-1041.00	Agricultural Sciences Teachers, Postsecondary

SOC Code and Title		O*NET-SOC Code and Title	
25-1042	Biological Science Teachers, Postsecondary	25-1042.00	Biological Science Teachers, Postsecondary
25-1043	Forestry and Conservation Science Teachers, Postsecondary	25-1043.00	Forestry and Conservation Science Teachers, Postsecondary
25-1051	Atmospheric, Earth, Marine, and Space Sciences Teachers, Postsecondary	25-1051.00	Atmospheric, Earth, Marine, and Space Sciences Teachers, Postsecondary
25-1052	Chemistry Teachers, Postsecondary	25-1052.00	Chemistry Teachers, Postsecondary
25-1053	Environmental Science Teachers, Postsecondary	25-1053.00	Environmental Science Teachers, Postsecondary
25-1054	Physics Teachers, Postsecondary	25-1054.00	Physics Teachers, Postsecondary
25-1061	Anthropology and Archeology Teachers, Postsecondary	25-1061.00	Anthropology and Archeology Teachers, Postsecondary
25-1062	Area, Ethnic, and Cultural Studies Teachers, Postsecondary	25-1062.00	Area, Ethnic, and Cultural Studies Teachers, Postsecondary
25-1063	Economics Teachers, Postsecondary	25-1063.00	Economics Teachers, Postsecondary
25-1064	Geography Teachers, Postsecondary	25-1064.00	Geography Teachers, Postsecondary
25-1065	Political Science Teachers, Postsecondary	25-1065.00	Political Science Teachers, Postsecondary
25-1066	Psychology Teachers, Postsecondary	25-1066.00	Psychology Teachers, Postsecondary
25-1067	Sociology Teachers, Postsecondary	25-1067.00	Sociology Teachers, Postsecondary
25-1069	Social Sciences Teachers, Postsecondary, All Other	25-1069.99	Social Sciences Teachers, Postsecondary, All Other
25-1071	Health Specialties Teachers, Postsecondary	25-1071.00	Health Specialties Teachers, Postsecondary
25-1072	Nursing Instructors and Teachers, Postsecondary	25-1072.00	Nursing Instructors and Teachers, Postsecondary
25-1081	Education Teachers, Postsecondary	25-1081.00	Education Teachers, Postsecondary
25-1082	Library Science Teachers, Postsecondary	25-1082.00	Library Science Teachers, Postsecondary
25-1111	Criminal Justice and Law Enforcement Teachers, Postsecondary	25-1111.00	Criminal Justice and Law Enforcement Teachers, Postsecondary
25-1112	Law Teachers, Postsecondary	25-1112.00	Law Teachers, Postsecondary
25-1113	Social Work Teachers, Postsecondary	25-1113.00	Social Work Teachers, Postsecondary
25-1121	Art, Drama, and Music Teachers, Postsecondary	25-1121.00	Art, Drama, and Music Teachers, Postsecondary
25-1122	Communications Teachers, Postsecondary	25-1122.00	Communications Teachers, Postsecondary
25-1123	English Language and Literature Teachers, Postsecondary	25-1123.00	English Language and Literature Teachers, Postsecondary
25-1124	Foreign Language and Literature Teachers, Postsecondary	25-1124.00	Foreign Language and Literature Teachers, Postsecondary
25-1125	History Teachers, Postsecondary	25-1125.00	History Teachers, Postsecondary
25-1126	Philosophy and Religion Teachers, Postsecondary	25-1126.00	Philosophy and Religion Teachers, Postsecondary
25-1191	Graduate Teaching Assistants	25-1191.00	Graduate Teaching Assistants
25-1192	Home Economics Teachers, Postsecondary	25-1192.00	Home Economics Teachers, Postsecondary
25-1193	Recreation and Fitness Studies Teachers, Postsecondary	25-1193.00	Recreation and Fitness Studies Teachers, Postsecondary
25-1194	Vocational Education Teachers, Postsecondary	25-1194.00	Vocational Education Teachers, Postsecondary

SOC Code and Title		O*NET-SOC Code and Title	
25-1199	Postsecondary Teachers, All Other	25-1199.99	Postsecondary Teachers, All Other
25-2011	Preschool Teachers, Except Special Education	25-2011.00	Preschool Teachers, Except Special Education
25-2012	Kindergarten Teachers, Except Special Education	25-2012.00	Kindergarten Teachers, Except Special Education
25-2021	Elementary School Teachers, Except Special Education	25-2021.00	Elementary School Teachers, Except Special Education
25-2022	Middle School Teachers, Except Special and Vocational Education	25-2022.00	Middle School Teachers, Except Special and Vocational Education
25-2023	Vocational Education Teachers, Middle School	25-2023.00	Vocational Education Teachers, Middle School
25-2031	Secondary School Teachers, Except Special and Vocational Education	25-2031.00	Secondary School Teachers, Except Special and Vocational Education
25-2032	Vocational Education Teachers, Secondary School	25-2032.00	Vocational Education Teachers, Secondary School
25-2041	Special Education Teachers, Preschool, Kindergarten, and Elementary School	25-2041.00	Special Education Teachers, Preschool, Kindergarten, and Elementary School
25-2042	Special Education Teachers, Middle School	25-2042.00	Special Education Teachers, Middle School
25-2043	Special Education Teachers, Secondary School	25-2043.00	Special Education Teachers, Secondary School
25-3011	Adult Literacy, Remedial Education, and GED Teachers and Instructors	25-3011.00	Adult Literacy, Remedial Education, and GED Teachers and Instructors
25-3021	Self-Enrichment Education Teachers	25-3021.00	Self-Enrichment Education Teachers
25-3099	Teachers and Instructors, All Other	25-3099.99	Teachers and Instructors, All Other
25-4011	Archivists	25-4011.00	Archivists
25-4012	Curators	25-4012.00	Curators
25-4013	Museum Technicians and Conservators	25-4013.00	Museum Technicians and Conservators
25-4021	Librarians	25-4021.00	Librarians
25-4031	Library Technicians	25-4031.00	Library Technicians
25-9011	Audio-Visual Collections Specialists	25-9011.00	Audio-Visual Collections Specialists
25-9021	Farm and Home Management Advisors	25-9021.00	Farm and Home Management Advisors
25-9031	Instructional Coordinators	25-9031.00	Instructional Coordinators
25-9041	Teacher Assistants	25-9041.00	Teacher Assistants
25-9099	Education, Training, and Library Workers, All Other	25-9099.99	Education, Training, and Library Workers, All Other
27-1011	Art Directors	27-1011.00	Art Directors
27-1012	Craft Artists	27-1012.00	Craft Artists
27-1013	Fine Artists, Including Painters, Sculptors, and Illustrators	27-1013.00	Fine Artists, Including Painters, Sculptors, and Illustrators
27-1013	Fine Artists, Including Painters, Sculptors, and Illustrators	27-1013.01	Painters and Illustrators
27-1013	Fine Artists, Including Painters, Sculptors, and Illustrators	27-1013.02	Sketch Artists
27-1013	Fine Artists, Including Painters, Sculptors, and Illustrators	27-1013.03	Cartoonists

SOC Code and Title		O*NET-SOC Code and Title	
27-1013	Fine Artists, Including Painters, Sculptors, and Illustrators	27-1013.04	Sculptors
27-1014	Multi-Media Artists and Animators	27-1014.00	Multi-Media Artists and Animators
27-1019	Artists and Related Workers, All Other	27-1019.99	Artists and Related Workers, All Other
27-1021	Commercial and Industrial Designers	27-1021.00	Commercial and Industrial Designers
27-1022	Fashion Designers	27-1022.00	Fashion Designers
27-1023	Floral Designers	27-1023.00	Floral Designers
27-1024	Graphic Designers	27-1024.00	Graphic Designers
27-1025	Interior Designers	27-1025.00	Interior Designers
27-1026	Merchandise Displayers and Window Trimmers	27-1026.00	Merchandise Displayers and Window Trimmers
27-1027	Set and Exhibit Designers	27-1027.00	Set and Exhibit Designers
27-1027	Set and Exhibit Designers	27-1027.01	Set Designers
27-1027	Set and Exhibit Designers	27-1027.02	Exhibit Designers
27-1029	Designers, All Other	27-1029.99	Designers, All Other
27-2011	Actors	27-2011.00	Actors
27-2012	Producers and Directors	27-2012.00	Producers and Directors
27-2012	Producers and Directors	27-2012.01	Producers
27-2012	Producers and Directors	27-2012.02	Directors—Stage, Motion Pictures, Television, and Radio
27-2012	Producers and Directors	27-2012.03	Program Directors
27-2012	Producers and Directors	27-2012.04	Talent Directors
27-2012	Producers and Directors	27-2012.05	Technical Directors/Managers
27-2021	Athletes and Sports Competitors	27-2021.00	Athletes and Sports Competitors
27-2022	Coaches and Scouts	27-2022.00	Coaches and Scouts
27-2023	Umpires, Referees, and Other Sports Officials	27-2023.00	Umpires, Referees, and Other Sports Officials
27-2031	Dancers	27-2031.00	Dancers
27-2032	Choreographers	27-2032.00	Choreographers
27-2041	Music Directors and Composers	27-2041.00	Music Directors and Composers
27-2041	Music Directors and Composers	27-2041.01	Music Directors
27-2041	Music Directors and Composers	27-2041.02	Music Arrangers and Orchestrators
27-2041	Music Directors and Composers	27-2041.03	Composers
27-2042	Musicians and Singers	27-2042.00	Musicians and Singers
27-2042	Musicians and Singers	27-2042.01	Singers
27-2042	Musicians and Singers	27-2042.02	Musicians, Instrumental
27-2099	Entertainers and Performers, Sports and Related Workers, All Other	27-2099.99	Entertainers and Performers, Sports and Related Workers, All Other
27-3011	Radio and Television Announcers	27-3011.00	Radio and Television Announcers
27-3012	Public Address System and Other Announcers	27-3012.00	Public Address System and Other Announcers

SOC Code and Title		O*NET-SOC Code and Title	
27-3021	Broadcast News Analysts	27-3021.00	Broadcast News Analysts
27-3022	Reporters and Correspondents	27-3022.00	Reporters and Correspondents
27-3031	Public Relations Specialists	27-3031.00	Public Relations Specialists
27-3041	Editors	27-3041.00	Editors
27-3042	Technical Writers	27-3042.00	Technical Writers
27-3043	Writers and Authors	27-3043.00	Writers and Authors
27-3043	Writers and Authors	27-3043.01	Poets and Lyricists
27-3043	Writers and Authors	27-3043.02	Creative Writers
27-3043	Writers and Authors	27-3043.03	Caption Writers
27-3043	Writers and Authors	27-3043.04	Copy Writers
27-3091	Interpreters and Translators	27-3091.00	Interpreters and Translators
27-3099	Media and Communication Workers, All Other	27-3099.99	Media and Communication Workers, All Other
27-4011	Audio and Video Equipment Technicians	27-4011.00	Audio and Video Equipment Technicians
27-4012	Broadcast Technicians	27-4012.00	Broadcast Technicians
27-4013	Radio Operators	27-4013.00	Radio Operators
27-4014	Sound Engineering Technicians	27-4014.00	Sound Engineering Technicians
27-4021	Photographers	27-4021.00	Photographers
27-4021	Photographers	27-4021.01	Professional Photographers
27-4021	Photographers	27-4021.02	Photographers, Scientific
27-4031	Camera Operators, Television, Video, and Motion Picture	27-4031.00	Camera Operators, Television, Video, and Motion Picture
27-4032	Film and Video Editors	27-4032.00	Film and Video Editors
27-4099	Media and Communication Equipment Workers, All Other	27-4099.99	Media and Communication Equipment Workers, All Other
29-1011	Chiropractors	29-1011.00	Chiropractors
29-1021	Dentists, General	29-1021.00	Dentists, General
29-1022	Oral and Maxillofacial Surgeons	29-1022.00	Oral and Maxillofacial Surgeons
29-1023	Orthodontists	29-1023.00	Orthodontists
29-1024	Prosthodontists	29-1024.00	Prosthodontists
29-1029	Dentists, All Other Specialists	29-1029.99	Dentists, All Other Specialists
29-1031	Dietitians and Nutritionists	29-1031.00	Dietitians and Nutritionists
29-1041	Optometrists	29-1041.00	Optometrists
29-1051	Pharmacists	29-1051.00	Pharmacists
29-1061	Anesthesiologists	29-1061.00	Anesthesiologists
29-1062	Family and General Practitioners	29-1062.00	Family and General Practitioners
29-1063	Internists, General	29-1063.00	Internists, General
29-1064	Obstetricians and Gynecologists	29-1064.00	Obstetricians and Gynecologists

SOC Code and Title		O*NET-SOC Code and Title	
29-1065	Pediatricians, General	29-1065.00	Pediatricians, General
29-1066	Psychiatrists	29-1066.00	Psychiatrists
29-1067	Surgeons	29-1067.00	Surgeons
29-1069	Physicians and Surgeons, All Other	29-1069.99	Physicians and Surgeons, All Other
29-1071	Physician Assistants	29-1071.00	Physician Assistants
29-1081	Podiatrists	29-1081.00	Podiatrists
29-1111	Registered Nurses	29-1111.00	Registered Nurses
29-1121	Audiologists	29-1121.00	Audiologists
29-1122	Occupational Therapists	29-1122.00	Occupational Therapists
29-1123	Physical Therapists	29-1123.00	Physical Therapists
29-1124	Radiation Therapists	29-1124.00	Radiation Therapists
29-1125	Recreational Therapists	29-1125.00	Recreational Therapists
29-1126	Respiratory Therapists	29-1126.00	Respiratory Therapists
29-1127	Speech-Language Pathologists	29-1127.00	Speech-Language Pathologists
29-1129	Therapists, All Other	29-1129.99	Therapists, All Other
29-1131	Veterinarians	29-1131.00	Veterinarians
29-1199	Health Diagnosing and Treating Practitioners, All Other	29-1199.99	Health Diagnosing and Treating Practitioners, All Other
29-2011	Medical and Clinical Laboratory Technologists	29-2011.00	Medical and Clinical Laboratory Technologists
29-2012	Medical and Clinical Laboratory Technicians	29-2012.00	Medical and Clinical Laboratory Technicians
29-2021	Dental Hygienists	29-2021.00	Dental Hygienists
29-2031	Cardiovascular Technologists and Technicians	29-2031.00	Cardiovascular Technologists and Technicians
29-2032	Diagnostic Medical Sonographers	29-2032.00	Diagnostic Medical Sonographers
29-2033	Nuclear Medicine Technologists	29-2033.00	Nuclear Medicine Technologists
29-2034	Radiologic Technologists and Technicians	29-2034.00	Radiologic Technologists and Technicians
29-2034	Radiologic Technologists and Technicians	29-2034.01	Radiologic Technologists
29-2034	Radiologic Technologists and Technicians	29-2034.02	Radiologic Technicians
29-2041	Emergency Medical Technicians and Paramedics	29-2041.00	Emergency Medical Technicians and Paramedics
29-2051	Dietetic Technicians	29-2051.00	Dietetic Technicians
29-2052	Pharmacy Technicians	29-2052.00	Pharmacy Technicians
29-2053	Psychiatric Technicians	29-2053.00	Psychiatric Technicians
29-2054	Respiratory Therapy Technicians	29-2054.00	Respiratory Therapy Technicians
29-2055	Surgical Technologists	29-2055.00	Surgical Technologists
29-2056	Veterinary Technologists and Technicians	29-2056.00	Veterinary Technologists and Technicians
29-2061	Licensed Practical and Licensed Vocational Nurses	29-2061.00	Licensed Practical and Licensed Vocational Nurses
29-2071	Medical Records and Health Information Technicians	29-2071.00	Medical Records and Health Information Technicians
29-2081	Opticians, Dispensing	29-2081.00	Opticians, Dispensing
29-2091	Orthotists and Prosthetists	29-2091.00	Orthotists and Prosthetists

SOC Code and Title		O*NET-SOC Code and Title	
29-2099	Health Technologists and Technicians, All Other	29-2099.99	Health Technologists and Technicians, All Other
29-9011	Occupational Health and Safety Specialists	29-9011.00	Occupational Health and Safety Specialists
29-9012	Occupational Health and Safety Technicians	29-9012.00	Occupational Health and Safety Technicians
29-9091	Athletic Trainers	29-9091.00	Athletic Trainers
29-9099	Healthcare Practitioners and Technical Workers, All Other	29-9099.99	Healthcare Practitioners and Technical Workers, All Other
31-1011	Home Health Aides	31-1011.00	Home Health Aides
31-1012	Nursing Aides, Orderlies, and Attendants	31-1012.00	Nursing Aides, Orderlies, and Attendants
31-1013	Psychiatric Aides	31-1013.00	Psychiatric Aides
31-2011	Occupational Therapist Assistants	31-2011.00	Occupational Therapist Assistants
31-2012	Occupational Therapist Aides	31-2012.00	Occupational Therapist Aides
31-2021	Physical Therapist Assistants	31-2021.00	Physical Therapist Assistants
31-2022	Physical Therapist Aides	31-2022.00	Physical Therapist Aides
31-9011	Massage Therapists	31-9011.00	Massage Therapists
31-9091	Dental Assistants	31-9091.00	Dental Assistants
31-9092	Medical Assistants	31-9092.00	Medical Assistants
31-9093	Medical Equipment Preparers	31-9093.00	Medical Equipment Preparers
31-9094	Medical Transcriptionists	31-9094.00	Medical Transcriptionists
31-9095	Pharmacy Aides	31-9095.00	Pharmacy Aides
31-9096	Veterinary Assistants and Laboratory Animal Caretakers	31-9096.00	Veterinary Assistants and Laboratory Animal Caretakers
31-9099	Healthcare Support Workers, All Other	31-9099.99	Healthcare Support Workers, All Other
33-1011	First-Line Supervisors/Managers of Correctional Officers	33-1011.00	First-Line Supervisors/Managers of Correctional Officers
33-1012	First-Line Supervisors/Managers of Police and Detectives	33-1012.00	First-Line Supervisors/Managers of Police and Detectives
33-1021	First-Line Supervisors/Managers of Fire Fighting and Prevention Workers	33-1021.00	First-Line Supervisors/Managers of Fire Fighting and Prevention Workers
33-1021	First-Line Supervisors/Managers of Fire Fighting and Prevention Workers	33-1021.01	Municipal Fire Fighting and Prevention Supervisors
33-1021	First-Line Supervisors/Managers of Fire Fighting and Prevention Workers	33-1021.02	Forest Fire Fighting and Prevention Supervisors
33-1099	First-Line Supervisors/Managers, Protective Service Workers, All Other	33-1099.99	First-Line Supervisors/Managers, Protective Service Workers, All Other
33-2011	Fire Fighters	33-2011.00	Fire Fighters
33-2011	Fire Fighters	33-2011.01	Municipal Fire Fighters
33-2011	Fire Fighters	33-2011.02	Forest Fire Fighters
33-2021	Fire Inspectors and Investigators	33-2021.00	Fire Inspectors and Investigators
33-2021	Fire Inspectors and Investigators	33-2021.01	Fire Inspectors

SOC Code and Title		O*NET-SOC Code and Title	
33-2021	Fire Inspectors and Investigators	33-2021.02	Fire Investigators
33-2022	Forest Fire Inspectors and Prevention Specialists	33-2022.00	Forest Fire Inspectors and Prevention Specialists
33-3011	Bailiffs	33-3011.00	Bailiffs
33-3012	Correctional Officers and Jailers	33-3012.00	Correctional Officers and Jailers
33-3021	Detectives and Criminal Investigators	33-3021.00	Detectives and Criminal Investigators
33-3021	Detectives and Criminal Investigators	33-3021.01	Police Detectives
33-3021	Detectives and Criminal Investigators	33-3021.02	Police Identification and Records Officers
33-3021	Detectives and Criminal Investigators	33-3021.03	Criminal Investigators and Special Agents
33-3021	Detectives and Criminal Investigators	33-3021.04	Child Support, Missing Persons, and Unemployment Insurance Fraud Investigators
33-3021	Detectives and Criminal Investigators	33-3021.05	Immigration and Customs Inspectors
33-3031	Fish and Game Wardens	33-3031.00	Fish and Game Wardens
33-3041	Parking Enforcement Workers	33-3041.00	Parking Enforcement Workers
33-3051	Police and Sheriff's Patrol Officers	33-3051.00	Police and Sheriff's Patrol Officers
33-3051	Police and Sheriff's Patrol Officers	33-3051.01	Police Patrol Officers
33-3051	Police and Sheriff's Patrol Officers	33-3051.02	Highway Patrol Pilots
33-3051	Police and Sheriff's Patrol Officers	33-3051.03	Sheriffs and Deputy Sheriffs
33-3052	Transit and Railroad Police	33-3052.00	Transit and Railroad Police
33-9011	Animal Control Workers	33-9011.00	Animal Control Workers
33-9021	Private Detectives and Investigators	33-9021.00	Private Detectives and Investigators
33-9031	Gaming Surveillance Officers and Gaming Investigators	33-9031.00	Gaming Surveillance Officers and Gaming Investigators
33-9032	Security Guards	33-9032.00	Security Guards
33-9091	Crossing Guards	33-9091.00	Crossing Guards
33-9092	Lifeguards, Ski Patrol, and Other Recreational Protective Service Workers	33-9092.00	Lifeguards, Ski Patrol, and Other Recreational Protective Service Workers
33-9099	Protective Service Workers, All Other	33-9099.99	Protective Service Workers, All Other
35-1011	Chefs and Head Cooks	35-1011.00	Chefs and Head Cooks
35-1012	First-Line Supervisors/Managers of Food Preparation and Serving Workers	35-1012.00	First-Line Supervisors/Managers of Food Preparation and Serving Workers
35-2011	Cooks, Fast Food	35-2011.00	Cooks, Fast Food
35-2012	Cooks, Institution and Cafeteria	35-2012.00	Cooks, Institution and Cafeteria
35-2013	Cooks, Private Household	35-2013.00	Cooks, Private Household
35-2014	Cooks, Restaurant	35-2014.00	Cooks, Restaurant
35-2015	Cooks, Short Order	35-2015.00	Cooks, Short Order
35-2019	Cooks, All Other	35-2019.99	Cooks, All Other
35-2021	Food Preparation Workers	35-2021.00	Food Preparation Workers
35-3011	Bartenders	35-3011.00	Bartenders

SOC Code and Title		O*NET-SOC Code and Title	
35-3021	Combined Food Preparation and Serving Workers, Including Fast Food	35-3021.00	Combined Food Preparation and Serving Workers, Including Fast Food
35-3022	Counter Attendants, Cafeteria, Food Concession, and Coffee Shop	35-3022.00	Counter Attendants, Cafeteria, Food Concession, and Coffee Shop
35-3031	Waiters and Waitresses	35-3031.00	Waiters and Waitresses
35-3041	Food Servers, Nonrestaurant	35-3041.00	Food Servers, Nonrestaurant
35-9011	Dining Room and Cafeteria Attendants and Bartender Helpers	35-9011.00	Dining Room and Cafeteria Attendants and Bartender Helpers
35-9021	Dishwashers	35-9021.00	Dishwashers
35-9031	Hosts and Hostesses, Restaurant, Lounge, and Coffee Shop	35-9031.00	Hosts and Hostesses, Restaurant, Lounge, and Coffee Shop
35-9099	Food Preparation and Serving Related Workers, All Other	35-9099.99	Food Preparation and Serving Related Workers, All Other
37-1011	First-Line Supervisors/Managers of Housekeeping and Janitorial Workers	37-1011.00	First-Line Supervisors/Managers of Housekeeping and Janitorial Workers
37-1011	First-Line Supervisors/Managers of Housekeeping and Janitorial Workers	37-1011.01	Housekeeping Supervisors
37-1011	First-Line Supervisors/Managers of Housekeeping and Janitorial Workers	37-1011.02	Janitorial Supervisors
37-1012	First-Line Supervisors/Managers of Landscaping, Lawn Service, and Groundskeeping Workers	37-1012.00	First-Line Supervisors/Managers of Landscaping, Lawn Service, and Groundskeeping Workers
37-1012	First-Line Supervisors/Managers of Landscaping, Lawn Service, and Groundskeeping Workers	37-1012.01	Lawn Service Managers
37-1012	First-Line Supervisors/Managers of Landscaping, Lawn Service, and Groundskeeping Workers	37-1012.02	First-Line Supervisors and Manager/Supervisors—Landscaping Workers
37-2011	Janitors and Cleaners, Except Maids and Housekeeping Cleaners	37-2011.00	Janitors and Cleaners, Except Maids and Housekeeping Cleaners
37-2012	Maids and Housekeeping Cleaners	37-2012.00	Maids and Housekeeping Cleaners
37-2019	Building Cleaning Workers, All Other	37-2019.99	Building Cleaning Workers, All Other
37-2021	Pest Control Workers	37-2021.00	Pest Control Workers
37-3011	Landscaping and Groundskeeping Workers	37-3011.00	Landscaping and Groundskeeping Workers
37-3012	Pesticide Handlers, Sprayers, and Applicators, Vegetation	37-3012.00	Pesticide Handlers, Sprayers, and Applicators, Vegetation
37-3013	Tree Trimmers and Pruners	37-3013.00	Tree Trimmers and Pruners
37-3019	Grounds Maintenance Workers, All Other	37-3019.99	Grounds Maintenance Workers, All Other
39-1011	Gaming Supervisors	39-1011.00	Gaming Supervisors
39-1012	Slot Key Persons	39-1012.00	Slot Key Persons
39-1021	First-Line Supervisors/Managers of Personal Service Workers	39-1021.00	First-Line Supervisors/Managers of Personal Service Workers
39-2011	Animal Trainers	39-2011.00	Animal Trainers

SOC Code and Title		O*NET-SOC Code and Title	
39-2021	Nonfarm Animal Caretakers	39-2021.00	Nonfarm Animal Caretakers
39-3011	Gaming Dealers	39-3011.00	Gaming Dealers
39-3012	Gaming and Sports Book Writers and Runners	39-3012.00	Gaming and Sports Book Writers and Runners
39-3019	Gaming Service Workers, All Other	39-3019.99	Gaming Service Workers, All Other
39-3021	Motion Picture Projectionists	39-3021.00	Motion Picture Projectionists
39-3031	Ushers, Lobby Attendants, and Ticket Takers	39-3031.00	Ushers, Lobby Attendants, and Ticket Takers
39-3091	Amusement and Recreation Attendants	39-3091.00	Amusement and Recreation Attendants
39-3092	Costume Attendants	39-3092.00	Costume Attendants
39-3093	Locker Room, Coatroom, and Dressing Room Attendants	39-3093.00	Locker Room, Coatroom, and Dressing Room Attendants
39-3099	Entertainment Attendants and Related Workers, All Other	39-3099.99	Entertainment Attendants and Related Workers, All Other
39-4011	Embalmers	39-4011.00	Embalmers
39-4021	Funeral Attendants	39-4021.00	Funeral Attendants
39-5011	Barbers	39-5011.00	Barbers
39-5012	Hairdressers, Hairstylists, and Cosmetologists	39-5012.00	Hairdressers, Hairstylists, and Cosmetologists
39-5091	Makeup Artists, Theatrical and Performance	39-5091.00	Makeup Artists, Theatrical and Performance
39-5092	Manicurists and Pedicurists	39-5092.00	Manicurists and Pedicurists
39-5093	Shampooers	39-5093.00	Shampooers
39-5094	Skin Care Specialists	39-5094.00	Skin Care Specialists
39-6011	Baggage Porters and Bellhops	39-6011.00	Baggage Porters and Bellhops
39-6012	Concierges	39-6012.00	Concierges
39-6021	Tour Guides and Escorts	39-6021.00	Tour Guides and Escorts
39-6022	Travel Guides	39-6022.00	Travel Guides
39-6031	Flight Attendants	39-6031.00	Flight Attendants
39-6032	Transportation Attendants, Except Flight Attendants and Baggage Porters	39-6032.00	Transportation Attendants, Except Flight Attendants and Baggage Porters
39-9011	Child Care Workers	39-9011.00	Child Care Workers
39-9021	Personal and Home Care Aides	39-9021.00	Personal and Home Care Aides
39-9031	Fitness Trainers and Aerobics Instructors	39-9031.00	Fitness Trainers and Aerobics Instructors
39-9032	Recreation Workers	39-9032.00	Recreation Workers
39-9041	Residential Advisors	39-9041.00	Residential Advisors
39-9099	Personal Care and Service Workers, All Other	39-9099.99	Personal Care and Service Workers, All Other
41-1011	First-Line Supervisors/Managers of Retail Sales Workers	41-1011.00	First-Line Supervisors/Managers of Retail Sales Workers
41-1012	First-Line Supervisors/Managers of Non-Retail Sales Workers	41-1012.00	First-Line Supervisors/Managers of Non-Retail Sales Workers
41-2011	Cashiers	41-2011.00	Cashiers

SOC Code and Title		O*NET-SOC Code and Title	
41-2012	Gaming Change Persons and Booth Cashiers	41-2012.00	Gaming Change Persons and Booth Cashiers
41-2021	Counter and Rental Clerks	41-2021.00	Counter and Rental Clerks
41-2022	Parts Salespersons	41-2022.00	Parts Salespersons
41-2031	Retail Salespersons	41-2031.00	Retail Salespersons
41-3011	Advertising Sales Agents	41-3011.00	Advertising Sales Agents
41-3021	Insurance Sales Agents	41-3021.00	Insurance Sales Agents
41-3031	Securities, Commodities, and Financial Services Sales Agents	41-3031.00	Securities, Commodities, and Financial Services Sales Agents
41-3031	Securities, Commodities, and Financial Services Sales Agents	41-3031.01	Sales Agents, Securities and Commodities
41-3031	Securities, Commodities, and Financial Services Sales Agents	41-3031.02	Sales Agents, Financial Services
41-3041	Travel Agents	41-3041.00	Travel Agents
41-3099	Sales Representatives, Services, All Other	41-3099.99	Sales Representatives, Services, All Other
41-4011	Sales Representatives, Wholesale and Manufacturing, Technical and Scientific Products	41-4011.00	Sales Representatives, Wholesale and Manufacturing, Technical and Scientific Products
41-4011	Sales Representatives, Wholesale and Manufacturing, Technical and Scientific Products	41-4011.01	Sales Representatives, Agricultural
41-4011	Sales Representatives, Wholesale and Manufacturing, Technical and Scientific Products	41-4011.02	Sales Representatives, Chemical and Pharmaceutical
41-4011	Sales Representatives, Wholesale and Manufacturing, Technical and Scientific Products	41-4011.03	Sales Representatives, Electrical/Electronic
41-4011	Sales Representatives, Wholesale and Manufacturing, Technical and Scientific Products	41-4011.04	Sales Representatives, Mechanical Equipment and Supplies
41-4011	Sales Representatives, Wholesale and Manufacturing, Technical and Scientific Products	41-4011.05	Sales Representatives, Medical
41-4011	Sales Representatives, Wholesale and Manufacturing, Technical and Scientific Products	41-4011.06	Sales Representatives, Instruments
41-4012	Sales Representatives, Wholesale and Manufacturing, Except Technical and Scientific Products	41-4012.00	Sales Representatives, Wholesale and Manufacturing, Except Technical and Scientific Products
41-9011	Demonstrators and Product Promoters	41-9011.00	Demonstrators and Product Promoters
41-9012	Models	41-9012.00	Models
41-9021	Real Estate Brokers	41-9021.00	Real Estate Brokers
41-9022	Real Estate Sales Agents	41-9022.00	Real Estate Sales Agents
41-9031	Sales Engineers	41-9031.00	Sales Engineers
41-9041	Telemarketers	41-9041.00	Telemarketers
41-9091	Door-To-Door Sales Workers, News and Street Vendors, and Related Workers	41-9091.00	Door-To-Door Sales Workers, News and Street Vendors, and Related Workers
41-9099	Sales and Related Workers, All Other	41-9099.99	Sales and Related Workers, All Other

SOC Code and Title		O*NET-SOC Code and Title	
43-1011	First-Line Supervisors/Managers of Office and Administrative Support Workers	43-1011.00	First-Line Supervisors/Managers of Office and Administrative Support Workers
43-1011	First-Line Supervisors/Managers of Office and Administrative Support Workers	43-1011.01	First-Line Supervisors, Customer Service
43-1011	First-Line Supervisors/Managers of Office and Administrative Support Workers	43-1011.02	First-Line Supervisors, Administrative Support
43-2011	Switchboard Operators, Including Answering Service	43-2011.00	Switchboard Operators, Including Answering Service
43-2021	Telephone Operators	43-2021.00	Telephone Operators
43-2021	Telephone Operators	43-2021.01	Directory Assistance Operators
43-2021	Telephone Operators	43-2021.02	Central Office Operators
43-2099	Communications Equipment Operators, All Other	43-2099.99	Communications Equipment Operators, All Other
43-3011	Bill and Account Collectors	43-3011.00	Bill and Account Collectors
43-3021	Billing and Posting Clerks and Machine Operators	43-3021.00	Billing and Posting Clerks and Machine Operators
43-3021	Billing and Posting Clerks and Machine Operators	43-3021.01	Statement Clerks
43-3021	Billing and Posting Clerks and Machine Operators	43-3021.02	Billing, Cost, and Rate Clerks
43-3021	Billing and Posting Clerks and Machine Operators	43-3021.03	Billing, Posting, and Calculating Machine Operators
43-3031	Bookkeeping, Accounting, and Auditing Clerks	43-3031.00	Bookkeeping, Accounting, and Auditing Clerks
43-3041	Gaming Cage Workers	43-3041.00	Gaming Cage Workers
43-3051	Payroll and Timekeeping Clerks	43-3051.00	Payroll and Timekeeping Clerks
43-3061	Procurement Clerks	43-3061.00	Procurement Clerks
43-3071	Tellers	43-3071.00	Tellers
43-4011	Brokerage Clerks	43-4011.00	Brokerage Clerks
43-4021	Correspondence Clerks	43-4021.00	Correspondence Clerks
43-4031	Court, Municipal, and License Clerks	43-4031.00	Court, Municipal, and License Clerks
43-4031	Court, Municipal, and License Clerks	43-4031.01	Court Clerks
43-4031	Court, Municipal, and License Clerks	43-4031.02	Municipal Clerks
43-4031	Court, Municipal, and License Clerks	43-4031.03	License Clerks
43-4041	Credit Authorizers, Checkers, and Clerks	43-4041.00	Credit Authorizers, Checkers, and Clerks
43-4041	Credit Authorizers, Checkers, and Clerks	43-4041.01	Credit Authorizers
43-4041	Credit Authorizers, Checkers, and Clerks	43-4041.02	Credit Checkers
43-4051	Customer Service Representatives	43-4051.00	Customer Service Representatives
43-4051	Customer Service Representatives	43-4051.01	Adjustment Clerks
43-4051	Customer Service Representatives	43-4051.02	Customer Service Representatives, Utilities
43-4061	Eligibility Interviewers, Government Programs	43-4061.00	Eligibility Interviewers, Government Programs
43-4061	Eligibility Interviewers, Government Programs	43-4061.01	Claims Takers, Unemployment Benefits
43-4061	Eligibility Interviewers, Government Programs	43-4061.02	Welfare Eligibility Workers and Interviewers
43-4071	File Clerks	43-4071.00	File Clerks
43-4081	Hotel, Motel, and Resort Desk Clerks	43-4081.00	Hotel, Motel, and Resort Desk Clerks

SOC Code and Title		O*NET-SOC Code and Title	
43-4111	Interviewers, Except Eligibility and Loan	43-4111.00	Interviewers, Except Eligibility and Loan
43-4121	Library Assistants, Clerical	43-4121.00	Library Assistants, Clerical
43-4131	Loan Interviewers and Clerks	43-4131.00	Loan Interviewers and Clerks
43-4141	New Accounts Clerks	43-4141.00	New Accounts Clerks
43-4151	Order Clerks	43-4151.00	Order Clerks
43-4161	Human Resources Assistants, Except Payroll and Timekeeping	43-4161.00	Human Resources Assistants, Except Payroll and Timekeeping
43-4171	Receptionists and Information Clerks	43-4171.00	Receptionists and Information Clerks
43-4181	Reservation and Transportation Ticket Agents and Travel Clerks	43-4181.00	Reservation and Transportation Ticket Agents and Travel Clerks
43-4181	Reservation and Transportation Ticket Agents and Travel Clerks	43-4181.01	Travel Clerks
43-4181	Reservation and Transportation Ticket Agents and Travel Clerks	43-4181.02	Reservation and Transportation Ticket Agents
43-4199	Information and Record Clerks, All Other	43-4199.99	Information and Record Clerks, All Other
43-5011	Cargo and Freight Agents	43-5011.00	Cargo and Freight Agents
43-5021	Couriers and Messengers	43-5021.00	Couriers and Messengers
43-5031	Police, Fire, and Ambulance Dispatchers	43-5031.00	Police, Fire, and Ambulance Dispatchers
43-5032	Dispatchers, Except Police, Fire, and Ambulance	43-5032.00	Dispatchers, Except Police, Fire, and Ambulance
43-5041	Meter Readers, Utilities	43-5041.00	Meter Readers, Utilities
43-5051	Postal Service Clerks	43-5051.00	Postal Service Clerks
43-5052	Postal Service Mail Carriers	43-5052.00	Postal Service Mail Carriers
43-5053	Postal Service Mail Sorters, Processors, and Processing Machine Operators	43-5053.00	Postal Service Mail Sorters, Processors, and Processing Machine Operators
43-5061	Production, Planning, and Expediting Clerks	43-5061.00	Production, Planning, and Expediting Clerks
43-5071	Shipping, Receiving, and Traffic Clerks	43-5071.00	Shipping, Receiving, and Traffic Clerks
43-5081	Stock Clerks and Order Fillers	43-5081.00	Stock Clerks and Order Fillers
43-5081	Stock Clerks and Order Fillers	43-5081.01	Stock Clerks, Sales Floor
43-5081	Stock Clerks and Order Fillers	43-5081.02	Marking Clerks
43-5081	Stock Clerks and Order Fillers	43-5081.03	Stock Clerks—Stockroom, Warehouse, or Storage Yard
43-5081	Stock Clerks and Order Fillers	43-5081.04	Order Fillers, Wholesale and Retail Sales
43-5111	Weighers, Measurers, Checkers, and Samplers, Recordkeeping	43-5111.00	Weighers, Measurers, Checkers, and Samplers, Recordkeeping
43-6011	Executive Secretaries and Administrative Assistants	43-6011.00	Executive Secretaries and Administrative Assistants
43-6012	Legal Secretaries	43-6012.00	Legal Secretaries
43-6013	Medical Secretaries	43-6013.00	Medical Secretaries
43-6014	Secretaries, Except Legal, Medical, and Executive	43-6014.00	Secretaries, Except Legal, Medical, and Executive
43-9011	Computer Operators	43-9011.00	Computer Operators

SOC-to-O*NET Cross-Reference Table

SOC Code and Title		O*NET-SOC Code and Title	
43-9021	Data Entry Keyers	43-9021.00	Data Entry Keyers
43-9022	Word Processors and Typists	43-9022.00	Word Processors and Typists
43-9031	Desktop Publishers	43-9031.00	Desktop Publishers
43-9041	Insurance Claims and Policy Processing Clerks	43-9041.00	Insurance Claims and Policy Processing Clerks
43-9041	Insurance Claims and Policy Processing Clerks	43-9041.01	Insurance Claims Clerks
43-9041	Insurance Claims and Policy Processing Clerks	43-9041.02	Insurance Policy Processing Clerks
43-9051	Mail Clerks and Mail Machine Operators, Except Postal Service	43-9051.00	Mail Clerks and Mail Machine Operators, Except Postal Service
43-9051	Mail Clerks and Mail Machine Operators, Except Postal Service	43-9051.01	Mail Machine Operators, Preparation and Handling
43-9051	Mail Clerks and Mail Machine Operators, Except Postal Service	43-9051.02	Mail Clerks, Except Mail Machine Operators and Postal Service
43-9061	Office Clerks, General	43-9061.00	Office Clerks, General
43-9071	Office Machine Operators, Except Computer	43-9071.00	Office Machine Operators, Except Computer
43-9071	Office Machine Operators, Except Computer	43-9071.01	Duplicating Machine Operators
43-9081	Proofreaders and Copy Markers	43-9081.00	Proofreaders and Copy Markers
43-9111	Statistical Assistants	43-9111.00	Statistical Assistants
43-9199	Office and Administrative Support Workers, All Other	43-9199.99	Office and Administrative Support Workers, All Other
45-1011	First-Line Supervisors/Managers of Farming, Fishing, and Forestry Workers	45-1011.00	First-Line Supervisors/Managers of Farming, Fishing, and Forestry Workers
45-1011	First-Line Supervisors/Managers of Farming, Fishing, and Forestry Workers	45-1011.01	First-Line Supervisors and Manager/Supervisors—Agricultural Crop Workers
45-1011	First-Line Supervisors/Managers of Farming, Fishing, and Forestry Workers	45-1011.02	First-Line Supervisors and Manager/Supervisors—Animal Husbandry Workers
45-1011	First-Line Supervisors/Managers of Farming, Fishing, and Forestry Workers	45-1011.03	First-Line Supervisors and Manager/Supervisors—Animal Care Workers, Except Livestock
45-1011	First-Line Supervisors/Managers of Farming, Fishing, and Forestry Workers	45-1011.04	First-Line Supervisors and Manager/Supervisors—Horticultural Workers
45-1011	First-Line Supervisors/Managers of Farming, Fishing, and Forestry Workers	45-1011.05	First-Line Supervisors and Manager/Supervisors—Logging Workers
45-1011	First-Line Supervisors/Managers of Farming, Fishing, and Forestry Workers	45-1011.06	First-Line Supervisors and Manager/Supervisors—Fishery Workers
45-2011	Agricultural Inspectors	45-2011.00	Agricultural Inspectors
45-2021	Animal Breeders	45-2021.00	Animal Breeders
45-2031	Farm Labor Contractors	45-2031.00	Farm Labor Contractors
45-2041	Graders and Sorters, Agricultural Products	45-2041.00	Graders and Sorters, Agricultural Products
45-2091	Agricultural Equipment Operators	45-2091.00	Agricultural Equipment Operators
45-2092	Farmworkers and Laborers, Crop, Nursery, and Greenhouse	45-2092.00	Farmworkers and Laborers, Crop, Nursery, and Greenhouse

SOC Code and Title		O*NET-SOC Code and Title	
45-2092	Farmworkers and Laborers, Crop, Nursery, and Greenhouse	45-2092.01	Nursery Workers
45-2092	Farmworkers and Laborers, Crop, Nursery, and Greenhouse	45-2092.02	General Farmworkers
45-2093	Farmworkers, Farm and Ranch Animals	45-2093.00	Farmworkers, Farm and Ranch Animals
45-2099	Agricultural Workers, All Other	45-2099.99	Agricultural Workers, All Other
45-3011	Fishers and Related Fishing Workers	45-3011.00	Fishers and Related Fishing Workers
45-3021	Hunters and Trappers	45-3021.00	Hunters and Trappers
45-4011	Forest and Conservation Workers	45-4011.00	Forest and Conservation Workers
45-4021	Fallers	45-4021.00	Fallers
45-4022	Logging Equipment Operators	45-4022.00	Logging Equipment Operators
45-4022	Logging Equipment Operators	45-4022.01	Logging Tractor Operators
45-4023	Log Graders and Scalers	45-4023.00	Log Graders and Scalers
45-4029	Logging Workers, All Other	45-4029.99	Logging Workers, All Other
47-1011	First-Line Supervisors/Managers of Construction Trades and Extraction Workers	47-1011.00	First-Line Supervisors/Managers of Construction Trades and Extraction Workers
47-1011	First-Line Supervisors/Managers of Construction Trades and Extraction Workers	47-1011.01	First-Line Supervisors and Manager/Supervisors—Construction Trades Workers
47-1011	First-Line Supervisors/Managers of Construction Trades and Extraction Workers	47-1011.02	First-Line Supervisors and Manager/Supervisors—Extractive Workers
47-2011	Boilermakers	47-2011.00	Boilermakers
47-2021	Brickmasons and Blockmasons	47-2021.00	Brickmasons and Blockmasons
47-2022	Stonemasons	47-2022.00	Stonemasons
47-2031	Carpenters	47-2031.00	Carpenters
47-2031	Carpenters	47-2031.01	Construction Carpenters
47-2031	Carpenters	47-2031.02	Rough Carpenters
47-2031	Carpenters	47-2031.03	Carpenter Assemblers and Repairers
47-2031	Carpenters	47-2031.04	Ship Carpenters and Joiners
47-2031	Carpenters	47-2031.05	Boat Builders and Shipwrights
47-2031	Carpenters	47-2031.06	Brattice Builders
47-2041	Carpet Installers	47-2041.00	Carpet Installers
47-2042	Floor Layers, Except Carpet, Wood, and Hard Tiles	47-2042.00	Floor Layers, Except Carpet, Wood, and Hard Tiles
47-2043	Floor Sanders and Finishers	47-2043.00	Floor Sanders and Finishers
47-2044	Tile and Marble Setters	47-2044.00	Tile and Marble Setters
47-2051	Cement Masons and Concrete Finishers	47-2051.00	Cement Masons and Concrete Finishers
47-2053	Terrazzo Workers and Finishers	47-2053.00	Terrazzo Workers and Finishers
47-2061	Construction Laborers	47-2061.00	Construction Laborers
47-2071	Paving, Surfacing, and Tamping Equipment Operators	47-2071.00	Paving, Surfacing, and Tamping Equipment Operators

SOC Code and Title		O*NET-SOC Code and Title	
47-2072	Pile-Driver Operators	47-2072.00	Pile-Driver Operators
47-2073	Operating Engineers and Other Construction Equipment Operators	47-2073.00	Operating Engineers and Other Construction Equipment Operators
47-2073	Operating Engineers and Other Construction Equipment Operators	47-2073.01	Grader, Bulldozer, and Scraper Operators
47-2073	Operating Engineers and Other Construction Equipment Operators	47-2073.02	Operating Engineers
47-2081	Drywall and Ceiling Tile Installers	47-2081.00	Drywall and Ceiling Tile Installers
47-2081	Drywall and Ceiling Tile Installers	47-2081.01	Ceiling Tile Installers
47-2081	Drywall and Ceiling Tile Installers	47-2081.02	Drywall Installers
47-2082	Tapers	47-2082.00	Tapers
47-2111	Electricians	47-2111.00	Electricians
47-2121	Glaziers	47-2121.00	Glaziers
47-2131	Insulation Workers, Floor, Ceiling, and Wall	47-2131.00	Insulation Workers, Floor, Ceiling, and Wall
47-2132	Insulation Workers, Mechanical	47-2132.00	Insulation Workers, Mechanical
47-2141	Painters, Construction and Maintenance	47-2141.00	Painters, Construction and Maintenance
47-2142	Paperhangers	47-2142.00	Paperhangers
47-2151	Pipelayers	47-2151.00	Pipelayers
47-2152	Plumbers, Pipefitters, and Steamfitters	47-2152.00	Plumbers, Pipefitters, and Steamfitters
47-2152	Plumbers, Pipefitters, and Steamfitters	47-2152.01	Pipe Fitters
47-2152	Plumbers, Pipefitters, and Steamfitters	47-2152.02	Plumbers
47-2152	Plumbers, Pipefitters, and Steamfitters	47-2152.03	Pipelaying Fitters
47-2161	Plasterers and Stucco Masons	47-2161.00	Plasterers and Stucco Masons
47-2171	Reinforcing Iron and Rebar Workers	47-2171.00	Reinforcing Iron and Rebar Workers
47-2181	Roofers	47-2181.00	Roofers
47-2211	Sheet Metal Workers	47-2211.00	Sheet Metal Workers
47-2221	Structural Iron and Steel Workers	47-2221.00	Structural Iron and Steel Workers
47-3011	Helpers—Brickmasons, Blockmasons, Stonemasons, and Tile and Marble Setters	47-3011.00	Helpers—Brickmasons, Blockmasons, Stonemasons, and Tile and Marble Setters
47-3012	Helpers—Carpenters	47-3012.00	Helpers—Carpenters
47-3013	Helpers—Electricians	47-3013.00	Helpers—Electricians
47-3014	Helpers—Painters, Paperhangers, Plasterers, and Stucco Masons	47-3014.00	Helpers—Painters, Paperhangers, Plasterers, and Stucco Masons
47-3015	Helpers—Pipelayers, Plumbers, Pipefitters, and Steamfitters	47-3015.00	Helpers—Pipelayers, Plumbers, Pipefitters, and Steamfitters
47-3016	Helpers—Roofers	47-3016.00	Helpers—Roofers
47-3019	Helpers, Construction Trades, All Other	47-3019.99	Helpers, Construction Trades, All Other
47-4011	Construction and Building Inspectors	47-4011.00	Construction and Building Inspectors

SOC Code and Title		O*NET-SOC Code and Title	
47-4021	Elevator Installers and Repairers	47-4021.00	Elevator Installers and Repairers
47-4031	Fence Erectors	47-4031.00	Fence Erectors
47-4041	Hazardous Materials Removal Workers	47-4041.00	Hazardous Materials Removal Workers
47-4041	Hazardous Materials Removal Workers	47-4041.01	Irradiated-Fuel Handlers
47-4051	Highway Maintenance Workers	47-4051.00	Highway Maintenance Workers
47-4061	Rail-Track Laying and Maintenance Equipment Operators	47-4061.00	Rail-Track Laying and Maintenance Equipment Operators
47-4071	Septic Tank Servicers and Sewer Pipe Cleaners	47-4071.00	Septic Tank Servicers and Sewer Pipe Cleaners
47-4091	Segmental Pavers	47-4091.00	Segmental Pavers
47-4099	Construction and Related Workers, All Other	47-4099.99	Construction and Related Workers, All Other
47-5011	Derrick Operators, Oil and Gas	47-5011.00	Derrick Operators, Oil and Gas
47-5012	Rotary Drill Operators, Oil and Gas	47-5012.00	Rotary Drill Operators, Oil and Gas
47-5013	Service Unit Operators, Oil, Gas, and Mining	47-5013.00	Service Unit Operators, Oil, Gas, and Mining
47-5021	Earth Drillers, Except Oil and Gas	47-5021.00	Earth Drillers, Except Oil and Gas
47-5021	Earth Drillers, Except Oil and Gas	47-5021.01	Construction Drillers
47-5021	Earth Drillers, Except Oil and Gas	47-5021.02	Well and Core Drill Operators
47-5031	Explosives Workers, Ordnance Handling Experts, and Blasters	47-5031.00	Explosives Workers, Ordnance Handling Experts, and Blasters
47-5041	Continuous Mining Machine Operators	47-5041.00	Continuous Mining Machine Operators
47-5042	Mine Cutting and Channeling Machine Operators	47-5042.00	Mine Cutting and Channeling Machine Operators
47-5049	Mining Machine Operators, All Other	47-5049.99	Mining Machine Operators, All Other
47-5051	Rock Splitters, Quarry	47-5051.00	Rock Splitters, Quarry
47-5061	Roof Bolters, Mining	47-5061.00	Roof Bolters, Mining
47-5071	Roustabouts, Oil and Gas	47-5071.00	Roustabouts, Oil and Gas
47-5081	Helpers—Extraction Workers	47-5081.00	Helpers—Extraction Workers
47-5099	Extraction Workers, All Other	47-5099.99	Extraction Workers, All Other
49-1011	First-Line Supervisors/Managers of Mechanics, Installers, and Repairers	49-1011.00	First-Line Supervisors/Managers of Mechanics, Installers, and Repairers
49-2011	Computer, Automated Teller, and Office Machine Repairers	49-2011.00	Computer, Automated Teller, and Office Machine Repairers
49-2011	Computer, Automated Teller, and Office Machine Repairers	49-2011.01	Automatic Teller Machine Servicers
49-2011	Computer, Automated Teller, and Office Machine Repairers	49-2011.02	Data Processing Equipment Repairers
49-2011	Computer, Automated Teller, and Office Machine Repairers	49-2011.03	Office Machine and Cash Register Servicers
49-2021	Radio Mechanics	49-2021.00	Radio Mechanics
49-2022	Telecommunications Equipment Installers and Repairers, Except Line Installers	49-2022.00	Telecommunications Equipment Installers and Repairers, Except Line Installers

SOC Code and Title		O*NET-SOC Code and Title	
49-2022	Telecommunications Equipment Installers and Repairers, Except Line Installers	49-2022.01	Central Office and PBX Installers and Repairers
49-2022	Telecommunications Equipment Installers and Repairers, Except Line Installers	49-2022.02	Frame Wirers, Central Office
49-2022	Telecommunications Equipment Installers and Repairers, Except Line Installers	49-2022.03	Communication Equipment Mechanics, Installers, and Repairers
49-2022	Telecommunications Equipment Installers and Repairers, Except Line Installers	49-2022.04	Telecommunications Facility Examiners
49-2022	Telecommunications Equipment Installers and Repairers, Except Line Installers	49-2022.05	Station Installers and Repairers, Telephone
49-2091	Avionics Technicians	49-2091.00	Avionics Technicians
49-2092	Electric Motor, Power Tool, and Related Repairers	49-2092.00	Electric Motor, Power Tool, and Related Repairers
49-2092	Electric Motor, Power Tool, and Related Repairers	49-2092.01	Electric Home Appliance and Power Tool Repairers
49-2092	Electric Motor, Power Tool, and Related Repairers	49-2092.02	Electric Motor and Switch Assemblers and Repairers
49-2092	Electric Motor, Power Tool, and Related Repairers	49-2092.03	Battery Repairers
49-2092	Electric Motor, Power Tool, and Related Repairers	49-2092.04	Transformer Repairers
49-2092	Electric Motor, Power Tool, and Related Repairers	49-2092.05	Electrical Parts Reconditioners
49-2092	Electric Motor, Power Tool, and Related Repairers	49-2092.06	Hand and Portable Power Tool Repairers
49-2093	Electrical and Electronics Installers and Repairers, Transportation Equipment	49-2093.00	Electrical and Electronics Installers and Repairers, Transportation Equipment
49-2094	Electrical and Electronics Repairers, Commercial and Industrial Equipment	49-2094.00	Electrical and Electronics Repairers, Commercial and Industrial Equipment
49-2095	Electrical and Electronics Repairers, Powerhouse, Substation, and Relay	49-2095.00	Electrical and Electronics Repairers, Powerhouse, Substation, and Relay
49-2096	Electronic Equipment Installers and Repairers, Motor Vehicles	49-2096.00	Electronic Equipment Installers and Repairers, Motor Vehicles
49-2097	Electronic Home Entertainment Equipment Installers and Repairers	49-2097.00	Electronic Home Entertainment Equipment Installers and Repairers
49-2098	Security and Fire Alarm Systems Installers	49-2098.00	Security and Fire Alarm Systems Installers
49-3011	Aircraft Mechanics and Service Technicians	49-3011.00	Aircraft Mechanics and Service Technicians
49-3011	Aircraft Mechanics and Service Technicians	49-3011.01	Airframe-and-Power-Plant Mechanics
49-3011	Aircraft Mechanics and Service Technicians	49-3011.02	Aircraft Engine Specialists
49-3011	Aircraft Mechanics and Service Technicians	49-3011.03	Aircraft Body and Bonded Structure Repairers
49-3021	Automotive Body and Related Repairers	49-3021.00	Automotive Body and Related Repairers
49-3022	Automotive Glass Installers and Repairers	49-3022.00	Automotive Glass Installers and Repairers
49-3023	Automotive Service Technicians and Mechanics	49-3023.00	Automotive Service Technicians and Mechanics
49-3023	Automotive Service Technicians and Mechanics	49-3023.01	Automotive Master Mechanics
49-3023	Automotive Service Technicians and Mechanics	49-3023.02	Automotive Specialty Technicians

SOC Code and Title		O*NET-SOC Code and Title	
49-3031	Bus and Truck Mechanics and Diesel Engine Specialists	49-3031.00	Bus and Truck Mechanics and Diesel Engine Specialists
49-3041	Farm Equipment Mechanics	49-3041.00	Farm Equipment Mechanics
49-3042	Mobile Heavy Equipment Mechanics, Except Engines	49-3042.00	Mobile Heavy Equipment Mechanics, Except Engines
49-3043	Rail Car Repairers	49-3043.00	Rail Car Repairers
49-3051	Motorboat Mechanics	49-3051.00	Motorboat Mechanics
49-3052	Motorcycle Mechanics	49-3052.00	Motorcycle Mechanics
49-3053	Outdoor Power Equipment and Other Small Engine Mechanics	49-3053.00	Outdoor Power Equipment and Other Small Engine Mechanics
49-3091	Bicycle Repairers	49-3091.00	Bicycle Repairers
49-3092	Recreational Vehicle Service Technicians	49-3092.00	Recreational Vehicle Service Technicians
49-3093	Tire Repairers and Changers	49-3093.00	Tire Repairers and Changers
49-9011	Mechanical Door Repairers	49-9011.00	Mechanical Door Repairers
49-9012	Control and Valve Installers and Repairers, Except Mechanical Door	49-9012.00	Control and Valve Installers and Repairers, Except Mechanical Door
49-9012	Control and Valve Installers and Repairers, Except Mechanical Door	49-9012.01	Electric Meter Installers and Repairers
49-9012	Control and Valve Installers and Repairers, Except Mechanical Door	49-9012.02	Valve and Regulator Repairers
49-9012	Control and Valve Installers and Repairers, Except Mechanical Door	49-9012.03	Meter Mechanics
49-9021	Heating, Air Conditioning, and Refrigeration Mechanics and Installers	49-9021.00	Heating, Air Conditioning, and Refrigeration Mechanics and Installers
49-9021	Heating, Air Conditioning, and Refrigeration Mechanics and Installers	49-9021.01	Heating and Air Conditioning Mechanics
49-9021	Heating, Air Conditioning, and Refrigeration Mechanics and Installers	49-9021.02	Refrigeration Mechanics
49-9031	Home Appliance Repairers	49-9031.00	Home Appliance Repairers
49-9031	Home Appliance Repairers	49-9031.01	Home Appliance Installers
49-9031	Home Appliance Repairers	49-9031.02	Gas Appliance Repairers
49-9041	Industrial Machinery Mechanics	49-9041.00	Industrial Machinery Mechanics
49-9042	Maintenance and Repair Workers, General	49-9042.00	Maintenance and Repair Workers, General
49-9043	Maintenance Workers, Machinery	49-9043.00	Maintenance Workers, Machinery
49-9044	Millwrights	49-9044.00	Millwrights
49-9045	Refractory Materials Repairers, Except Brickmasons	49-9045.00	Refractory Materials Repairers, Except Brickmasons
49-9051	Electrical Power-Line Installers and Repairers	49-9051.00	Electrical Power-Line Installers and Repairers
49-9052	Telecommunications Line Installers and Repairers	49-9052.00	Telecommunications Line Installers and Repairers
49-9061	Camera and Photographic Equipment Repairers	49-9061.00	Camera and Photographic Equipment Repairers
49-9062	Medical Equipment Repairers	49-9062.00	Medical Equipment Repairers

SOC Code and Title		O*NET-SOC Code and Title	
49-9063	Musical Instrument Repairers and Tuners	49-9063.00	Musical Instrument Repairers and Tuners
49-9063	Musical Instrument Repairers and Tuners	49-9063.01	Keyboard Instrument Repairers and Tuners
49-9063	Musical Instrument Repairers and Tuners	49-9063.02	Stringed Instrument Repairers and Tuners
49-9063	Musical Instrument Repairers and Tuners	49-9063.03	Reed or Wind Instrument Repairers and Tuners
49-9063	Musical Instrument Repairers and Tuners	49-9063.04	Percussion Instrument Repairers and Tuners
49-9064	Watch Repairers	49-9064.00	Watch Repairers
49-9069	Precision Instrument and Equipment Repairers, All Other	49-9069.99	Precision Instrument and Equipment Repairers, All Other
49-9091	Coin, Vending, and Amusement Machine Servicers and Repairers	49-9091.00	Coin, Vending, and Amusement Machine Servicers and Repairers
49-9092	Commercial Divers	49-9092.00	Commercial Divers
49-9093	Fabric Menders, Except Garment	49-9093.00	Fabric Menders, Except Garment
49-9094	Locksmiths and Safe Repairers	49-9094.00	Locksmiths and Safe Repairers
49-9095	Manufactured Building and Mobile Home Installers	49-9095.00	Manufactured Building and Mobile Home Installers
49-9096	Riggers	49-9096.00	Riggers
49-9097	Signal and Track Switch Repairers	49-9097.00	Signal and Track Switch Repairers
49-9098	Helpers—Installation, Maintenance, and Repair Workers	49-9098.00	Helpers—Installation, Maintenance, and Repair Workers
49-9099	Installation, Maintenance, and Repair Workers, All Other	49-9099.99	Installation, Maintenance, and Repair Workers, All Other
51-1011	First-Line Supervisors/Managers of Production and Operating Workers	51-1011.00	First-Line Supervisors/Managers of Production and Operating Workers
51-2011	Aircraft Structure, Surfaces, Rigging, and Systems Assemblers	51-2011.00	Aircraft Structure, Surfaces, Rigging, and Systems Assemblers
51-2011	Aircraft Structure, Surfaces, Rigging, and Systems Assemblers	51-2011.01	Aircraft Structure Assemblers, Precision
51-2011	Aircraft Structure, Surfaces, Rigging, and Systems Assemblers	51-2011.02	Aircraft Systems Assemblers, Precision
51-2011	Aircraft Structure, Surfaces, Rigging, and Systems Assemblers	51-2011.03	Aircraft Rigging Assemblers
51-2021	Coil Winders, Tapers, and Finishers	51-2021.00	Coil Winders, Tapers, and Finishers
51-2022	Electrical and Electronic Equipment Assemblers	51-2022.00	Electrical and Electronic Equipment Assemblers
51-2023	Electromechanical Equipment Assemblers	51-2023.00	Electromechanical Equipment Assemblers
51-2031	Engine and Other Machine Assemblers	51-2031.00	Engine and Other Machine Assemblers
51-2041	Structural Metal Fabricators and Fitters	51-2041.00	Structural Metal Fabricators and Fitters
51-2041	Structural Metal Fabricators and Fitters	51-2041.01	Metal Fabricators, Structural Metal Products
51-2041	Structural Metal Fabricators and Fitters	51-2041.02	Fitters, Structural Metal—Precision
51-2091	Fiberglass Laminators and Fabricators	51-2091.00	Fiberglass Laminators and Fabricators
51-2092	Team Assemblers	51-2092.00	Team Assemblers
51-2093	Timing Device Assemblers, Adjusters, and Calibrators	51-2093.00	Timing Device Assemblers, Adjusters, and Calibrators

SOC Code and Title		O*NET-SOC Code and Title	
51-2099	Assemblers and Fabricators, All Other	51-2099.99	Assemblers and Fabricators, All Other
51-3011	Bakers	51-3011.00	Bakers
51-3011	Bakers	51-3011.01	Bakers, Bread and Pastry
51-3011	Bakers	51-3011.02	Bakers, Manufacturing
51-3021	Butchers and Meat Cutters	51-3021.00	Butchers and Meat Cutters
51-3022	Meat, Poultry, and Fish Cutters and Trimmers	51-3022.00	Meat, Poultry, and Fish Cutters and Trimmers
51-3023	Slaughterers and Meat Packers	51-3023.00	Slaughterers and Meat Packers
51-3091	Food and Tobacco Roasting, Baking, and Drying Machine Operators and Tenders	51-3091.00	Food and Tobacco Roasting, Baking, and Drying Machine Operators and Tenders
51-3092	Food Batchmakers	51-3092.00	Food Batchmakers
51-3093	Food Cooking Machine Operators and Tenders	51-3093.00	Food Cooking Machine Operators and Tenders
51-4011	Computer-Controlled Machine Tool Operators, Metal and Plastic	51-4011.00	Computer-Controlled Machine Tool Operators, Metal and Plastic
51-4011	Computer-Controlled Machine Tool Operators, Metal and Plastic	51-4011.01	Numerical Control Machine Tool Operators and Tenders, Metal and Plastic
51-4012	Numerical Tool and Process Control Programmers	51-4012.00	Numerical Tool and Process Control Programmers
51-4021	Extruding and Drawing Machine Setters, Operators, and Tenders, Metal and Plastic	51-4021.00	Extruding and Drawing Machine Setters, Operators, and Tenders, Metal and Plastic
51-4022	Forging Machine Setters, Operators, and Tenders, Metal and Plastic	51-4022.00	Forging Machine Setters, Operators, and Tenders, Metal and Plastic
51-4023	Rolling Machine Setters, Operators, and Tenders, Metal and Plastic	51-4023.00	Rolling Machine Setters, Operators, and Tenders, Metal and Plastic
51-4031	Cutting, Punching, and Press Machine Setters, Operators, and Tenders, Metal and Plastic	51-4031.00	Cutting, Punching, and Press Machine Setters, Operators, and Tenders, Metal and Plastic
51-4031	Cutting, Punching, and Press Machine Setters, Operators, and Tenders, Metal and Plastic	51-4031.01	Sawing Machine Tool Setters and Set-Up Operators, Metal and Plastic
51-4031	Cutting, Punching, and Press Machine Setters, Operators, and Tenders, Metal and Plastic	51-4031.02	Punching Machine Setters and Set-Up Operators, Metal and Plastic
51-4031	Cutting, Punching, and Press Machine Setters, Operators, and Tenders, Metal and Plastic	51-4031.03	Press and Press Brake Machine Setters and Set-Up Operators, Metal and Plastic
51-4031	Cutting, Punching, and Press Machine Setters, Operators, and Tenders, Metal and Plastic	51-4031.04	Shear and Slitter Machine Setters and Set-Up Operators, Metal and Plastic
51-4032	Drilling and Boring Machine Tool Setters, Operators, and Tenders, Metal and Plastic	51-4032.00	Drilling and Boring Machine Tool Setters, Operators, and Tenders, Metal and Plastic
51-4033	Grinding, Lapping, Polishing, and Buffing Machine Tool Setters, Operators, and Tenders, Metal and Plastic	51-4033.00	Grinding, Lapping, Polishing, and Buffing Machine Tool Setters, Operators, and Tenders, Metal and Plastic
51-4033	Grinding, Lapping, Polishing, and Buffing Machine Tool Setters, Operators, and Tenders, Metal and Plastic	51-4033.01	Grinding, Honing, Lapping, and Deburring Machine Set-Up Operators
51-4033	Grinding, Lapping, Polishing, and Buffing Machine Tool Setters, Operators, and Tenders, Metal and Plastic	51-4033.02	Buffing and Polishing Set-Up Operators

SOC Code and Title	O*NET-SOC Code and Title
51-4034 Lathe and Turning Machine Tool Setters, Operators, and Tenders, Metal and Plastic	51-4034.00 Lathe and Turning Machine Tool Setters, Operators, and Tenders, Metal and Plastic
51-4035 Milling and Planing Machine Setters, Operators, and Tenders, Metal and Plastic	51-4035.00 Milling and Planing Machine Setters, Operators, and Tenders, Metal and Plastic
51-4041 Machinists	51-4041.00 Machinists
51-4051 Metal-Refining Furnace Operators and Tenders	51-4051.00 Metal-Refining Furnace Operators and Tenders
51-4052 Pourers and Casters, Metal	51-4052.00 Pourers and Casters, Metal
51-4061 Model Makers, Metal and Plastic	51-4061.00 Model Makers, Metal and Plastic
51-4062 Patternmakers, Metal and Plastic	51-4062.00 Patternmakers, Metal and Plastic
51-4071 Foundry Mold and Coremakers	51-4071.00 Foundry Mold and Coremakers
51-4072 Molding, Coremaking, and Casting Machine Setters, Operators, and Tenders, Metal and Plastic	51-4072.00 Molding, Coremaking, and Casting Machine Setters, Operators, and Tenders, Metal and Plastic
51-4072 Molding, Coremaking, and Casting Machine Setters, Operators, and Tenders, Metal and Plastic	51-4072.01 Plastic Molding and Casting Machine Setters and Set-Up Operators
51-4072 Molding, Coremaking, and Casting Machine Setters, Operators, and Tenders, Metal and Plastic	51-4072.02 Plastic Molding and Casting Machine Operators and Tenders
51-4072 Molding, Coremaking, and Casting Machine Setters, Operators, and Tenders, Metal and Plastic	51-4072.03 Metal Molding, Coremaking, and Casting Machine Setters and Set-Up Operators
51-4072 Molding, Coremaking, and Casting Machine Setters, Operators, and Tenders, Metal and Plastic	51-4072.04 Metal Molding, Coremaking, and Casting Machine Operators and Tenders
51-4072 Molding, Coremaking, and Casting Machine Setters, Operators, and Tenders, Metal and Plastic	51-4072.05 Casting Machine Set-Up Operators
51-4081 Multiple Machine Tool Setters, Operators, and Tenders, Metal and Plastic	51-4081.00 Multiple Machine Tool Setters, Operators, and Tenders, Metal and Plastic
51-4081 Multiple Machine Tool Setters, Operators, and Tenders, Metal and Plastic	51-4081.01 Combination Machine Tool Setters and Set-Up Operators, Metal and Plastic
51-4081 Multiple Machine Tool Setters, Operators, and Tenders, Metal and Plastic	51-4081.02 Combination Machine Tool Operators and Tenders, Metal and Plastic
51-4111 Tool and Die Makers	51-4111.00 Tool and Die Makers
51-4121 Welders, Cutters, Solderers, and Brazers	51-4121.00 Welders, Cutters, Solderers, and Brazers
51-4121 Welders, Cutters, Solderers, and Brazers	51-4121.01 Welders, Production
51-4121 Welders, Cutters, Solderers, and Brazers	51-4121.02 Welders and Cutters
51-4121 Welders, Cutters, Solderers, and Brazers	51-4121.03 Welder-Fitters
51-4121 Welders, Cutters, Solderers, and Brazers	51-4121.04 Solderers
51-4121 Welders, Cutters, Solderers, and Brazers	51-4121.05 Brazers
51-4122 Welding, Soldering, and Brazing Machine Setters, Operators, and Tenders	51-4122.00 Welding, Soldering, and Brazing Machine Setters, Operators, and Tenders
51-4122 Welding, Soldering, and Brazing Machine Setters, Operators, and Tenders	51-4122.01 Welding Machine Setters and Set-Up Operators

SOC Code and Title		O*NET-SOC Code and Title	
51-4122	Welding, Soldering, and Brazing Machine Setters, Operators, and Tenders	51-4122.02	Welding Machine Operators and Tenders
51-4122	Welding, Soldering, and Brazing Machine Setters, Operators, and Tenders	51-4122.03	Soldering and Brazing Machine Setters and Set-Up Operators
51-4122	Welding, Soldering, and Brazing Machine Setters, Operators, and Tenders	51-4122.04	Soldering and Brazing Machine Operators and Tenders
51-4191	Heat Treating Equipment Setters, Operators, and Tenders, Metal and Plastic	51-4191.00	Heat Treating Equipment Setters, Operators, and Tenders, Metal and Plastic
51-4191	Heat Treating Equipment Setters, Operators, and Tenders, Metal and Plastic	51-4191.01	Heating Equipment Setters and Set-Up Operators, Metal and Plastic
51-4191	Heat Treating Equipment Setters, Operators, and Tenders, Metal and Plastic	51-4191.02	Heat Treating, Annealing, and Tempering Machine Operators and Tenders, Metal and Plastic
51-4191	Heat Treating Equipment Setters, Operators, and Tenders, Metal and Plastic	51-4191.03	Heaters, Metal and Plastic
51-4192	Lay-Out Workers, Metal and Plastic	51-4192.00	Lay-Out Workers, Metal and Plastic
51-4193	Plating and Coating Machine Setters, Operators, and Tenders, Metal and Plastic	51-4193.00	Plating and Coating Machine Setters, Operators, and Tenders, Metal and Plastic
51-4193	Plating and Coating Machine Setters, Operators, and Tenders, Metal and Plastic	51-4193.01	Electrolytic Plating and Coating Machine Setters and Set-Up Operators, Metal and Plastic
51-4193	Plating and Coating Machine Setters, Operators, and Tenders, Metal and Plastic	51-4193.02	Electrolytic Plating and Coating Machine Operators and Tenders, Metal and Plastic
1-4193	Plating and Coating Machine Setters, Operators, and Tenders, Metal and Plastic	51-4193.03	Nonelectrolytic Plating and Coating Machine Setters and Set-Up Operators, Metal and Plastic
51-4193	Plating and Coating Machine Setters, Operators, and Tenders, Metal and Plastic	51-4193.04	Nonelectrolytic Plating and Coating Machine Operators and Tenders, Metal and Plastic
51-4194	Tool Grinders, Filers, and Sharpeners	51-4194.00	Tool Grinders, Filers, and Sharpeners
51-4199	Metal Workers and Plastic Workers, All Other	51-4199.99	Metal Workers and Plastic Workers, All Other
51-5011	Bindery Workers	51-5011.00	Bindery Workers
51-5011	Bindery Workers	51-5011.01	Bindery Machine Setters and Set-Up Operators
51-5011	Bindery Workers	51-5011.02	Bindery Machine Operators and Tenders
51-5012	Bookbinders	51-5012.00	Bookbinders
51-5021	Job Printers	51-5021.00	Job Printers
51-5022	Prepress Technicians and Workers	51-5022.00	Prepress Technicians and Workers
51-5022	Prepress Technicians and Workers	51-5022.01	Hand Compositors and Typesetters
51-5022	Prepress Technicians and Workers	51-5022.02	Paste-Up Workers
51-5022	Prepress Technicians and Workers	51-5022.03	Photoengravers
51-5022	Prepress Technicians and Workers	51-5022.04	Camera Operators
51-5022	Prepress Technicians and Workers	51-5022.05	Scanner Operators
51-5022	Prepress Technicians and Workers	51-5022.06	Strippers

SOC Code and Title	O*NET-SOC Code and Title
51-5022 Prepress Technicians and Workers	51-5022.07 Platemakers
51-5022 Prepress Technicians and Workers	51-5022.08 Dot Etchers
51-5022 Prepress Technicians and Workers	51-5022.09 Electronic Masking System Operators
51-5022 Prepress Technicians and Workers	51-5022.10 Electrotypers and Stereotypers
51-5022 Prepress Technicians and Workers	51-5022.11 Plate Finishers
51-5022 Prepress Technicians and Workers	51-5022.12 Typesetting and Composing Machine Operators and Tenders
51-5022 Prepress Technicians and Workers	51-5022.13 Photoengraving and Lithographing Machine Operators and Tenders
51-5023 Printing Machine Operators	51-5023.00 Printing Machine Operators
51-5023 Printing Machine Operators	51-5023.01 Precision Printing Workers
51-5023 Printing Machine Operators	51-5023.02 Offset Lithographic Press Setters and Set-Up Operators
51-5023 Printing Machine Operators	51-5023.03 Letterpress Setters and Set-Up Operators
51-5023 Printing Machine Operators	51-5023.04 Design Printing Machine Setters and Set-Up Operators
51-5023 Printing Machine Operators	51-5023.05 Marking and Identification Printing Machine Setters and Set-Up Operators
51-5023 Printing Machine Operators	51-5023.06 Screen Printing Machine Setters and Set-Up Operators
51-5023 Printing Machine Operators	51-5023.07 Embossing Machine Set-Up Operators
51-5023 Printing Machine Operators	51-5023.08 Engraver Set-Up Operators
51-5023 Printing Machine Operators	51-5023.09 Printing Press Machine Operators and Tenders
51-6011 Laundry and Dry-Cleaning Workers	51-6011.00 Laundry and Dry-Cleaning Workers
51-6011 Laundry and Dry-Cleaning Workers	51-6011.01 Spotters, Dry Cleaning
51-6011 Laundry and Dry-Cleaning Workers	51-6011.02 Precision Dyers
51-6011 Laundry and Dry-Cleaning Workers	51-6011.03 Laundry and Drycleaning Machine Operators and Tenders, Except Pressing
51-6021 Pressers, Textile, Garment, and Related Materials	51-6021.00 Pressers, Textile, Garment, and Related Materials
51-6021 Pressers, Textile, Garment, and Related Materials	51-6021.01 Pressers, Delicate Fabrics
51-6021 Pressers, Textile, Garment, and Related Materials	51-6021.02 Pressing Machine Operators and Tenders—Textile, Garment, and Related Materials
51-6021 Pressers, Textile, Garment, and Related Materials	51-6021.03 Pressers, Hand
51-6031 Sewing Machine Operators	51-6031.00 Sewing Machine Operators
51-6031 Sewing Machine Operators	51-6031.01 Sewing Machine Operators, Garment
51-6031 Sewing Machine Operators	51-6031.02 Sewing Machine Operators, Non-Garment
51-6041 Shoe and Leather Workers and Repairers	51-6041.00 Shoe and Leather Workers and Repairers
51-6042 Shoe Machine Operators and Tenders	51-6042.00 Shoe Machine Operators and Tenders
51-6051 Sewers, Hand	51-6051.00 Sewers, Hand
51-6052 Tailors, Dressmakers, and Custom Sewers	51-6052.00 Tailors, Dressmakers, and Custom Sewers
51-6052 Tailors, Dressmakers, and Custom Sewers	51-6052.01 Shop and Alteration Tailors

SOC Code and Title		O*NET-SOC Code and Title	
51-6052	Tailors, Dressmakers, and Custom Sewers	51-6052.02	Custom Tailors
51-6061	Textile Bleaching and Dyeing Machine Operators and Tenders	51-6061.00	Textile Bleaching and Dyeing Machine Operators and Tenders
51-6062	Textile Cutting Machine Setters, Operators, and Tenders	51-6062.00	Textile Cutting Machine Setters, Operators, and Tenders
51-6063	Textile Knitting and Weaving Machine Setters, Operators, and Tenders	51-6063.00	Textile Knitting and Weaving Machine Setters, Operators, and Tenders
51-6064	Textile Winding, Twisting, and Drawing Out Machine Setters, Operators, and Tenders	51-6064.00	Textile Winding, Twisting, and Drawing Out Machine Setters, Operators, and Tenders
51-6091	Extruding and Forming Machine Setters, Operators, and Tenders, Synthetic and Glass Fibers	51-6091.00	Extruding and Forming Machine Setters, Operators, and Tenders, Synthetic and Glass Fibers
51-6091	Extruding and Forming Machine Setters, Operators, and Tenders, Synthetic and Glass Fibers	51-6091.01	Extruding and Forming Machine Operators and Tenders, Synthetic or Glass Fibers
51-6092	Fabric and Apparel Patternmakers	51-6092.00	Fabric and Apparel Patternmakers
51-6093	Upholsterers	51-6093.00	Upholsterers
51-6099	Textile, Apparel, and Furnishings Workers, All Other	51-6099.99	Textile, Apparel, and Furnishings Workers, All Other
51-7011	Cabinetmakers and Bench Carpenters	51-7011.00	Cabinetmakers and Bench Carpenters
51-7021	Furniture Finishers	51-7021.00	Furniture Finishers
51-7031	Model Makers, Wood	51-7031.00	Model Makers, Wood
51-7032	Patternmakers, Wood	51-7032.00	Patternmakers, Wood
51-7041	Sawing Machine Setters, Operators, and Tenders, Wood	51-7041.00	Sawing Machine Setters, Operators, and Tenders, Wood
51-7041	Sawing Machine Setters, Operators, and Tenders, Wood	51-7041.01	Sawing Machine Setters and Set-Up Operators
51-7041	Sawing Machine Setters, Operators, and Tenders, Wood	51-7041.02	Sawing Machine Operators and Tenders
51-7042	Woodworking Machine Setters, Operators, and Tenders, Except Sawing	51-7042.00	Woodworking Machine Setters, Operators, and Tenders, Except Sawing
51-7042	Woodworking Machine Setters, Operators, and Tenders, Except Sawing	51-7042.01	Woodworking Machine Setters and Set-Up Operators, Except Sawing
51-7042	Woodworking Machine Setters, Operators, and Tenders, Except Sawing	51-7042.02	Woodworking Machine Operators and Tenders, Except Sawing
51-7099	Woodworkers, All Other	51-7099.99	Woodworkers, All Other
51-8011	Nuclear Power Reactor Operators	51-8011.00	Nuclear Power Reactor Operators
51-8012	Power Distributors and Dispatchers	51-8012.00	Power Distributors and Dispatchers
51-8013	Power Plant Operators	51-8013.00	Power Plant Operators
51-8013	Power Plant Operators	51-8013.01	Power Generating Plant Operators, Except Auxiliary Equipment Operators
51-8013	Power Plant Operators	51-8013.02	Auxiliary Equipment Operators, Power
51-8021	Stationary Engineers and Boiler Operators	51-8021.00	Stationary Engineers and Boiler Operators
51-8021	Stationary Engineers and Boiler Operators	51-8021.01	Boiler Operators and Tenders, Low Pressure

SOC Code and Title	O*NET-SOC Code and Title
51-8021 Stationary Engineers and Boiler Operators	51-8021.02 Stationary Engineers
51-8031 Water and Liquid Waste Treatment Plant and System Operators	51-8031.00 Water and Liquid Waste Treatment Plant and System Operators
51-8091 Chemical Plant and System Operators	51-8091.00 Chemical Plant and System Operators
51-8092 Gas Plant Operators	51-8092.00 Gas Plant Operators
51-8092 Gas Plant Operators	51-8092.01 Gas Processing Plant Operators
51-8092 Gas Plant Operators	51-8092.02 Gas Distribution Plant Operators
51-8093 Petroleum Pump System Operators, Refinery Operators, and Gaugers	51-8093.00 Petroleum Pump System Operators, Refinery Operators, and Gaugers
51-8093 Petroleum Pump System Operators, Refinery Operators, and Gaugers	51-8093.01 Petroleum Pump System Operators
51-8093 Petroleum Pump System Operators, Refinery Operators, and Gaugers	51-8093.02 Petroleum Refinery and Control Panel Operators
51-8093 Petroleum Pump System Operators, Refinery Operators, and Gaugers	51-8093.03 Gaugers
51-8099 Plant and System Operators, All Other	51-8099.99 Plant and System Operators, All Other
51-9011 Chemical Equipment Operators and Tenders	51-9011.00 Chemical Equipment Operators and Tenders
51-9011 Chemical Equipment Operators and Tenders	51-9011.01 Chemical Equipment Controllers and Operators
51-9011 Chemical Equipment Operators and Tenders	51-9011.02 Chemical Equipment Tenders
51-9012 Separating, Filtering, Clarifying, Precipitating, and Still Machine Setters, Operators, and Tenders	51-9012.00 Separating, Filtering, Clarifying, Precipitating, and Still Machine Setters, Operators, and Tenders
51-9021 Crushing, Grinding, and Polishing Machine Setters, Operators, and Tenders	51-9021.00 Crushing, Grinding, and Polishing Machine Setters, Operators, and Tenders
51-9022 Grinding and Polishing Workers, Hand	51-9022.00 Grinding and Polishing Workers, Hand
51-9023 Mixing and Blending Machine Setters, Operators, and Tenders	51-9023.00 Mixing and Blending Machine Setters, Operators, and Tenders
51-9031 Cutters and Trimmers, Hand	51-9031.00 Cutters and Trimmers, Hand
51-9032 Cutting and Slicing Machine Setters, Operators, and Tenders	51-9032.00 Cutting and Slicing Machine Setters, Operators, and Tenders
51-9032 Cutting and Slicing Machine Setters, Operators, and Tenders	51-9032.01 Fiber Product Cutting Machine Setters and Set-Up Operators
51-9032 Cutting and Slicing Machine Setters, Operators, and Tenders	51-9032.02 Stone Sawyers
51-9032 Cutting and Slicing Machine Setters, Operators, and Tenders	51-9032.03 Glass Cutting Machine Setters and Set-Up Operators
51-9032 Cutting and Slicing Machine Setters, Operators, and Tenders	51-9032.04 Cutting and Slicing Machine Operators and Tenders
51-9041 Extruding, Forming, Pressing, and Compacting Machine Setters, Operators, and Tenders	51-9041.00 Extruding, Forming, Pressing, and Compacting Machine Setters, Operators, and Tenders

SOC Code and Title		O*NET-SOC Code and Title	
51-9041	Extruding, Forming, Pressing, and Compacting Machine Setters, Operators, and Tenders	51-9041.01	Extruding, Forming, Pressing, and Compacting Machine Setters and Set-Up Operators
51-9041	Extruding, Forming, Pressing, and Compacting e Machine Setters, Operators, and Tenders	51-9041.02	Extruding, Forming, Pressing, and Compacting Machine Operators and Tenders
51-9051	Furnace, Kiln, Oven, Drier, and Kettle Operators and Tenders	51-9051.00	Furnace, Kiln, Oven, Drier, and Kettle Operators and Tenders
51-9061	Inspectors, Testers, Sorters, Samplers, and Weighers	51-9061.00	Inspectors, Testers, Sorters, Samplers, and Weighers
51-9061	Inspectors, Testers, Sorters, Samplers, and Weighers	51-9061.01	Materials Inspectors
51-9061	Inspectors, Testers, Sorters, Samplers, and Weighers	51-9061.02	Mechanical Inspectors
51-9061	Inspectors, Testers, Sorters, Samplers, and Weighers	51-9061.03	Precision Devices Inspectors and Testers
51-9061	Inspectors, Testers, Sorters, Samplers, and Weighers	51-9061.04	Electrical and Electronic Inspectors and Testers
51-9061	Inspectors, Testers, Sorters, Samplers, and Weighers	51-9061.05	Production Inspectors, Testers, Graders, Sorters, Samplers, Weighers
51-9071	Jewelers and Precious Stone and Metal Workers	51-9071.00	Jewelers and Precious Stone and Metal Workers
51-9071	Jewelers and Precious Stone and Metal Workers	51-9071.01	Jewelers
51-9071	Jewelers and Precious Stone and Metal Workers	51-9071.02	Silversmiths
51-9071	Jewelers and Precious Stone and Metal Workers	51-9071.03	Model and Mold Makers, Jewelry
51-9071	Jewelers and Precious Stone and Metal Workers	51-9071.04	Bench Workers, Jewelry
51-9071	Jewelers and Precious Stone and Metal Workers	51-9071.05	Pewter Casters and Finishers
51-9071	Jewelers and Precious Stone and Metal Workers	51-9071.06	Gem and Diamond Workers
51-9081	Dental Laboratory Technicians	51-9081.00	Dental Laboratory Technicians
51-9082	Medical Appliance Technicians	51-9082.00	Medical Appliance Technicians
51-9083	Ophthalmic Laboratory Technicians	51-9083.00	Ophthalmic Laboratory Technicians
51-9083	Ophthalmic Laboratory Technicians	51-9083.01	Precision Lens Grinders and Polishers
51-9083	Ophthalmic Laboratory Technicians	51-9083.02	Optical Instrument Assemblers
51-9111	Packaging and Filling Machine Operators and Tenders	51-9111.00	Packaging and Filling Machine Operators and Tenders
51-9121	Coating, Painting, and Spraying Machine Setters, Operators, and Tenders	51-9121.00	Coating, Painting, and Spraying Machine Setters, Operators, and Tenders
51-9121	Coating, Painting, and Spraying Machine Setters, Operators, and Tenders	51-9121.01	Coating, Painting, and Spraying Machine Setters and Set-Up Operators
51-9121	Coating, Painting, and Spraying Machine Setters, Operators, and Tenders	51-9121.02	Coating, Painting, and Spraying Machine Operators and Tenders
51-9122	Painters, Transportation Equipment	51-9122.00	Painters, Transportation Equipment
51-9123	Painting, Coating, and Decorating Workers	51-9123.00	Painting, Coating, and Decorating Workers
51-9131	Photographic Process Workers	51-9131.00	Photographic Process Workers
51-9131	Photographic Process Workers	51-9131.01	Photographic Retouchers and Restorers
51-9131	Photographic Process Workers	51-9131.02	Photographic Reproduction Technicians
51-9131	Photographic Process Workers	51-9131.03	Photographic Hand Developers
51-9131	Photographic Process Workers	51-9131.04	Film Laboratory Technicians

SOC Code and Title	O*NET-SOC Code and Title
51-9132 Photographic Processing Machine Operators	51-9132.00 Photographic Processing Machine Operators
51-9141 Semiconductor Processors	51-9141.00 Semiconductor Processors
51-9191 Cementing and Gluing Machine Operators and Tenders	51-9191.00 Cementing and Gluing Machine Operators and Tenders
51-9192 Cleaning, Washing, and Metal Pickling Equipment Operators and Tenders	51-9192.00 Cleaning, Washing, and Metal Pickling Equipment Operators and Tenders
51-9193 Cooling and Freezing Equipment Operators and Tenders	51-9193.00 Cooling and Freezing Equipment Operators and Tenders
51-9194 Etchers and Engravers	51-9194.00 Etchers and Engravers
51-9194 Etchers and Engravers	51-9194.01 Precision Etchers and Engravers, Hand or Machine
51-9194 Etchers and Engravers	51-9194.02 Engravers/Carvers
51-9194 Etchers and Engravers	51-9194.03 Etchers
51-9194 Etchers and Engravers	51-9194.04 Pantograph Engravers
51-9194 Etchers and Engravers	51-9194.05 Etchers, Hand
51-9194 Etchers and Engravers	51-9194.06 Engravers, Hand
51-9195 Molders, Shapers, and Casters, Except Metal and Plastic	51-9195.00 Molders, Shapers, and Casters, Except Metal and Plastic
51-9195 Molders, Shapers, and Casters, Except Metal and Plastic	51-9195.01 Precision Mold and Pattern Casters, except Nonferrous Metals
51-9195 Molders, Shapers, and Casters, Except Metal and Plastic	51-9195.02 Precision Pattern and Die Casters, Nonferrous Metals
51-9195 Molders, Shapers, and Casters, Except Metal and Plastic	51-9195.03 Stone Cutters and Carvers
51-9195 Molders, Shapers, and Casters, Except Metal and Plastic	51-9195.04 Glass Blowers, Molders, Benders, and Finishers
51-9195 Molders, Shapers, and Casters, Except Metal and Plastic	51-9195.05 Potters
51-9195 Molders, Shapers, and Casters, Except Metal and Plastic	51-9195.06 Mold Makers, Hand
51-9195 Molders, Shapers, and Casters, Except Metal and Plastic	51-9195.07 Molding and Casting Workers
51-9196 Paper Goods Machine Setters, Operators, and Tenders	51-9196.00 Paper Goods Machine Setters, Operators, and Tenders
51-9197 Tire Builders	51-9197.00 Tire Builders
51-9198 Helpers—Production Workers	51-9198.00 Helpers—Production Workers
51-9198 Helpers—Production Workers	51-9198.01 Production Laborers
51-9198 Helpers—Production Workers	51-9198.02 Production Helpers
51-9199 Production Workers, All Other	51-9199.99 Production Workers, All Other
53-1011 Aircraft Cargo Handling Supervisors	53-1011.00 Aircraft Cargo Handling Supervisors

SOC Code and Title		O*NET-SOC Code and Title	
53-1021	First-Line Supervisors/Managers of Helpers, Laborers, and Material Movers, Hand	53-1021.00	First-Line Supervisors/Managers of Helpers, Laborers, and Material Movers, Hand
53-1031	First-Line Supervisors/Managers of Transportation and Material-Moving Machine and Vehicle Operators	53-1031.00	First-Line Supervisors/Managers of Transportation and Material-Moving Machine and Vehicle Operators
53-2011	Airline Pilots, Copilots, and Flight Engineers	53-2011.00	Airline Pilots, Copilots, and Flight Engineers
53-2012	Commercial Pilots	53-2012.00	Commercial Pilots
53-2021	Air Traffic Controllers	53-2021.00	Air Traffic Controllers
53-2022	Airfield Operations Specialists	53-2022.00	Airfield Operations Specialists
53-3011	Ambulance Drivers and Attendants, Except Emergency Medical Technicians	53-3011.00	Ambulance Drivers and Attendants, Except Emergency Medical Technicians
53-3021	Bus Drivers, Transit and Intercity	53-3021.00	Bus Drivers, Transit and Intercity
53-3022	Bus Drivers, School	53-3022.00	Bus Drivers, School
53-3031	Driver/Sales Workers	53-3031.00	Driver/Sales Workers
53-3032	Truck Drivers, Heavy and Tractor-Trailer	53-3032.00	Truck Drivers, Heavy and Tractor-Trailer
53-3032	Truck Drivers, Heavy and Tractor-Trailer	53-3032.01	Truck Drivers, Heavy
53-3032	Truck Drivers, Heavy and Tractor-Trailer	53-3032.02	Tractor-Trailer Truck Drivers
53-3033	Truck Drivers, Light or Delivery Services	53-3033.00	Truck Drivers, Light or Delivery Services
53-3041	Taxi Drivers and Chauffeurs	53-3041.00	Taxi Drivers and Chauffeurs
53-3099	Motor Vehicle Operators, All Other	53-3099.99	Motor Vehicle Operators, All Other
53-4011	Locomotive Engineers	53-4011.00	Locomotive Engineers
53-4012	Locomotive Firers	53-4012.00	Locomotive Firers
53-4013	Rail Yard Engineers, Dinkey Operators, and Hostlers	53-4013.00	Rail Yard Engineers, Dinkey Operators, and Hostlers
53-4021	Railroad Brake, Signal, and Switch Operators	53-4021.00	Railroad Brake, Signal, and Switch Operators
53-4021	Railroad Brake, Signal, and Switch Operators	53-4021.01	Train Crew Members
53-4021	Railroad Brake, Signal, and Switch Operators	53-4021.02	Railroad Yard Workers
53-4031	Railroad Conductors and Yardmasters	53-4031.00	Railroad Conductors and Yardmasters
53-4041	Subway and Streetcar Operators	53-4041.00	Subway and Streetcar Operators
53-4099	Rail Transportation Workers, All Other	53-4099.99	Rail Transportation Workers, All Other
53-5011	Sailors and Marine Oilers	53-5011.00	Sailors and Marine Oilers
53-5011	Sailors and Marine Oilers	53-5011.01	Able Seamen
53-5011	Sailors and Marine Oilers	53-5011.02	Ordinary Seamen and Marine Oilers
53-5021	Captains, Mates, and Pilots of Water Vessels	53-5021.00	Captains, Mates, and Pilots of Water Vessels
53-5021	Captains, Mates, and Pilots of Water Vessels	53-5021.01	Ship and Boat Captains
53-5021	Captains, Mates, and Pilots of Water Vessels	53-5021.02	Mates—Ship, Boat, and Barge
53-5021	Captains, Mates, and Pilots of Water Vessels	53-5021.03	Pilots, Ship
53-5022	Motorboat Operators	53-5022.00	Motorboat Operators
53-5031	Ship Engineers	53-5031.00	Ship Engineers
53-6011	Bridge and Lock Tenders	53-6011.00	Bridge and Lock Tenders

SOC Code and Title		O*NET-SOC Code and Title	
53-6021	Parking Lot Attendants	53-6021.00	Parking Lot Attendants
53-6031	Service Station Attendants	53-6031.00	Service Station Attendants
53-6041	Traffic Technicians	53-6041.00	Traffic Technicians
53-6051	Transportation Inspectors	53-6051.00	Transportation Inspectors
53-6051	Transportation Inspectors	53-6051.01	Aviation Inspectors
53-6051	Transportation Inspectors	53-6051.02	Public Transportation Inspectors
53-6051	Transportation Inspectors	53-6051.03	Marine Cargo Inspectors
53-6051	Transportation Inspectors	53-6051.04	Railroad Inspectors
53-6051	Transportation Inspectors	53-6051.05	Motor Vehicle Inspectors
53-6051	Transportation Inspectors	53-6051.06	Freight Inspectors
53-6099	Transportation Workers, All Other	53-6099.99	Transportation Workers, All Other
53-7011	Conveyor Operators and Tenders	53-7011.00	Conveyor Operators and Tenders
53-7021	Crane and Tower Operators	53-7021.00	Crane and Tower Operators
53-7031	Dredge Operators	53-7031.00	Dredge Operators
53-7032	Excavating and Loading Machine and Dragline Operators	53-7032.00	Excavating and Loading Machine and Dragline Operators
53-7032	Excavating and Loading Machine and Dragline Operators	53-7032.01	Excavating and Loading Machine Operators
53-7032	Excavating and Loading Machine and Dragline Operators	53-7032.02	Dragline Operators
53-7033	Loading Machine Operators, Underground Mining	53-7033.00	Loading Machine Operators, Underground Mining
53-7041	Hoist and Winch Operators	53-7041.00	Hoist and Winch Operators
53-7051	Industrial Truck and Tractor Operators	53-7051.00	Industrial Truck and Tractor Operators
53-7061	Cleaners of Vehicles and Equipment	53-7061.00	Cleaners of Vehicles and Equipment
53-7062	Laborers and Freight, Stock, and Material Movers, Hand	53-7062.00	Laborers and Freight, Stock, and Material Movers, Hand
53-7062	Laborers and Freight, Stock, and Material Movers, Hand	53-7062.01	Stevedores, Except Equipment Operators
53-7062	Laborers and Freight, Stock, and Material Movers, Hand	53-7062.02	Grips and Set-Up Workers, Motion Picture Sets, Studios, and Stages
53-7062	Laborers and Freight, Stock, and Material Movers, Hand	53-7062.03	Freight, Stock, and Material Movers, Hand
53-7063	Machine Feeders and Offbearers	53-7063.00	Machine Feeders and Offbearers
53-7064	Packers and Packagers, Hand	53-7064.00	Packers and Packagers, Hand
53-7071	Gas Compressor and Gas Pumping Station Operators	53-7071.00	Gas Compressor and Gas Pumping Station Operators
53-7071	Gas Compressor and Gas Pumping Station Operators	53-7071.01	Gas Pumping Station Operators
53-7071	Gas Compressor and Gas Pumping Station Operators	53-7071.02	Gas Compressor Operators
53-7072	Pump Operators, Except Wellhead Pumpers	53-7072.00	Pump Operators, Except Wellhead Pumpers
53-7073	Wellhead Pumpers	53-7073.00	Wellhead Pumpers

SOC Code and Title		O*NET-SOC Code and Title	
53-7081	Refuse and Recyclable Material Collectors	53-7081.00	Refuse and Recyclable Material Collectors
53-7111	Shuttle Car Operators	53-7111.00	Shuttle Car Operators
53-7121	Tank Car, Truck, and Ship Loaders	53-7121.00	Tank Car, Truck, and Ship Loaders
53-7199	Material Moving Workers, All Other	53-7199.99	Material Moving Workers, All Other
55-1011	Air Crew Officers	55-1011.00	Air Crew Officers
55-1012	Aircraft Launch and Recovery Officers	55-1012.00	Aircraft Launch and Recovery Officers
55-1013	Armored Assault Vehicle Officers	55-1013.00	Armored Assault Vehicle Officers
55-1014	Artillery and Missile Officers	55-1014.00	Artillery and Missile Officers
55-1015	Command and Control Center Officers	55-1015.00	Command and Control Center Officers
55-1016	Infantry Officers	55-1016.00	Infantry Officers
55-1017	Special Forces Officers	55-1017.00	Special Forces Officers
55-1019	Military Officer Special and Tactical Operations Leaders/Managers, All Other	55-1019.99	Military Officer Special and Tactical Operations Leaders/Managers, All Other
55-2011	First-Line Supervisors/Managers of Air Crew Members	55-2011.00	First-Line Supervisors/Managers of Air Crew Members
55-2012	First-Line Supervisors/Managers of Weapons Specialists/Crew Members	55-2012.00	First-Line Supervisors/Managers of Weapons Specialists/Crew Members
55-2013	First-Line Supervisors/Managers of All Other Tactical Operations Specialists	55-2013.00	First-Line Supervisors/Managers of All Other Tactical Operations Specialists
55-3011	Air Crew Members	55-3011.00	Air Crew Members
55-3012	Aircraft Launch and Recovery Specialists	55-3012.00	Aircraft Launch and Recovery Specialists
55-3013	Armored Assault Vehicle Crew Members	55-3013.00	Armored Assault Vehicle Crew Members
55-3014	Artillery and Missile Crew Members	55-3014.00	Artillery and Missile Crew Members
55-3015	Command and Control Center Specialists	55-3015.00	Command and Control Center Specialists
55-3016	Infantry	55-3016.00	Infantry
55-3017	Radar and Sonar Technicians	55-3017.00	Radar and Sonar Technicians
55-3018	Special Forces	55-3018.00	Special Forces
55-3019	Military Enlisted Tactical Operations and Air/Weapons Specialists and Crew Members, All Other	55-3019.99	Military Enlisted Tactical Operations and Air/Weapons Specialists and Crew Members, All Other

INDEX

Use this index to locate the jobs described in this book and their associated titles. Each job's SOC number appears in parentheses, followed by its page reference.

Index

Standard Occupational Classification Manual

© JIST Works

Index